MW00443152

Leaders and International Conflict

Chiozza and Goemans seek to explain why and when political leaders decide to initiate international crises and wars. They argue that the fate of leaders and the way leadership changes shapes leaders' decisions to initiate international conflict. Leaders who anticipate regular removal from office, through elections for example, have little to gain and much to lose from international conflict, whereas leaders who anticipate a forcible removal from office, e.g. through coup or revolution, have little to lose and much to gain from conflict. This theory is tested against an extensive analysis of more than 80 years of international conflict and with an intensive historical examination of Central American leaders from 1848 to 1918. *Leaders and International Conflict* highlights the political nature of the choice between war and peace and will appeal to all scholars of international relations and comparative politics.

GIACOMO CHIOZZA is Assistant Professor in the Department of Political Science at Vanderbilt University and studies international relations and international security. He is an expert on the study of attitudes towards US power and the study of political leaders in conflict processes. He is the author of *Anti-Americanism and the American World Order* (2009) and of several articles published in academic journals, including the *Journal of Conflict Resolution*, the *American Journal of Political Science*, and the *European Journal of International Relations*. In 2008–09 he served as a member of the American Political Science Association Presidential Task Force on US Standing in World Politics. Professor Chiozza holds a Ph.D. from Duke University.

H. E. GOEMANS is Associate Professor of Political Science at the University of Rochester and studies international relations with a focus on conflict. He is the author of *War and Punishment: the Causes of War Termination and the First World War* (2000) and has authored and co-authored articles in the *American Political Science Review*, the *American Journal of Political Science*, the *Journal of Politics*, *International Organization*, the *Journal of Conflict Resolution*, and the *Journal of Peace Research*. Professor Goemans holds a Ph.D. from the University of Chicago.

Leaders and International Conflict

GIACOMO CHIOZZA AND
H. E. GOEMANS

CAMBRIDGE
UNIVERSITY PRESS

CAMBRIDGE UNIVERSITY PRESS
Cambridge, New York, Melbourne, Madrid, Cape Town,
Singapore, São Paulo, Delhi, Tokyo, Mexico City

Cambridge University Press
The Edinburgh Building, Cambridge CB2 8RU, UK

Published in the United States of America by Cambridge University Press, New York

www.cambridge.org
Information on this title: www.cambridge.org/9781107660731

First published 2011

Printed in the United Kingdom at the University Press, Cambridge

A catalogue record for this publication is available from the British Library

Library of Congress Cataloguing in Publication data
Chiozza, Giacomo.
Leaders and international conflict / Giacomo Chiozza and H. E. Goemans.
    p.   cm.
Includes bibliographical references and index.
ISBN 978-1-107-01172-4 (hardback)
1. Politics and war.   2. Political leadership.   3. International relations.   4. Politics
and war – Case studies.   5. Political leadership – Case studies.   6. International
relations – Case studies.   I. Goemans, H. E. (Hein Erich), 1957–   II. Title.
JZ6385.C55   2011
303.6′6 – dc23   2011020738

ISBN 978-1-107-01172-4 Hardback
ISBN 978-1-107-66073-1 Paperback

Contents

Tables

Figures

Acknowledgments

We would like to thank Jeffrey Arnold, Carol Atkinson, Rand Blimes, Tim Büthe, Kevin Clarke, Eugene Gholz, Ron Hassner, Susan Hyde, Brenton Kenkel, Deborah Larson, Jeffrey Lewis, Nikolay Marinov, Sandra Morton, Michael Peress, Dan Posner, Norrin Ripsman, Bruce Russett, Ken Schultz, Glenn Scrimshaw, Curt Signorino, Duncan Snidal, Randy Stone, Marc Trachtenberg, R. Harrison Wagner and in particular Alexandre Debs and Arnd Plagge. Muhammet Bas provided extremely helpful research assistance.

We have benefited from the comments of the participants at the Peace Studies Program at Cornell University, the University of Chicago, PIPES, the University of California, Berkeley, UCLA, the University of Texas at Austin, Yale University.

Mistakes, omissions, and other assorted infelicities are our own responsibility.

Online appendices

Online appendices have been supplied as supplementary material for Chapters 3, 4, and 6. Please find the online appendices at:
http://sites.google.com/site/giacomochiozza/
or
http://www.rochester.edu/college/faculty/hgoemans/research.htm/
Links to these sites can also be found on the book's homepage at:
www.cambridge.org/9781107660731

1 | *Leaders*

Joaquim Alberto Chissano, the second President of Mozambique, stepped down from power on February 2, 2005 after serving his country for 19 years. During his rule, Mozambique experienced economic progress, democratic development, and pacification. The civil war that had ravaged the country for 16 years came to an end in 1992 when a UN-sponsored peace accord was signed in Rome between President Chissano and the Renamo leader, Afonso Dhlakama. Elections were held two years later and again in 1999, which Chissano and the Frelimo party won. In 2004, President Chissano announced that he would not run for a third term, even though Mozambique's constitution would allow him to do so. Rather, he voluntarily retired and let a successor be selected. For all his services to his country, President Chissano was awarded the first Mo Ibrahim Prize for Achievement in African Leadership, a great honor meant to celebrate his outstanding contributions to peace, prosperity and democracy, but also... *a lot of money*: 5 million US dollars over 10 years and 200,000 US dollars annually for life thereafter, in addition to up to 200,000 US dollars a year for 10 years towards the winner's public interest activities and good causes.

The prize is the brainchild of Dr. Mo Ibrahim, a Sudanese businessman and telecommunications mogul, who, after selling his main business, set up a charity foundation devoted to fostering democratic governance and economic development in Africa. But rather than funding health care projects or civil works, Dr. Ibrahim's foundation adopted a revolutionary approach to charity: to promote development by changing the incentives that drive political leaders in office.

Aid and development projects, two of the traditional approaches of charity organizations, are discounted, because they do not directly address the political sources of the persistent stagnation and underdevelopment of African societies and economies. Aid and development projects do not alter how leaders govern their countries. Development and prosperity, in Dr. Ibrahim's view, flow from good governance; and good governance depends on how leaders strike a balance between private gains and public benefits to pursue their political careers.

The assumption that underlies the Mo Ibrahim Prize is that the fate of leaders once they are *out of office* is a key determinant of how they run their countries. The assumption runs as follows: When leaders face impoverishment and retribution once they are out of office, they would be doggedly determined to enrich themselves, squash any opposition, trample over any legal restraint in order to cling onto power. Power is their lifeline. When leaders can expect a safe retirement, however, they would take a different perspective on how to govern. In a recent interview with the *Financial Times*, Dr. Ibrahim explained that

African leaders [. . .] look to retirement as they would to the edge of a cliff, beyond which lies a dizzying fall towards retribution and relative poverty. "We don't have financial institutions for ex-presidents to go and run, or boards of great companies. There is life after office in other parts of the world. I just read that Tony Blair was paid half a million pounds to make a speech in China. People like Blair always have a place in society, they have secure financial futures," he says. Ibrahim believes he has created an attractive alternative to clinging on to power.[1]

In this book, we show that Dr. Ibrahim's intuition identified a fundamental factor that drives leaders' performance in office. Not just with respect to good governance, but also with respect to international conflict, leaders and their political incentives make a difference. We argue that the fate of leaders and the political processes of

[1] The interview was published on February 15, 2008 in the celebrated series *Lunch with the FT*, and is available at www.ft.com/cms/s/0/c6a7d87a-d93b-11dc-bd4d-0000779fd2ac.html. See also BBC News, June 3, 2005, "Is There Life after the Presidency?" http://news.bbc.co.uk/2/hi/africa/4607269.stm, which quotes the National Democratic Institute to say "many African presidents cling to power beyond constitutionality and democratically tolerable limits, in part because life after the presidency is seen to offer little in compensation to the riches, stature and security of being in power." In the feedback below the article, one respondent from Zimbabwe wrote: "Former presidents should be respected because of what they did for a country. However at the same time, when Mugabe becomes a former president, my views will change." Finally, Mengistu Haile Mariam, the former leader of Ethiopia, who was deposed in 1991 and fled to Zimbabwe, lamented to his interviewer: "African leaders are unlucky. There are very few who can live among their people after they lose power... I worked so hard, so tirelessly for Ethiopia. It grieves me that I cannot grow old on Ethiopian soil" (quoted in Baker (2004, 1492)).

leadership turnover shape leaders' decisions to initiate international conflict. We explain *why* and *when* political leaders decide to initiate international crises and wars. Our theory of conflict presents a new and, we believe, powerful way to look at the fundamental question of international relations: what are the causes of war and the conditions for peace? Our answer simply reformulates a famous dictum about war by the historian E. H. Carr (1946, 109): "War lurks in the background of international politics just as revolution lurks in the background of domestic politics," argued Carr. In our theory, war lurks in the background of international politics *because* revolution – a forcible or violent removal from office – lurks in the background of domestic politics. As the domestic political conditions that create stable and peaceful processes of leadership turnover improve, therefore, the scourge of war will also fade.

Our leader theory of international conflict sheds new light on the momentous finding of a small, but growing, group of scholars that has documented a profound transformation in the nature of war over the twentieth century and beyond. Mary Kaldor (1999), Robert Jervis (2002), Jeffrey Record (2002) and, above all, John Mueller (2004) have pointed out that modern war, the type of interstate war that developed from the Napoleonic revolution, has been in decline, a rarer and rarer occurrence, soon to become a relic of the past. Incredible though this claim might sound while the wars in Afghanistan and Iraq are raging, there has been a marked decline in the number of conflicts which we might legitimately call interstate wars. Instead, we have been experiencing, directly or indirectly, new forms of warfare, increasing instances of internationalized civil war, asymmetric warfare, or insurgent warfare where the boundaries between what is war and what is violent crime and terrorism are vanishing (Gleditsch *et al.*, 2002). These scholars argue that technological transformations, democratic institutions, the memories of the carnage of World War I, and new attitudes about violence in modern societies all contribute to make war between modern developed nations an anachronism. In their view, war can no longer serve as a viable mechanism to solve international disputes.

Our argument explains this empirical trend, while eschewing any teleological undertones that might creep into alternative explanations. We argue that the taming of political violence in leadership succession significantly contributes to the taming of international political violence. What remains of warfare when the risk of violent and forcible removal from office is reduced to nil is what modern, civilized, and decent societies have to do to police thugs and to protect their citizens and innocent populations from the violent actions of bandits, criminals, and brigands.

1.1 The central question

Now, as always, states fight wars. As one of the most destructive forms of human behavior, war and its study lie at the very heart of the discipline of international relations. It is not surprising, therefore, that much theoretical work has been done to explain the causes of war initiation. What is surprising, however, is the relative paucity of effort to understand and explain why and when leaders decide to engage their country in war. In theories that explain war as the result of impersonal forces such as capitalism, the offense–defense balance or multipolarity, leaders appear irrelevant. However, almost all wars begin because of conscious decisions by leaders. This book, therefore, seeks to answer the question: why and when do leaders go to war?

1.2 The central argument

Our answer starts from what is by now the conventional wisdom. The fundamental cause of international conflict is that the opposing parties have incompatible demands: each side demands more than the other side is willing to concede. From the perspective of the political leaders in charge of the conduct of foreign affairs, an explanation of international conflict thus requires an explanation of why and when leaders demand more than their opponent is willing to concede. We propose that a leader's international demands crucially depend on his calculations of the *private* costs and benefits of international conflict. Such private benefits can severely shrink or altogether eliminate any bargaining range created for unitary rational actors by the costs of war. This argument by itself is not new. A significant literature in international relations and comparative politics argues that leaders choose policy with an eye to one particular private benefit: their continued stay in office. Theories of diversionary war – which we discuss in detail in the next chapter – for example, argue that leaders seek to initiate international conflict when they face a high probability of losing office. We argue that such a focus on just the leader's tenure in office is too narrow. Our fundamental innovation is to argue that leaders consider a broader range of private costs and benefits. Specifically, leaders choose policy with an eye not only on the probability, but also the *manner* and *consequences* of losing office. For perhaps less than obvious reasons, the manner and consequences of losing office turn out to be closely related. Leaders who lose office as a result of a lost election, term limits or voluntary retirement – more broadly, in a regular manner – rarely suffer subsequent personal punishment. Leaders who lose office in a violent or forcible manner such as a coup or revolution, however, almost always suffer additional punishment in the form of exile, imprisonment or death.

Starting from this broader range of potential costs and benefits, we argue in Chapter 2 that leaders who anticipate a regular removal from office – e.g. term limits, elections, etc. – have little to gain and much to lose from international conflict. They have little to gain because even victory does not decrease their probability of a regular removal from office. They have much to lose because defeat increases the probability of a forcible removal from office, with all its unpleasant consequences. Leaders with a high risk of a regular removal from office, we argue, become *less* likely to initiate international conflict. In a nutshell, we identify a mechanism for peace: international *peace* obtains because of such leaders' domestic political insecurity.

In marked contrast, leaders who anticipate a forcible removal from office – e.g. a looming revolt, revolution or coup – have little to lose and much to gain from international conflict. The ability to choose the time, place, and circumstances of conflict initiation gives leaders a golden opportunity to neutralize dangerous rivals who threaten a revolt or coup. More importantly, with an already high risk of a forcible removal from office – with its unpleasant associated consequences – potential defeat is less of a deterrent for such leaders: their punishment is truncated. Leaders with a high risk of a forcible removal from office, therefore, become *more* likely to initiate international conflict. In a nutshell, we argue that such leaders are, literally, *fighting for survival*.

1.3 Leaders in the study of international politics

We next briefly describe the historical arc of research on leaders in international relations. Since Waltz (1954) introduced the three "images" of international relations, scholars have based their explanations of international relations in general and international conflict in particular on one of these three images or levels of analysis (Singer, 1961).[2] While scholars accept the usefulness of the three images to structure their research, at various times the field as a whole favored one image over the others. In the 1960s and 1970s, for example, following the path-breaking work of Snyder, Bruck and Sapin (1962), a majority of scholars in the field focused on individuals and leaders and their psychological attributes to explain international relations. (A decade earlier Leites (1951) blazed this trail with his work on the organizational code of the politburo.) The seminal work of Waltz (1979) forced a major shift in focus, as the field by and large switched its focus to the international system. The discovery of the 'democratic peace' in the late 1980s – early 1990s (Doyle, 1983a, b; Russett, 1993) brought another shift in focus, this time to the state and its attributes. In the wake of the rational choice revolution and its emphasis on methodological individualism, in the last five years scholars such as Bueno de Mesquita *et al.* (2003) have brought the field full circle by a renewed focus on the role of leaders. This time, however, the focus is not so much on the psychological attributes of leaders as on their incentive structures and institutional constraints.

In particular, Bueno de Mesquita *et al.* (ibid.) build a general theory of politics, the *selectorate theory*, that explains the balance between the production of public goods – policies that benefit everyone in a society such as civil freedoms, national security, and economic prosperity – and the production of private benefits for rulers and their supporters. They define the selectorate as the set of people who potentially have a say in the selection of leaders, while the winning coalition is the set of people whose support the leader needs to retain to remain in power. In their theory, the balance between the provision of public and private goods depends upon the size of the selectorate and the size of the winning coalition. Bueno de Mesquita *et al.* (ibid.) show that in societies where leaders are selected by large winning coalitions

[2] The first image proposes that the attributes of individuals are central to explanations of international relations; the second gives pride of place to the attributes of states; while the third seeks explanations for international relations in the attributes of the international system. Of course, other political scientists have proposed different levels of analysis. Wolfers (1962, 3–24) proposed two, Jervis (1976, 15) four, and Rosenau (1966) five levels of analysis.

with large selectorates, leaders find it more efficient to resort to the production of public goods rather than private benefits to remain in power. In a concise summary of their theory, Morrow *et al.* (2008, 394) claim that "Democratic politics in our theory is a competition in competence to produce public goods; autocratic politics centers on the purchase of the loyalty of key supporters."

Like Bueno de Mesquita *et al.* (2003), we too place leaders at the center of our analytical approach. As they do, we postulate that political leaders are the central node that mediates the political and military dynamics that underlie the threat and use of force in the international arena. In our theory, however, it is not just staying power *per se* that matters; it is the personal fate that leaders would envision for themselves when they are *out of office*. As a consequence, while recognizing that Bueno de Mesquita *et al.* (ibid.) offer a fundamental contribution to the study of politics, we do not privilege coalition building as the key explanatory factor of leaders' policy choices. Nor do we evaluate how specific personal characteristics of leaders, from their cognitive styles to their educational and military backgrounds, affect their decisions about war and peace (Hermann, 1977; Horowitz, McDermott and Stam, 2005).

Rather, we assess how leadership turnover, and what happens when the leaders no longer control the levers of power, shapes leaders' decisions about international conflict. Our theory cuts across the important comparison between the conflict patterns of democratic and non-democratic countries, the fundamental question in international relations theory in the last 20 years. We echo Samuel Huntington's famous opening statement in his celebrated treatise, *Political Order in Changing Societies*, in downplaying the importance of the form of government to understand politics. When it comes to decisions about international conflict, the most important political distinction among countries concerns how leaders are selected, replaced, and treated when in retirement.

1.3.1 Is *war costly* for leaders?

In our previous research on leaders and conflict, we established two empirical facts. First, we showed that leaders are more likely to initiate an international conflict when they face a low *overall* risk of losing office (Chiozza and Goemans, 2003). In other words, contrary to traditional theories of diversionary war, we showed that when leaders are more likely to lose office they become less likely to initiate international conflict.[3] Second, we showed that the assumption that war is *ex post* inefficient which underpins the foremost rational-choice explanation for war, the bargaining model of war, does not hold for leaders (Chiozza and Goemans, 2004b).

The assumption that war is *ex post* inefficient is incompatible with our claim that leaders can obtain private benefits from war. The assumption posits that "[a]s long as both sides suffer some costs for fighting, then war is always inefficient *ex post*" for rational unitary-actors (Fearon, 1995, 383). The assumption that war is *ex post* inefficient simply means that the "pie" at stake between two actors will be smaller after a war than before war, because war shrinks the available pie.[4] Hence *both* sides could gain if they could come to an agreement that would avoid such costs of war; there would be more pie to divide. Rational unitary actor explanations of war must then explain what impedes bargains that avoid the costs of war. Fearon (ibid., 381) proposed that three – and only three – mechanisms could form the basis for rational explanations for conflict between *unitary* rational actors. Private information (and incentives to misrepresent such information), commitment problems, and issue indivisibilities explain why unitary rational actors sometimes end up in *ex post* inefficient conflict.[5]

We posit that even though their country-as-a-whole will surely suffer as a result of war, under certain circumstances war may pay for leaders. Fearon (ibid., 379, fn. 1) explicitly recognized this could form the basis of alternative mechanisms to explain war, but did not explore this possibility.[6] To explore the potential of this approach, we assessed

---

[3] In our previous research (Chiozza and Goemans, 2003) we deliberately considered only the overall probability of losing office, and did not distinguish between the probability of a regular and the probability of a forcible removal from office.

[4] The intuition is powerful: of course war destroys lives, industries, productive capacity. However, as Burk (1982) and others have shown, sometimes war provides a boost to the domestic economy that could not be achieved by any other means.

[5] Powell (2006) shows that issue indivisibilities reduce to commitment problems.

[6] As we will briefly discuss in Chapter 6, in almost all the unitary rational-actor explanations of war, it is unclear what the potential benefits of war could be, except "more is better." This omission has important implications for future research.

whether Fearon's crucial assumption that war is costly also applies to contending leaders (Chiozza and Goemans, 2004b). If war is costly also for leaders, we are back to Fearon's basic explanations. If, however, war is not necessarily *ex post* inefficient for dueling leaders, then there exists room for new leader-level explanations for war.

To that end, in our 2004 article we examined whether contending leaders are worse off after fighting a war than they would otherwise be after fighting a crisis or staying out of conflict altogether. Under the war-is-costly assumption, the tenure-pie to be divided among the opposing leaders must be strictly smaller after war than after a crisis that did not escalate to war. Operationally, the hazard of losing office for winners and losers in wars must be higher than the hazard of losing office for winners and losers in crises and than that of leaders who remained at peace. War would not be negative-sum, for example, if leaders did not face a higher hazard after a draw – which by definition includes both sides – in a war than after a draw in a crisis. When we tested the empirical record about how international conflict affected leaders' hold on power, we found that leaders' tenure prospects were not systematically shortened by international conflict. Moreover, we found that wars are not more politically harmful to leaders than are crises short of war. In other words, war does not seem to necessarily be *ex post* inefficient for leaders. If leaders do not necessarily stand to suffer political consequences from conflict, therefore, a leader perspective on conflict potentially covers a larger spectrum of mechanisms than those built on private information and incentives to misrepresent or commitment problems (Fearon, 1995; Powell, 2006).

We do not seek to supplant rational unitary actor explanations for war, rather, we aim to offer additional rational explanations. Specifically, we argue that leaders sometimes go to war because they can obtain private benefits from international conflict. In Chapter 2, we explain what leaders have to gain and what they have to lose from international conflict. More precisely, we show that there exists a class of political leaders, those who are at risk of being forcibly removed from power, that might use international conflict as their last gamble to save their personal survival. These leaders *fight for survival.*

The mechanisms that explain war in the bargaining model of war continue to be operative. More transparency, more reliable information, and greater role of third parties certainly help reduce the risk of war (Walter, 2002). These mechanisms, however, need to be complemented. For some leaders, only conflict can interrupt the political dynamics that might lead to their forcible or violent removal. When the noose of the executioner is getting closer, international conflict is a more palatable alternative. We illustrate this theoretical claim empirically in Chapters 3, 4, and 5.

In the next chapter, we develop our theory and discuss in detail the most prominent competing leader-level theory, the theory of diversionary war. In Chapters 3 and 4 we test our theory with the help of *Archigos*, our new data set on leaders.[7] In Chapter 3 we examine first whether international conflict indeed does bestow private costs and benefits on leaders. To that end we assess how international conflict affected the hazard and manner of losing office for the leaders in our sample between 1919 and 2003. In Chapter 4 we test our central claim that as the risk of a forcible removal from office increases, so does the probability of conflict initiation. Although Chapters 3 and 4 use some fairly advanced statistical models, we have made an effort to ensure that our arguments and exposition is not cluttered by unnecessary technical details and jargon. For maximum readability we have moved the technical discussions to several appendices, available on the web at the addresses listed on p. xi. In Chapter 5 we leave the data behind to present a detailed historical examination of Central American leaders between 1840 and 1918. We focus on Central America in order to examine the behavior of leaders who face a high risk of a forcible removal from office to trace our causal mechanism up close. *Archigos* indicates that Haiti and the Dominican Republic and the five states of Central America experienced the most forcible removals from office between 1875 and 1919. We examine Central America rather than Hispaniola because the historiography on the latter region before the nineteenth century is very meagre indeed. The history of Central America between 1875 and 1919 displays a striking pattern, whereby a change in the regional ideological balance of power increased the risk of a leader's forcible removal from office. As a result, such leaders repeatedly invaded their neighbors and went to war. We sum up our conclusions and review the explanatory power of our leader-level approach in Chapter 6.

---

[7] We very briefly describe the data in Appendix A. We earlier introduced the data set to the academic community in Goemans, Gleditsch and Chiozza (2009).

1.4 Conclusions

With our new theoretical and empirical focus on leaders, we aim to open up new avenues of research on international conflict. Leader-level theories not only can offer new, but also more powerful explanations for international conflict than state- or system-level theories of war (see Chapter 6). Above all, however, we favor a focus on leaders, because this approach highlights the political nature of the choice between war and peace.

2 | *Why and when do leaders fight?*

The decisive means for politics is violence.... Anyone who fails to see this is, indeed, a political infant.

Max Weber

In this chapter we present a new theory which explains why and when leaders seek or avoid international conflict. In our theory, the strategic interaction that leads to or away from war is to be found at the domestic, rather than the international level. To provide the reader a roadmap of the first half of this chapter, we briefly sketch the main logic of our theory. We begin generically with a leader and an opposition locked in a competition over power and policy. An exogenous shock (temporarily) changes the domestic balance of forces in favor of the leader's political opposition. Leaders who worry mainly about a regular, peaceful, removal from office are willing and able to make credible political concessions to the opposition because they can reasonably assume a safe retirement and even the possibility of returning to office. For such leaders, an increase in the risk of a regular removal from office makes them less likely to initiate international conflict. Those leaders who must worry about a *forcible* removal from office, unfortunately, cannot credibly commit to concessions. Because concessions that weaken their power increase their risk of a forcible removal from office and subsequent personal punishment, such leaders have incentives to try to take back any concessions they made once the tide swings back in their favor. In turn, the opposition has every incentive to capitalize on its (temporary) advantage and try to overthrow the leader. Leaders then can use international conflict as a means to fight against their domestic opposition – for example, if rebels concentrate forces across the border[1] – or to seek gains from conflict that can

---

[1] As Grégoire noted in 1791, spreading the French Revolution might be necessary to protect it from its opponents: "When my neighbor keeps a nest of vipers, I

be used to bolster their domestic position. A (temporary) shock and increase in the risk of a forcible removal from office therefore increases the probability of international conflict.

In the second part of this chapter we discuss the most prominent current competing leader-central theories of international conflict, collectively known as the theory of diversionary war. As we will show, the singular "theory" is inappropriate, because the various existing versions of diversionary war each articulate a different logic. Although different versions suggest different mechanisms, we show they share common flaws: they fail to convincingly explain why and when international conflict benefits leaders, and fail to consider the full range of potential costs of international conflict.

Our main theoretical innovation is twofold. First, we argue that leaders care not just about the probability, but also the manner and associated consequences of losing office. This allows us, second, to distinguish two distinct political processes whereby leaders lose office. In the first, leaders lose office through peaceful, regular processes and can look forward to peaceful, perhaps prosperous, retirement. In the second, leaders lose office through the threat or use of force and must fear for their personal safety afterwards. Whether a leader is likely to find himself removed by the first or the second process fundamentally affects the choice for or against international conflict. Since these two processes are fundamental for our theory, we first elaborate our logic on the processes whereby leaders lose office.

2.1 How leaders are removed from office

In his classic article on rationalist explanations for war between *unitary* actors, James Fearon (1995, 379, fn. 1) notes in passing that "war may be rational for ... leaders if they will enjoy various benefits of war without suffering costs imposed on the population." It is on these *private* benefits and costs of war that we focus. A leader's private costs and benefits are not limited to his time in office. Instead, leaders consider not just the probability, but also the *manner* and *consequences* of losing power (Goemans, 2000b, 37). The potential private costs of international conflict thus are not limited to just the loss of office.

have the right to smother them lest I become their victim" (quoted in Walt (1997, 79)).

Leaders can lose office in a variety of ways – e.g. in a regular and peaceful or an irregular and potentially violent manner – and the manner in which they lose office is significantly associated with their subsequent fate. Some leaders can look forward to a profitable retirement. For example, in their tax filings for the 2008 presidential campaign, the Clintons revealed they had made over $109 million since leaving office in 2001.[2] Other leaders must deal with a very real threat of exile, imprisonment or even death after they are removed from office. Saddam Hussein, for one, seems to have been well aware that nothing good awaited him once he lost power. In their policy decisions, we argue, leaders take these potential private benefits and costs into account.

Our recognition that leaders can lose office through *two* distinct processes allows us to explain and improve upon the poor empirical record of diversionary wars.[3] As noted above, we propose that leaders can lose office as the result of a *"regular"* process involving their country's established norms, procedures, and institutions. Removal in a regular manner is thus typified by defeat in elections, voluntary retirement, and term limits. Alternatively, leaders can lose office through the threat or use of force by what we call an *"irregular"* or *"forcible"* process. This second process typically culminates in coups, insurrections, and revolutions.[4]

The distinction between these two processes in itself is not new; indeed, it constitutes a cornerstone in research about regime type in comparative politics. Thus Popper (1963, 124) claims:

---

[2] *The New York Times*, April 5, 2008, "Clintons Made $109 Million in Last 8 Years." As President George W. Bush put it when asked about his plans after he leaves the White House, "I'll give some speeches, just to replenish the ol' coffers." ("In Book, Bush Peeks Ahead To His Legacy," *The New York Times*, September 2, 2007, p. 1.) For a broader discussion of the prospect of retiring leaders, see "Into the sunset. How ex-leaders adjust to life with less power." *Financial Times*, Thursday, December 27, 2007, p. 7.

[3] The failure to disaggregate the different ways leaders lose office implicitly assumes that voluntary retirements, term limits, the natural death of leaders, coups, and revolutions and foreign interventions to overthrow the leader all result from effactually similar political processes. In other words, a policy choice such as international conflict initiation has the same effect on the probability of voluntary retirement, the probability of losing office as a result of term limits or illness, the probability of a coup or a revolution, and the probability of removal as the result of a foreign invasion.

[4] For a fascinating and insightful discussion of the tactics of coups, see Farcau (1994).

we may distinguish two main types of government. The first type consists of governments of which we can get rid without bloodshed – for example, by way of general elections; that is to say, the social institutions provide means by which the rulers may be dismissed by the ruled, and the social traditions ensure that these institutions will not easily be destroyed by those who are in power. The second type consists of governments which the ruled cannot get rid of except by way of a successful revolution – that is to say, in most cases, not at all. I suggest the term "democracy" as a short-hand label for a government of the first type, and the term "tyranny" or "dictatorship" for the second.

More recently, Przeworski *et al.* (2000, 15) very similarly distinguish between democracy and dictatorship by differentiating between

(1) regimes that allow some, even if limited, regularized competition among conflicting visions and interests; and
(2) regimes in which some values or interests enjoy a monopoly buttressed by the threat or the actual use of force.

The limited, regularized competition of Przeworski *et al.* (ibid.) corresponds to our regular process. The removal of leaders of regimes who rely on the "threat or actual use of force" typically requires the threat or actual use of force by either domestic or foreign opponents, and therefore corresponds to our second, forcible, process.

The difference between these two processes, according to Riker (1982, 6–7, emphasis added), stems from the presence or absence of institutions to protect politicians and leaders after they lose office:

Almost everything... that we think of as civil liberties (the rights of a speedy trial, habeas corpus, and security against unreasonable search and seizure, for example) originated to *protect politicians who feared prosecution if and when they lost office.* Thus the historic purpose of these fundamental democratic liberties has been not to provide freedom as an end in itself, but to render effective both political participation and the process of choice in voting.

Leaders of countries which do not rely on such well-established norms, rules, and procedures lack institutional protections and shields after they lose office against subsequent, sometimes severe, punishment. Riker's argument thus suggests a close institutional link between the manner and consequences of losing office. Leaders lose office in a regular manner because they can afford to. Leaders lose office in an irregular manner, because holding on to power provides their only protection against potential punishment; the only way to remove them from office is by the use or threat of force.

We have gone into some detail about these two processes because they fundamentally structure a leader's incentive for or against war. In contrast to the earlier literature in comparative politics and the currently dominant approach in international relations, we do not rely on regime type as an indicator of the regular and irregular removal from office, but model these processes directly. This strategy has several important advantages. First, by focusing on these two fundamental processes *directly*, we isolate their effects and do not conflate them with other potentially important institutional factors of different regimes which could affect international conflict in different, potentially offsetting ways. Second, our focus on the two fundamental processes allows us to empirically examine any residual effects of regime type on war, whereby other institutional factors could potentially systematically affect international conflict.

In the next section we provide some basic rationalist underpinnings to explain the domestic use of force, as in failed or successful attempts to forcibly remove a leader. A better understanding of the causes of attempts to forcibly remove a leader enables us to explain why and when international conflict can mitigate those dangers.

2.1.1 Explaining the forcible removal from office

The threat or use of force to remove a leader raises the *ex post* inefficiency puzzle discussed in Chapter 1, but places it in the context of domestic politics. If both the leader and the opposition seek to control their country's resources, why would they use force if violence decreases a country's total resources? In other words, what prevents a deal which avoids the costs of the use of force? Not surprisingly, Fearon (2004, 289–90) argues there basically exist two rationalist explanations of insurgencies, revolts and coups: (1) private information and incentives to misrepresent and (2) commitment problems. We agree with Fearon that commitment problems constitute powerful explanations for coups, insurgencies, and revolts.[5]

---

[5] Fearon (2004, 290) finds private information-based explanations less convincing, as do we. It is unclear, moreover, how international conflict would reveal the relative strength of the leader versus coup plotters. See also Acemoglu and Robinson (2000, 2001, 2006); Fearon (2004); Powell (2006).

Fearon (ibid., 290) succinctly describes how a commitment problem might produce civil conflict:

a temporary shock to government capabilities or legitimacy gives coup plotters or rebels a window of opportunity. During such moments, the ruler might want to commit to paying the junior officers more, or giving more autonomy to a region, but such commitments are rendered incredible by the knowledge that the shock is temporary.

Coup plotters or rebels will therefore try to lock in and extend their temporary advantage by fighting and taking over the government.[6] (See Fearon (ibid.) for a formal model along these lines.) A strength of Fearon's argument is that it encompasses a variety of empirical pathways that trigger the commitment problem and thus domestic conflict. As a result, his model does a good job explaining the civil wars in his sample.

However, and as should be obvious, temporary shocks in the domestic balance of power – as in mid-term elections – by no means always or even most of the time trigger such pernicious commitment problems. Temporary shocks are common, but coups, civil wars, and revolutions are not. Leaders who worry only about a regular removal from office can accede to demands of the opposition for more power or for policy concessions, because they can expect to regain power and pursue policy priorities of their own if and when the tide swings back in their favor. Coups, civil wars, and revolutions are unlikely in such systems, because the opposition does not face strong incentives to take advantage of any temporary power-swing in their favor. After all, if leaders lose office through a regular process, the opposition also has the same regular process as a way to gain power. Thus, the opposition can reasonably anticipate they will be winners in the future, as a result of the next election or other regular transfers of power (Przeworski, 1991). The combination of the costs of domestic violence with the reasonable chance of gaining power in the foreseeable future makes the opposition in systems characterized by regular removals from office relatively unwilling to use force to gain power. In contrast, in systems

---

[6] Note that the logic of this commitment problem suggests an additional reason to punish such leaders after they lose office. In the formal literature, commitment problems are typically solved by "extermination" of one side. Simply put, when one player is removed from the game, there is no more commitment problem. Even out of office, a surviving leader might regain his strength and present the new leader with the same commitment problem.

where leaders typically lose office by the use of force, the opposition can anticipate the leader will try to stay in office as long as he can, if only to avoid personal punishment.[7] Cut off from any other reasonable prospects of gaining power, the opposition has incentives to make the most of any significant temporary advantage and launch a coup attempt, insurgency or civil war. Thus, countries which lack the institutions and safeguards to credibly protect leaders after they lose office will easily be caught in "coup-traps" where one leader after another loses office through forcible means.

In the next section we explain what leaders who fear a forcible removal from office have to gain from international conflict, and what leaders who need worry only about a regular removal from office have to lose from international conflict.

2.1.2 Fighting and gambling for survival

We argued above that in countries that lack institutional protections for their former leaders, a temporary shock in the leader's capabilities or legitimacy creates a commitment problem which increases his risk of a forcible removal from office. International conflict can "solve" this commitment problem in two basic ways. First, in the formal literature, commitment problems are almost always "solved" by the elimination of one player (Fearon, 2004; Powell, 2006). If one player is removed from the game, by definition the commitment problem goes away. International conflict can solve the problem in this way if it increases the probability the leader (completely) defeats his *domestic* opponents. Second, the commitment problem would be solved if its cause, a temporary shock in favor of the opposition, can be quickly reversed. International conflict can reverse the temporary shock because victory can quickly bring the leader increased legitimacy and capabilities.[8] We explain and explore these solutions in more detail below.

---

[7] Note that the opposition might also be concerned by any former leader's future attempt to regain power. Since it is difficult for any such leader to credibly commit not to return to office, the opposition can perhaps most easily solve this commitment problem by eliminating the former leader altogether.

[8] Simply put, we argue that leaders rationally go to war when war pays. This innocuous, perhaps obvious claim, nevertheless highlights more than one fundamental confusion in the field. Recent research, particularly on the democratic peace, misinterprets the finding that democratic leaders are overall more likely to lose office (Bueno de Mesquita, Siverson and Woller, 1992;

International conflict can increase a leader's probability of victory against his *domestic* opponents in at least two ways.[9] First, simply sending soldiers to fight can increase a leader's chances against his opponents. We refer to this as *fighting for survival*. Second, victory in international conflict increases the leader's legitimacy and capabilities and thereby both increases the probability of victory against his domestic opponents and addresses the shock that produced the commitment problem in the first place. Because conflict initiation increases the probability of victory (Bueno de Mesquita, Siverson and Woller, 1992), leaders who seek to lower their risk of a forcible removal this way have incentives to initiate conflict. We refer to this as *gambling for survival*. We first explain how simply sending troops to fight in an international conflict can improve a leader's chances against his domestic opponents.[10]

The ability of Challengers – leaders who initiated the conflict – to pick the time and place of their conflict can help to significantly

Chiozza and Goemans, 2004b) to mean that democratic leaders are also more likely to lose office as a result of international conflict (Debs and Goemans, 2010). In other words, scholars tend to confuse the unconditional probability of losing office and the probability of losing office *conditional* on (the outcome of) a conflict. As we will briefly elaborate in the conclusion, it surely does not come as a surprise that leaders go to war when we include "war" as a positive contribution in their utility function. However, other explanations often leave completely unexplored why war pays.

[9] It is important to again stress that our focus here is on probability of success of attempts to irregularly remove the leader *conditional on the outcome of conflict*. The overall – unconditional – potential benefits of overthrowing the leader center around direct control over policy-making, which produces better protection of the military's (corporate) interests, the interests of allied elites, and the satisfaction of personal ambitions (O'Kane, 1983, 1993; Londregan and Poole, 1990; Belkin and Schofer, 2003, 2005; Acemoglu and Robinson, 2006). The overall potential costs include an increased probability of the loss of one's job, freedom or life, and an increased probability of civil war.

[10] We mention in passing a common practice of the late Middle Ages: to send troops abroad in order to have them live off their neighbor's land and save the costs of maintaining the troops, and the dangers of having them stationed back home. Thus, for example, in late 1791 the minister of finance of the French National Assembly wrote: "We must maintain a state of war; the return of our soldiers would increase the disorder everywhere and ruin us." In turn, Roland noted, "It is necessary to march the thousands of men whom we have under arms as far away as their legs will carry them, or else they will come back and cut our throats" (both quoted in Walt (1997, 82, fn. 114, see also 111)). This practice seems to have died out after the French Revolution.

decrease the probability of a forcible removal from office. The initiation of or participation in international conflict can provide leaders with unique opportunities to deal with the actors most likely to remove them forcibly from office: rebels and potential coup plotters. Examples where the explicit goal of international conflict was to deal with domestic rebels abound in history (see Walt (1997) and Chapter 6). At the end of December 1791, when France began to prepare for war with Austria, Hérault de Séchelles sums up the logic particularly succinctly:

[I]n time of war measures can be taken that would appear too stern in time of peace. War will justify all your steps; for, in brief, it is at home that war must be made on rebels before it is carried abroad.

(quoted in Clapham (1899, 136); see also Walt (1997, 65–8))

To deal with potential coup plotters in the military, the leader can send them to the front to fight and die for the country. In *The Sign of the Broken Sword*, G.K. Chesterton neatly encapsulates one way how picking an international conflict offers leaders an opportunity to get rid of potential opponents. In the short story, Father Brown asks Flambeau:

"Where would a wise man hide a leaf? In the forest." The other did not answer. "If there were no forest, he would make a forest. And if he wished to hide a dead leaf, he would make a dead forest." There was still no reply, and the priest added still more mildly and quietly: "And if a man had to hide a dead body, he would make a field of dead bodies to hide it in."

Lest this sounds far-fetched, an historical example makes the point. Following the ancient example of King David and Uriah the Hittite,[11] Idi Amin, the leader of Uganda, apparently used the same strategy to eliminate opposition from within the armed forces. In 1977 Great Britain broke off diplomatic relations and together with the United

---

[11] The bible, 2 Samuel 11, tells the story of King David, Bathsheba, and Uriah. David seduced and impregnated Bathsheba, the wife of Uriah the Hittite. Uriah was a prominent military officer who could thus pose a threat to David. To deal with this threat, David sent Uriah to the front at Rabbah and instructed his commander, Joab: "Put Uriah in the front line where the fighting is fiercest. Then withdraw from him so he will be struck down and die" (Barker, 1995, 433–4). David's plan worked, Uriah was killed in the battle and David took Bathsheba for his wife. Undoubtedly, Chesterton was well aware of the story of Uriah the Hittite.

States, imposed harsh economic sanctions on Idi Amin's Uganda. These dramatically worsened an already faltering economy and, worsening his ability to buy off his core supporters in the military, created unrest among those (former) supporters (Omara-Otunnu, 1987, 139–41). Determined to maintain control, Amin began to purge his inner circle, most prominently his long-time second in command, Vice-President and Commander of the Armed Forces, General Idris Mustafa Adrisi (Smith, 1980, 176–8; Avirgan and Honey, 1982, 48–51). After Adrisi suffered a highly suspicious car accident, his supporters in the army, particularly the crack Simba (Lion) Regiment, and the Chui (Leopard) Regiment, began an open revolt. While the revolt was brutally suppressed, survivors fled across the border into Tanzania (ibid., 178). The 1978 war between Uganda and Tanzania started when Amin sent his soldiers in pursuit of the rebels. Contemporaries agree that Amin's primary goal of the invasion was to deal with a threat from his *own* military forces. Milton Obote, the former president of Uganda, in exile in Tanzania, put it bluntly at the time: the invasion "was a desperate measure to extricate Amin from the consequences of the failure of his *own* plots against his *own* army" (quoted in Avirgan and Honey (1982, 52), emphases in original). By going after some of his remaining core supporters, Amin risked antagonizing the very forces underpinning his brutal regime. Thus, he tried to blame the Tanzanian forces for the executions of rebels from the Simba Regiment. After the Tanzanian forces recaptured the Kagera Salient, they found "[s]cattered in the bush . . . the bodies of 120 Ugandan soldiers. There had been no Tanzanian troops in the area before, and there was no sign that Tanzanian artillery had landed there" (ibid., 69). The conclusion was inescapable: "The Tanzanian commanders deduced the corpses had been dumped to look as if they were battle fatalities, although they were actually executed mutineers" (Kamau and Cameron, 1979, 306).

Conflict can also allow leaders to undermine potential rivals and the sources of their power in more subtle ways. Gordon Tullock (1987, 29) offers a particularly striking example how Mao used the Korean War to deal with domestic military rivals:

When Mao Tse-Tung seized control of China, he actually was the head of an organization in which there were in essence 5 armies all of which had been built up by one leader from practically nothing and which were to a considerable extent loyal to that leader. Mao may have been able to deal with this by ordinary methods, but the Korean War gave him a wonderful opportunity. He in essence drafted from each of these armies specific units to send to the Korean War. These units were then rotated back to China on a regular basis, but were not returned to their original army. As a result at the end of the Korean War the 5 major armies had melded into one. Mao was then able to remove the four most important generals from their positions of personal power.

The examples above seem to raise a question: why would military leaders who plan to overthrow the leader obey orders to go to the front and thus have their coup plans foiled? First, a failure to obey orders immediately identifies these officers as committed plotters. Once positively identified, they can relatively easily be isolated and rendered harmless. Second, their unique position makes it extremely difficult for military leaders and soldiers alike to disobey orders to deploy. Military leaders would lose their legitimacy if, called upon, they would forego their duty. As a result, potential coup plotters are caught in a Catch-22 situation. Obey orders, and a coup or rebellion becomes much more difficult, if not impossible, to stage. Once at the front, after all, military leaders have other pressing and immediate concerns. Do not obey orders and identify yourself as a committed plotter and, moreover, lose legitimacy.[12]

The mere act of sending troops to fight, and initiating a conflict can also boost a leader's legitimacy if his initial reluctance to do so undermined his legitimacy and increased the probability of a revolt. An example along these lines stems from the War of the Pacific 1879–84,

---

[12] Schroeder (1994, 177–9) describes how the Directorate's fears about Napoleon's ambitions and potential plans for a military takeover created such a Catch-22 situation, which led to Napoleon's invasion of Egypt in 1798:

> Following the collapse of the peace talks at Lille, the Directors, particularly Reubell, again took up the idea of a cross-Channel invasion. . . . But Bonaparte, given command of the proposed invasion force, soon decided that he would not sacrifice his popularity in this hopeless enterprise. With invasion infeasible and revolutionary subversion and raids on British commerce clearly inadequate, the idea of undermining Britain's will and capacity to fight by seizing Egypt and threatening the route to India seemed more attractive. Other purposes, however, were at least as important. The Directors wanted Bonaparte out of France, while Bonaparte was eager for action and hoped to see the government decay further in his absence.

The example also highlights how confident military leaders might gain added prestige and power from success, and thereby turn the tables.

between Chile, Peru, and Bolivia. Prominent Chileans (Subercaseaux, 1936, Ch. XXXVI, 369), Chilean newspapers (Sater, 1986, 9–10), and international diplomats warned of an insurrection or coup if Chilean President Anibal Pinto failed to take military action against Bolivia, and Pinto himself was well aware of the dangers (Pinto, 1921; 1922, 362, entry of April 1879). As the Bolivian envoy, José Antonio de Lavalle (1979, 62) wrote in his memoirs, "it was impossible, completely impossible [for Chilean President Pinto], to arrive at a peaceful solution, although Pinto's government would have been disposed to go to any lengths to avoid this end. However, if [the dispute] had been resolved peacefully, Pinto would have been violently overthrown and the war would still have taken place." In his book on the War of the Pacific, the historian William Sater (1986, 15–16) concurs, "Aware of Lima's activities, the war party so inflamed the public that Pinto had little choice . . . [T]he president faced two options: either enforce Chile's treaty obligations or be overthrown."[13] To be sure, defeat in this war would not have boded well, but Pinto's immediate concern was an impending revolt that could only be forestalled by going to war.

Domestic pressures for war played a similar role in the Yom Kippur War of 1973. Five years after the Six Day War, Sadat had not made good on any promises to reverse its outcome, and the army continued to grow each year as general mobilization remained in place. The enormous demands on "Egypt's economic and human resources [created] increasing internal pressure with every day that passed" (El-Gamasy, 1993, 175) (see also Rubinstein (1977, 215–18, 223, 282–3)). Sadat knew "that his popularity was at stake, [and as a result he] made a series of statements with which he tried to reassure the people that the decision for war was beyond question or discussion" (El-Gamasy, 1993, 140–1). On September 30, 1973, Sadat addressed the National Defense Council with a stark warning:

Each of you has had his say. Fine, I now want to tell you that our economy today is at zero and we have commitments till the end of the year which we will not be able to fulfill with the banks. When 1974 arrives in two

---

[13] This example is invoked by Mansfield and Snyder (2005) as an example of diversionary war because of impending elections. It is important to note, however, that these were congressional elections; presidential elections were two years away.

months time, we won't have a loaf of bread for our people. And I can't ask any Arab for a single dollar because the Arabs tell us that they are paying compensation for [lost] Suez canal revenues and that's enough. If there's no war, there's nothing.

(Sadat quoted in ibid., 186)

Even the Israelis apparently recognized the domestic pressures on Sadat. Israeli head of military intelligence, General Eliahu Za'ira, told the chiefs of staff that "the possibility exists that Egypt and Syria might carry out a military operation as a palliative to distract attention away from poor domestic political conditions in both countries or as a spectacle for local public consumption" (quoted in ibid., 190).[14]

Sending troops across the border can decrease a leader's probability of forcible removal from office in yet another way. An invasion across the border increases the probability of decisively defeating domestic rebels. Invading troops can pre-empt or disrupt an invasion of exiles who organized in safety across the border (see Chapter 5). Similarly, troops in pursuit of fleeing rebels can cross the border and invade another country to deal the rebels a final, decisive, defeat. In a revealing interview, Amin claimed that the 1978 war between Uganda and Tanzania alluded to above was the result of his attempt to deal with rebels across the border: "It was not Uganda's intention to invade Tanzania, we took it merely as a precautionary measure to prevent exiles from infiltrating into Uganda" (cited in Kamau and Cameron (1979, 304)). In passing, Kamau and Cameron (ibid., 301) note that the invasion of Tanzania would lower Amin's risk of a forcible removal also because he apparently hoped that the opportunity to plunder would at least temporarily buy off any rebellious soldiers: "Capture of the Kagera Salient would preempt the return of rebels and exiles – and with trade sanctions against Uganda beginning to bite, it would provide his soldiers with a chance of easy plunder." In a more recent example, exiled Hutu militants and the Banjamulenge threatened the stability of Paul Kagame's Rwandan regime, and to deal with that

---

[14] Anecdotal evidence suggests that personal survival motives of Nasser also lay at the root of the Six Day War. Major-General Indar Jit Rikhye, the commander of the UN peacekeeping forces in the Sinai, maintains that fear of a coup by the military, and especially General Hakim Amer, convinced Nasser to stand firm and (prepare to) attack Israel in 1967 (WGBH, 2007) (see also Rikhye (1978, 167–8), Thant (1978, 482), and Mor (1991, 361, 368–9), El-Gamasy (1993, 84–5), James (2005, 33)).

threat Rwanda invaded the Congo. We believe that "international" conflicts of this sort are fairly common. Recent research by Gleditsch, Salehyan and Schultz (2008) found that among countries involved in a civil war between 1946 to 2001, about 22 percent of all their MID initiations were the result of such externalizations of domestic conflict.

These examples show not only that conflict initiation and participation can improve a leader's chances against his domestic opposition and thus decrease the probability of a forcible removal from office. They have another striking feature in common. Although the leader initiates an *international* conflict, the enemy is domestic in character. More importantly, *defeat of the international opponents is not required to lower the risk of a forcible removal from office.* To be sure, the international opponent may fight back, and even stage a counter-invasion, and thus the initial attack can backfire. But the intended enemy is a domestic faction. Rightly in our opinion, such behavior does count as international conflict.[15] This surprising feature, whereby "international" conflict may not be aimed at the defeat of an international opponent, distinguishes our *fighting for survival* explanation of international conflict from earlier explanations.

We now turn to discuss how victory against the *international* opponent can increase a leader's probability of victory against his domestic opponents and reverse the temporary shock that produced a commitment problem. Victory in an international conflict can bring leaders the increased prestige, legitimacy, capabilities, and resources to either reverse the temporary shock which introduced the commitment problem or increase the leader's chances against his domestic opponents. Moreover, if coups are caused by a "tipping" process (Fearon, 2004), victory decreases the probability of a coup, because victory inhibits attempts to coordinate to remove the leader (Kuran, 1991; Goemans, 2000b). Because of the leader's demonstrated success and increased legitimacy, fewer people will believe that a sufficient number of others will join in the coup to make it successful. This belief, in turn, makes a coup both more costly and less likely to succeed. Finally, leaders who seek to obtain the benefits of victory have incentives to initiate

---

[15] Our focus here is on the initiation of conflict. It might be argued that targets not only lack the advantages of initiators outlined above, but that they suffer through an indirect pathway, whereby being a target increases the risk of defeat and, as a result, the risk of a forcible removal from office.

conflict not just in the hope of obtaining the benefits of victory, but additionally because the opportunity to pick the time and place of conflict increases the probability of victory (Reiter and Stam, 1998).

Levy and Vakili (1992) show how a (temporary?) domestic political shock against the Argentine Navy led to the 1982 Falklands War against Great Britain. The Argentine Navy apparently thought they could halt the slide in their domestic power, and perhaps even improve their domestic political position by attacking the Falklands. Levy and Vakili (1992, 131, 133–4) persuasively argue how intra-military conflict – particularly among the army and air force on one side and the navy on the other – forced Galtieri's hand in the Malvinas/Falklands War of 1982. (See also Makin (1985, 145), *Los Angeles Times*, May 9, 1982, pp. A1, A5: "Argentina's Tough Stance Laid to Navy" and in particular, *Los Angeles Times*, May 16, 1982, pp. G1–G2: "About the Politics of Personality".)

Though the recovery of the islands would bring prestige to the military as a whole, the navy had a particular interest in the Malvinas operation. Successful invasion would not only extend their power into the South Atlantic, but also give them a disproportionate share of the glory on the basis of their primary operational responsibility for the military operation. This would be an opportunity to increase their influence within the military and perhaps even replace the army as the traditionally dominant service, at a time when the priority given to the internal war against subversion had diminished the navy's role.[16]

Saddam Hussein's personal survival played a crucial role in his wars against Iran in 1980 and against Kuwait in 1991 (and arguably also against the United States in 2003). Relatively fresh to the presidency, in 1980, Saddam Hussein worried about the threats to his survival after the Iranian Revolution and increased Shi'a restiveness in Iraq.[17]

---

[16] Other sources also indicate the military were worried about a return to civilian rule and the possibility of investigations into those responsible for the disappearances of dissidents under their brutal rule. Victory, they hoped, would silence such calls for justice and revenge. See *The Washington Post*, January 28, 1982, pp. A1, A18: "'The Final Stage'," *The Washington Post*, February 12, 1982, pp. A33–A34: "Catholic Church, in New Stance, Criticizes Government," *Los Angeles Times*, April 25, 1982, p. F1: "Argentina's Military May Well Have Made Its Fatal Mistake."

[17] Freedman and Karsh (1993, 29) note that: "Saddam had a paranoiac obsession with personal and political survival, . . . He had never lost sight of his

Khomeini declared that "the people and Army of Iraq must turn their back on the Baath regime and overthrow it" (quoted in Walt (1997, 239)). A failed Iranian-sponsored assassination attempt on Tariq Aziz (Iraq's Deputy Prime Minister) led Saddam to clamp down hard on the Iraqi Shi'a minority. Freedman and Karsh (1993, 20, see also 19) argue that:

As these measures failed Saddam invaded Iran, as a pre-emptive strike to shore up his personal rule. He apparently believed that a limited campaign would suffice to convince the revolutionary regime in Tehran to desist from its attempts to overthrow him, and did not intend to engage in a prolonged drawn-out conflict. If he entertained aspirations beyond the containment of the Iranian danger – as he may have done – they were not the reasons for launching the war but were incidental.

Although Saddam survived, "the protracted war against Iran had somewhat loosed Saddam's grip over the officer corps, the main potential threat to his personal rule" (ibid., 29). From November 1988 on, he faced several attempts on his life, most worrisomely in January 1990, when "he narrowly escaped an assassination attempt by army officers while he was riding in his car through Baghdad" (ibid., 19–20). Strikingly, Saddam Hussein himself acknowledged he was *fighting for survival* in 1990. As reported in *The New York Times*, "Mr. Hussein told his interrogator on one occasion that a principal reason for invading was his belief that he needed to keep his army occupied. One senior intelligence official familiar with that interview said Mr. Hussein seemed to suggest that he distrusted what his restive officer corps might do if they were not otherwise distracted."[18] But Saddam probably was also *gambling for survival*, hoping to gain resources from a victory against Kuwait to jump-start the long overdue reconstruction of Iraq. With his economy in a shambles, Saddam needed the spoils of victory to offer at least modest prospects for the civilian population

predecessors' fate. When in July 1958 the pro-Western Hashemite dynasty . . . was overthrown by a military coup headed by General Abdal-Karim Qassem, the mutilated body of the Iraqi regent was dragged by a raging mob in the streets of Baghdad. Five years later, Qassem's bullet-ridden corpse was screened on television to the entire nation. Saddam was determined to use whatever means were required to avoid a similar fate."

[18] *The New York Times*, July 2, 2004. Section A, p. 1: "Hussein, In Jail, Reportedly Said Little of Value." See also Freedman and Karsh (1993, 54).

and for employment for the hundreds of thousands of returning and idle soldiers. As noted by Freedman and Karsh (ibid., 62):

> By adding Kuwait's fabulous wealth to the depleted Iraqi treasury, Saddam hoped to slash Iraq's foreign debt and launch the ambitious reconstruction programmes he had promised his people in the wake of the war with Iran. Given Iraq's historic claim to Kuwait, its occupation could lift Saddam's national prestige by portraying him as the liberator of usurped Iraqi lands. Last but not least, the capture of Kuwait could make Iraq the leading power in the Arab world and give it a decisive say in the the world oil market. In short, in one stroke his position would be permanently secured.

It is not difficult to find other examples of leaders who recognize the potential benefits of both fighting and gambling for their personal survival. However, leaders also recognize international conflict can threaten their survival as well.

In their decision for international conflict, leaders not only weigh the dangers of inaction against the potential benefits of fighting and victory, they must also consider the costs of potential defeat. In a nutshell, we argue that defeat carries a significant risk of a forcible removal from office. This provides little deterrent to leaders who already face a high risk of a forcible removal from office, as their punishment is *truncated*. On the other hand, the dangers of a forcible removal from office, and subsequent exile, jail, or death, as a result of defeat serve as a stark deterrent for leaders who worry only about a regular removal from office.

Two historical examples show how defeat undermined the leader's legitimacy, "tipped" the domestic opposition against the leader, and led to his removal in a coup. The first example stems from the Greek war against Turkey in 1920–2. The gross incompetence shown by the royalist leadership in Greece undermined its legitimacy and gave the liberalist opposition the political cover and support to oust the royalists. Colonels Plastiras and Gonatas overthrew King Constantine I in September 1922 after a series of disastrous Greek defeats in Asia Minor. While Constantine was allowed to go into exile, many of the former civilian leaders were executed in front of a firing squad. As *The Washington Post* (December 3, 1922, p. 27 "Palliates Greek Executions") reports, the Greek people:

> called aloud for the punishment of those whom they rightly blamed for the death and maiming of their sons and brothers, of sweethearts and of fathers, who had been sacrificed by the incompetence, the neglect, and the

cowardly intrigues of their officers in the pursuit of foolish and hopeless enterprises undertaken for no other purpose than to keep in office and in power those wretched, dishonest and corrupt politicians who have from time immemorial been the curse and the blight of an industrious, thrifty, and, in many respects, admirable people. If Dictator Gonatis [sic], now at the head of the revolutionary government, had not brought these men to justice, it is more than probable that his administration would have been unset, and that Athens and, indeed, all Greece, would have become a prey to anarchy of the most sanguinary character.

Bolivia's defeats in the Chaco War (1932–5) produced a very similar dynamic. After the disastrous performance of the Bolivian forces against Paraguay, General (and Vice-President) José Luis Tejada Sorzano forced the Bolivian civilian leader Daniel Salamanca to resign, threatening to hold *him* responsible for the outcome and sign *any* peace treaty with Paraguay (Farcau, 1996, 206), thereby absolving the military.[19] Tejada Sorzano, in turn, was overthrown by Colonels Toro and Busch, who blamed him for the terms of the peace treaty with Bolivia and the misery and poverty of the returning soldiers. The *Los Angeles Times* (May 19, 1936, p. A4 "Bolivia Goes Haywire") describes the motives behind the overthrow of Tejada Sorzano as follows:

The Chacoan peace has never been popular either with the army or with the large portion of the civilian population who felt themselves cheated because of the advantages gained by Paraguay. To the army the war had come to mean steady jobs providing at least food and clothing for all able-bodied males and home work for the women in the field, mines and civil pursuits. With the war ended and the repatriation of thousands of prisoners from

---

[19] It is noteworthy that the coup leaders made an effort to minimize the potential costs of the coup and make this transition appear regular and constitutional. As Farcau (1996, 206) notes:

Apart from an almost traditional desire by all Latin American armed forces to cloak their periodic seizures of power with a thin screen of legality, the Bolivian military had a more practical reason for wanting the transfer of power to appear as natural as possible. A much-needed loan of four hundred thousand pounds sterling was pending in London, and the conspirators feared that a coup d'état would risk losing this loan as well as future ones and arms purchases abroad. Thus they were willing to go some lengths, although it is impossible to say whether they really would have signed "any" peace treaty with Paraguay or not, to obtain Salamanca's signature.

Paraguay under way the labor market was glutted. Professional soldiers were disgruntled, thoroughly dissatisfied with the result and, worse than all, idle. The country was unable to absorb the rank and file. Former soldiers found themselves on their own resources which were nil. The Sorzano government, having negotiated the unpopular treaty, was blamed for resultant conditions and turned out of office by leaders of a provisional government composed of army officers and civilians.[20]

Defeat in an international conflict increases the risk of a forcible removal from office in a second way, because defeat weakens the military which, in countries that lack protections for leaders, typically also doubles as the leader's repressive apparatus. With such a weakened repressive apparatus, the leader's probability of victory against revolutionaries and insurgents decreases and the probability of a forcible removal from office increases. Third, in all-out war, defeat may leave the country and its leaders at the mercy of their foreign opponents. This has two effects. First, the foreign opponent may choose to remove the leader and replace him with someone more to their liking.[21] In Hitler's conquest of Europe, for example, the leaders of many – but not all – of the subjugated countries were forcibly removed from office. Second, the victor may overhaul, change, replace or otherwise not honor the established norms, procedures, and institutions that guide the process of regular removal. Indeed, it is often impossible for the victor to credibly guarantee the safety of their defeated foes, which can extend the duration of wars (Goemans, 2000b). Such a shock to the system will forcefully introduce the commitment problem discussed above, as leaders can obtain credible guarantees about their safety from neither domestic nor foreign opponents and defeat significantly weakened the leader's capabilities and legitimacy.

Leaders can rationally choose to go to war and *gamble for survival* when, compared to the baseline of staying at peace, the probability and consequences of victory outweigh the probability and consequences of

---

[20] See also *The New York Times*, May 18, 1936, pp. 1 and 9, "Bolivian Coup Puts The Army In Power; President Ousted."

[21] Between 1919 and 2003, 478 leaders were removed in an irregular manner. Most of these were at the hands of domestic forces, but 43 leaders were removed by foreign forces. Irregular removal from office is overwhelmingly the result of the threat or use of force as exemplified in coups, (popular) revolts, and assassinations.

defeat.[22] For leaders who already face a high probability of a forcible removal from office, and whose punishment is thus truncated, a large decrease in the probability of forcible removal in case of victory can outweigh a small increase in the probability of a forcible removal in case of defeat. The similarity to the well-known gambling for resurrection mechanism (Richards *et al.*, 1993; Downs and Rocke, 1994; Smith, 1996, 1998; Goemans and Fey, 2009) should be obvious. What distinguishes our mechanism, however, is that in our theory leaders act to save their lives, rather than just their job.[23]

We have so far emphasized how the risk of a forcible removal from office structures leaders' incentives for or against international conflict.[24] We developed two novel mechanisms to explain why

---

[22] The "gambling for survival" explanation of conflict initiation fits seamlessly with the argument in Goemans (2000b) on the causes of war termination. Goemans (ibid.) argues that decisions to continue or terminate war depend in part on the anticipated consequences for the leader's personal fate. Thucydides (1972, Book Eight, 593) illustrates how the overriding concern for their personal safety informed the Oligarchs' calculations whether to continue the war and the terms they would accept. "What they wanted in the first place was to preserve the oligarchy and keep control over the allies as well; if this was impossible, their next aim was to hold on to the fleet and fortifications of Athens and retain independence; but if this also proved beyond them, they were certainly not going to find themselves in the position of being the first people to be destroyed by a reconstituted democracy, and preferred instead to call in the enemy, give up the fleet and the fortifications, and make any sort of terms at all for the future of Athens, provided that they themselves at any rate had their lives guaranteed to them."
Rothenberg (2007, 62) argues that the Directory that came to power in 1795 had no interest in making peace with France's enemies for similar reasons.

[23] A simple example illustrates the logic of gambling for resurrection. Suppose the leader has the opportunity to initiate an international conflict in which his country has a 60% chance of defeat and a 40% chance of victory. Suppose furthermore that victory pays him an additional 1,000 days in office, whereas defeat would cost him 1,000 days in office. On the face of it, this would seem like a bad gamble: the expected value of international conflict is a loss of 200 days in office. Now suppose the leader calculates he has only 100 days in office left. Now the gamble is one between a 60% chance of losing 100 days and a 40% chance of gaining 1,000 days. The expected value of this gamble is a gain of 340 days in office. Because the leader expects to have only 100 days in office, his stake is only those 100 and not the full 1,000 days. Now the expected value of international conflict is greater than the expected value of staying at peace, and the leader rationally initiates conflict.

[24] It might seem that leaders who fear an imminent irregular removal from office could choose to exit in a regular manner and voluntarily resign. However, as we noted, such leaders typically live in countries that lack protections for

leaders can rationally choose to initiate international conflict: *fighting* and *gambling for survival*. Leaders, however, can also lose office through the regular process of elections, term limits, and voluntary retirements. We now turn to examine how prospects of a regular loss of office structure leaders' incentive to initiate or abstain from international conflict.

2.1.3 *International conflict and regular removals*

The regular process of leader removal is structured by norms, procedures, and institutions such as regularly scheduled elections. These institutions are largely unaffected by the onset or continuation of conflict, but can be fundamentally affected by their outcome, in particular by defeat in war. Nevertheless, two factors explain why Challengers – leaders who initiated the conflict – lower their probability of a regular removal from office. First, Challengers enjoy the benefits of picking the time and place of their conflicts. By carefully timing their initiation, for example, before important elections, leaders can gain the benefits of any "rallying around the flag," however short this effect may be (DeRouen Jr., 2000). Second, in times of war, scheduled elections often are postponed until after the war, as was the case in Britain in both world wars. We therefore expect that Challengers enjoy a lower hazard of a regular removal from office. Challenging could also affect the probability of a regular removal from office through a second, *indirect*, pathway.[25]

leaders who stepped down. It is therefore difficult for potential successors to credibly commit not to punish the former ruler or his family for their misdeeds in office. Pinochet of Chile, for example, before turning over power, tried to obtain iron-clad guarantees for his security. Even he, however, subsequently faced trouble as he was pursued by the Spanish and Chilean courts. Moreover, if potential successors could credibly commit to the former leader's safety, that would introduce a moral hazard problem, since departing dictators would face even less constraints on their actions.

[25] Targets – leaders who were attacked – do not choose the time and place of conflict. As a result, they may be more likely to suffer defeat and through this indirect pathway suffer an increased probability of a regular removal from office. Along a more direct pathway, Targets might enjoy a somewhat lower probability of a regular loss of office if the conflict lasts and elections are postponed. We are unable to *ex ante* specify which effect dominates, and thus make no predictions. Traditional theories of diversionary conflict posit that an increased risk in international conflict, be it as an initiator or a target, triggers

Scholars have proposed that Victory and Defeat reveal the foreign policy competence of leaders, and thereby influence the potential benefits of replacing the leader (Richards *et al.*, 1993; Smith, 1996, 1998). By this logic, there would be few benefits in removing victorious leaders with demonstrated competence, but large benefits in removing defeated leaders who demonstrated foreign policy incompetence. Thus, Victory should lower the hazard of a regular removal from office. It is important to keep in mind, though, that the process of regular removal is influenced not just by foreign policy competence, but also by regular domestic politics. Thus, Winston Churchill, Bülent Ecevit, and George H. W. Bush lost office in elections after their victories in World War II, the 1974 Cyprus War, and Gulf War I. In all three instances, foreign competence was trumped by (perceived) economic incompetence.[26] Thus, in elections contested on several dimensions, foreign policy competence is only one factor to weigh in decisions to replace the leader. Moreover, the question always remains of how much credit a leader can claim for victory. Sometimes, finally, the outcome of conflict has little to do with competence, but everything with blind luck, as Frederick the Great learned to his advantage in the Seven Years War. Mussolini's son-in-law and Italian Foreign Minister, Count Ciano, noted more cynically in 1942, "As always, victory finds a hundred fathers, but defeat is an orphan" (Ciano, 2002, 546, diary entry of September 9, 1942).[27] With these caveats in mind, it

---

a rallying-around-the-flag effect and thus a decreased risk of losing office. Inheritors – leaders who inherited the conflict from a former leader – should not be held "culpable" for the war and therefore not significantly different from leaders who remained at peace (Croco, 2008).

[26] Complicating things further still are extra-rational factors. Whether the people interpret the outcome as a victory or defeat can depend on several factors (Johns, 2006; Johnson and Tierney, 2006).

[27] Farcau (2000, 51) provides a fascinating example from the 1879–84 War of the Pacific between Chile, Peru, and Bolivia how victory can actually endanger a leader's hold on office:

President Pinto [of Chile] found himself in a position at the outbreak of the war similar to that of U.S. President James K. Polk during the war with Mexico earlier in the century. Both chief executives were obliged to fight a largely unplanned war with senior generals, all of whom were members of the opposition party and very likely candidates for the presidency in their own right in the coming elections, particularly if they should manage to secure noteworthy victories in the war. Each president was thus placed in a no-win situation in which a defeat in the war would redound to his own disgrace as

nevertheless seems reasonable to hypothesize that victory should lower the probability of a regular removal from office.

Crucially, for our arguments, we claim that leaders who are defeated in an international conflict will be removed in a forcible manner and not in a regular manner. First, the victor often decides to replace the leader, a forcible removal from office *par excellence*. Second, as we argued in the previous section, the victor almost always overthrows the norms, rules, and institutions that previously guided the regular transfer of power. As a result, leaders and their domestic opposition find themselves inescapably in the commitment problem outlined in section 2.1.1. With the regular process aborted, leaders should, highly counter-intuitively, face a *lower* risk of a regular removal from office after defeat, because that process is crowded out by the dramatically increased risk of a forcible removal.

Consider now how defeat affects leaders subject to a regular process compared to leaders subject to the forcible process of leader removal. For the latter, defeat may increase their probability of a forcible removal, but it was already relatively high, and their punishment is truncated. For the former, anticipating a regular removal and a safe retirement, defeat dramatically increases their risks of a forcible removal from office and exile, imprisonment or death. Thus, for leaders subject to the regular process, their punishment is anything but truncated. In other words, leaders who normally need to worry little about an irregular removal have relatively little to gain but much to lose from international conflict. For such leaders, Challenging and Victory may somewhat decrease their hazard of a regular removal from office, but Defeat significantly increases their hazard of an irregular removal from office, with its associated unpleasant consequences. For these leaders, thus, international conflict constitutes a dangerous gamble. Should, then, the security conditions of their countries call for the use of force, these leaders will be more inclined to initiate conflict when they are secure in office. Their firm control of power would serve as

author of the nation's war policy, while victory, under the guidance of a general who was a partisan of the opposition, would almost certainly lead to defeat for the president's party in the next general elections...Chile's President Pinto, however, came up with a unique solution for his political dilemma, albeit one that seriously handicapped the armed forces in their struggle with the external enemy and might easily have led to defeat in the war.

an insurance policy against the risks that conflict engenders. In other words, leaders who would normally rely on the regular process of leader replacement will seek to avoid wars when they face a high risk of losing office in a regular manner. Our reconsideration of the private costs and benefits of international conflict thus offers a novel explanation for why democratic leaders go to war early in their tenure when they are most secure in office (Gaubatz, 1991; Smith, 1996; Chiozza and Goemans, 2003).

2.2 Competing leader-level explanations of international conflict

Above we presented our new theory of conflict initiation which focused on how conflict affects the leader's manner of losing office. Current leader-central explanations of international conflict, as articulated in various strands of "diversionary conflict," consider a significantly smaller range of potential costs and benefits. Below, we disentangle the various strands of diversionary war by a focus on their conceptions of the leader's costs and benefits of international conflict. The first strand proposes that leaders gain from international conflict because it triggers in- and out-group bias among the populace, which in turn produces (temporary) increased support for the leader. The second strand argues that international conflict allows some leaders to reveal their competence in ways not otherwise possible, and thereby gain additional support. We do not examine the latest leader-level explanation for war, which revolves around audience costs, because this has proven prohibitively difficult to empirically examine with real-world data on leaders (Schultz, 2001b).

2.2.1 In- and out-group bias

The first theoretical articulations of diversionary conflict build on the well-known work of Simmel (1898, 1955) and Coser (1956). This strand in the literature postulated the "in-group/out-group" hypothesis. According to the first variant of this hypothesis, when a state becomes involved in an international crisis, in-group – in particular, national – identities become salient. This, in turn, produces in-group bias and greater cohesion among in-group members. In the literature on diversionary war, this effect has become known as "rallying around the flag," whereby the people supposedly put aside their differences with their leaders to support them in times of crisis (Mueller, 1973; Levy, 1989). Rallying around the flag, then, is argued to bolster a leader's chances to remain in office. A second variant emphasizes the out-group bias that international conflict supposedly triggers among in-group members. Specifically, out-group bias supposedly allows leaders to blame and scapegoat foreign enemies for their policy failures (Clark, 2003). Because of their psychological foundations, we classify theories that rely on the in-group/out-group hypothesis as *psychological* explanations of diversionary conflict.

Psychological explanations of diversionary conflict thus suggest that as people perceive a foreign threat, they become more likely to support their leader, bolstering his time in office, which becomes the reason why a leader might provoke a foreign crisis in the first place. These psychological explanations postulate a fully reciprocal relationship: as leaders become more likely to lose office, they become more likely to initiate an international conflict, while at the same time as an international conflict becomes more likely – and in-group identity becomes more salient, or the out-group more hated – leaders become less likely to lose office. Thus, the central hypothesis of psychological explanations of diversionary conflict posits a fully reciprocal relationship. As the leader's risk of losing office increases, the probability of conflict initiation increases, while at the same time, as the risk of international conflict increases, the probability of losing office decreases. Note that for this effect to obtain, it is not necessary that a war has already broken out; a foreign threat, or a threat of international conflict should be enough to produce the in- or out-group bias that produces "rallying around the flag."

A third, slightly more sophisticated, psychological variant posits that the people only rally around their leader at low and intermediate levels of pre-existing *domestic* inter-group conflict (Coser, 1956). At high levels of domestic inter-group conflict, the emergence of a foreign threat only further exacerbates domestic conflict, and thus endangers the leader's hold on power. Hence, in cases of extreme domestic inter-group conflict, such as civil war, leaders have a *dis*-incentive to initiate international conflict. However, once we "take out" such high levels of domestic inter-group conflict – by controlling for the endogenous risk of civil war – the risk of losing office should again monotonically increase the probability of conflict initiation.

The third psychological variant posits a curvilinear – inverse "U"-shaped – relationship between domestic inter-group conflict and the gains to be had by international conflict initiation. Controlling for civil war – the highest level of domestic inter-group conflict – a linear, and again reciprocal, relationship between the risk of losing office and international conflict initiation should remain.

In the following section, we offer a brief critique of both the fundamental theoretical mechanisms and the large statistical literature that purports to test this strand of the literature.

2.2.2 Evaluation

In both their theoretical conception and in the many empirical attempts to test them, psychological explanations of diversionary conflict suffer from several fundamental flaws. First, while psychological research has indeed found that an increased threat to the group produces in-*group* and – to a lesser degree (Brewer, 1999) – out-*group* bias (Labianca, Brass and Gray, 1998, 56), to the best of our knowledge, no psychological research shows whether this in turn translates into greater political support for group leaders. The relationship between greater affinity for other group members (in-group bias) and political support for the leader therefore remains an unexamined assumption. Similarly, while out-group bias might turn a foreign enemy into a convenient scapegoat, it remains unclear whether this produces greater political support for the leader.

Second, even if this psychological mechanism translates into greater political support for the leader, it is unclear how long this support lasts. (As we will see below, research on "rallying around the flag" suggests that any support is short in duration (DeRouen Jr., 2000).) Moreover, scholars in this strand of the literature have failed to examine the potential downside of international conflict. In particular, it is unclear when and why a short boost in tenure is worth the risk of an increased probability of losing office as a result of defeat.

Given these theoretical flaws, it is perhaps not surprising that the in-group/out-group hypothesis enjoys only mixed empirical support. Note, first, that this strand of the literature posits a broad and *general* theory of international conflict: leaders should initiate international conflict whenever they feel insecure in office. This broad and general theory dramatically over-predicts international conflict. Between 1919 and 2003, 1,977 leaders held and lost office. All of these leaders at some time in their tenure must have faced a high risk of losing office and thus had incentives to initiate conflict. However, in this same time span leaders initiated significantly fewer than 500 international conflicts (International Crisis Behavior Project, 2007).

Moreover, almost all empirical examinations of the in-group/out-group hypothesis suffer from two fundamental flaws: first, the failure to model the reciprocal, endogenous relationship between the loss of office and international conflict initiation and second, the near exclusive reliance on states, rather than leaders, as the unit of analysis.

First, almost all empirical research based on the psychological explanations examines only how a leader's popularity or approval affects international conflict initiation *or* how international conflict affects the leader's popularity. Until Chiozza and Goemans (2003), no one had estimated a system of equations that combined these, as explicitly suggested by psychological theories of diversionary war. Typically, scholars obtain indicators of a leader's popularity and include these in their regressions on international conflict. A regression which simply examines the effect of the president's or prime-minister's popularity as measured in public opinion polls on the probability of conflict, however, ignores the theoretical expectation that the leader's popularity is in turn affected by the risk of international conflict. Coefficients on variables which purport to capture the leader's risk of losing office will therefore be irretrievably biased.

Second, while diversionary conflict is theoretically pitched at the level of the leader, most empirical studies, by far, have instead relied on country-level data and use regime type as their main explanatory variable.[28] These studies, as well as those that do explicitly focus on leaders, find at best mixed support for the hypothesized diversionary behavior (Ostrom and Job, 1986; Morgan and Bickers, 1992; James

---

[28] Almost every possible regime type has been suggested as particularly prone to engage in diversionary war, including regimes in transition, unstable, autocratic, democratic, and oligarchic regimes (Wilkenfeld, 1968; Hazelwood, 1975; Lebow, 1981; Domke, 1988; Levy, 1989; Downs and Rocke, 1994; Miller, 1995; Smith, 1996; Gelpi, 1997; Bueno de Mesquita *et al.*, 1999; Mansfield and Snyder, 2005). None of the hypotheses linking regime type with the diversionary use of force, however, has met with general quantitative empirical support (Zinnes and Wilkenfeld, 1971; Mansfield and Snyder, 1995, 2005; Gelpi, 1997; Leeds and Davis, 1997; Miller, 1999).

and Hristoulas, 1994; Meernik, 1994; DeRouen Jr., 1995; Meernik and Waterman, 1996; Fordham, 1998a, b; Gowa, 1998; Morgan and Anderson, 1999). Meernik and Waterman (1996, 573), for example, "find little evidence of any kind of link between domestic political conditions in the United States and uses of force or international crises" (see also Lian and Oneal (1993); Meernik (1994); Gowa (1998); Lai and Reiter (2005)). Studies on leaders tend to overwhelmingly rely on US presidents – not the average leader by any measure – term-limited after 1952, with a fixed term of office, and ruling a superpower. In a particularly interesting analysis, Stoll (1984) examined whether US presidents are more likely to use force when they are up for re-election. He found that if the United States was not already involved in a conflict, in their re-election year US presidents were actually less likely to resort to the use of force (see also Gaubatz (1991)). When Morgan and Anderson (1999, 799) extended the analysis beyond the United States to Great Britain, they found that "the level of public support for the British government is in fact associated with the probability that Britain threatens, displays, or uses force abroad" (see also Lai and Reiter (2005)). In short, while some studies do find diversionary behavior, just as many reject their diversionary hypothesis.

There has been much less empirical research on the second stage of the relation between tenure and international conflict, the stage which posits that international conflict, or the risk of international conflict, decreases the probability of losing office. Several studies have investigated whether the popular standing of American presidents increases in time of war and international conflict (Ostrom and Job, 1986; Morgan and Bickers, 1992; Lian and Oneal, 1993). In general, however, the evidence for the "rally-around-the-flag" phenomenon has again been decidedly mixed (Mueller, 1973; Brace and Hinckley, 1992; Lian and Oneal, 1993; DeRouen Jr., 1995; Oneal and Bryan, 1995; James and Rioux, 1998; DeRouen Jr., 2000; Baker and Oneal, 2001).

In earlier work (Chiozza and Goemans, 2003), we presented the initial data and a two-stage method to assess the postulated logic of the psychological explanation of diversionary conflict. There, we focused on the risk of losing office and thus collapsed the regular and forcible manner of losing office into one overall category. We found that as the risk of losing office increases, the probability of conflict initiation strongly and significantly *decreases*. Moreover, as the risk of a crisis increases, the probability of losing office also increases. In other words, approaching conflict led to no discernible rallying around the flag, and instead worsened the leader's hold on office. In short, our findings strongly contradicted the psychological variant of diversionary war. We now turn to the more modern rationalist explanations of diversionary conflict.

2.2.3 Competence

The second main strand in the literature on diversionary conflict proposes a rationalist mechanism that has become known as "gambling for resurrection", as we described above (Richards *et al.*, 1993; Downs and Rocke, 1994; Smith, 1996; Bueno de Mesquita *et al.*, 1999; Mansfield and Snyder, 2005; Goemans and Fey, 2009). International conflict, in this framework, constitutes a *high variance* strategy. The leader prefers the higher variance in his probability of staying in office associated with international conflict, because the lower variance associated with peace leaves him very likely to lose office.

At the heart of this rationalist explanation lies the assumption that, relative to peace, victory decreases the leader's probability of losing office. Victory in an international conflict decreases a leader's probability of losing office, because international conflict supposedly allows leaders to reveal their "competence" (or cover up incompetence) in ways not otherwise possible (Richards *et al.*, 1993, 511; Hess and Orphanides, 1995, 829; Smith, 1996, 134).[29] Typically, leaders have private information about their competence and incentives to misrepresent it; the only way to credibly reveal competence is by demonstrated success.[30] In the case of foreign policy competence, as Downs and Rocke (1994, 362) put it, "the constituency must base its decision to retain an executive on the outcome of a conflict." Competent leaders are thought to be more likely to gain victory, therefore victory allows

---

[29] Downs and Rocke (1994, 365) alternatively consider leaders with private information about the costs and benefits of international conflict, and voters who assess whether the leader acted as they would have, if they had the same information.

[30] Note that this does not mean that only competent leaders enjoy success; sometimes incompetent leaders obtain successes. Because competent leaders are more likely to obtain successes than incompetent leaders, successful but unbeknownst to the public incompetent leaders are rewarded with longer tenure.

the constituency to update its belief about the leader's competence. Since the constituency generally benefits from competent leadership, it will reward victorious and competent leaders with longer tenure.

Because victory pays, and *the punishment of leaders is truncated at the loss of office*, leaders rationally initiate international conflict in a "gamble for resurrection." In other words, as in current strands of the literature, the higher the risk of losing office, the more likely leaders are to initiate international conflict. However, while in the psychological explanations international conflict pays because of "rallying around the flag," and little attention is given to the potential costs of international conflict, in the rationalist leader-level literature, the benefits of international conflict must be traced to the benefits of victory, while the potential costs of war are truncated.

While almost all of the literature on the diversionary use of force focuses on conflict *initiation*, recently Smith (1996) has argued that diversionary incentives are more likely to be reflected in the selection of targets in international conflict. Almost all of the literature on the diversionary use of force has focused only on the strategic interaction between leaders and citizens relevant to the leader's tenure; scholars rarely consider how this domestic interaction affects international interactions. However, as Bueno de Mesquita and Siverson (1995) argued, leaders select their international conflict strategically and therefore could well take into account the relevant domestic circumstances of potential opponents. In his discussion of endogenous crisis formation, Smith (1996) was the first to examine how the domestic political diversionary incentives of leaders affect the potential conflict incentives of other leaders. (More recently, Clark (2003) and Tarar (2006) have developed models that incorporate the strategic interaction between not just leaders and the domestic audience, but also a foreign opponent.) In a nutshell, Smith (1996, 149) suggested that "other nations avoid creating crises when democracies are likely to intervene," but this argument can be broadened to all types of leaders who feel diversionary pressures.[31] Because they gain a private benefit from conflict – the increased likelihood of staying in power – diversionary leaders can credibly demand a premium in interstate bargaining. *Ceteris paribus*, other leaders would thus gain less from a peaceful

---

[31] Smith (1996, 149) proposes a curvilinear relationship between the risk of losing office and the probability of becoming a target.

settlement with diversionary leaders, while international conflict would be more likely (because the bargaining range shrinks). In other words, given the ability of potential foreign opponents to read and play against a leader's diversionary incentives, leaders could have dis-incentives to target other leaders with diversionary incentives.

This strategic interaction formulation of diversionary conflict thus postulates that leaders with the strongest diversionary incentives – because they face a high probability of losing office – will get the fewest opportunities to exploit those incentives. In other words, this variant argues that the higher the probability of losing office, the less likely leaders are to become *targets* in international crises.

While Smith (1996) introduced strategic interaction between leaders and their foreign opponents, he built his insights on the assumption that diversionary conflict can pay because it enables constituents to learn more about the leader's competence. In other words, the assumption that victory increases the overall tenure of leaders is also fundamental to the strategic interaction strand in the rationalist literature on diversionary conflict.

Note, however, that the logic of strategic interaction could also operate in tandem with the earlier psychological explanations for diversionary conflict. In other words, if diversionary conflict pays because of a rally-around-the-flag effect, other leaders still would want to avoid leaders with diversionary incentives. This variant thus posits a reciprocal relationship between the loss of office and becoming a target in an international conflict.

Since this variant again postulates a *reciprocal* relationship, leaders should be less likely to be targeted as their risk of losing office increases, while at the same time the probability of losing office decreases as the risk of becoming a target increases. In the next section, we evaluate the contemporary rationalist approach to diversionary conflict.

2.2.4 Evaluation

The gambling for resurrection and strategic interaction rationalist formulations of diversionary conflict offer elegant mechanisms, but fail empirically on two fronts. First, we showed in Chiozza and Goemans (2003) that as the risk of losing office increases, contrary to the prediction of gambling for resurrection, the probability of conflict initiation *decreases*. Second, and as we argue here to be of central importance, the mechanism's fundamental assumption that punishment of leaders is truncated at the mere loss of office is false and misleading. As shown in Goemans (2008) (and also in Chapter 3), about a quarter of all leaders lose office as the result of the threat or use of force. Of the leaders who lost office in such a forcible manner, fully 80 percent suffered some form of punishment in the form of exile, imprisonment or death. Of the leaders who lost office in a regular manner, in stark contrast, only 7 percent suffered such punishment. Gambling for resurrection becomes a doubtful proposition if, compared to staying at peace, a leader significantly increases the probability of a fate much worse than merely losing office.

Several scholars have attempted to test empirically the rationalist strategic interaction approach to diversionary conflict as first suggested by Smith (1996). Specifically, scholars examined whether states avoid targeting democracies whose leaders might have diversionary incentives. Gaubatz (1991) was the first to note that democratic leaders initiate foreign conflict *early* in their tenure, when they are most secure and least in need of diversionary conflict to stay in office. Miller (1995) finds that under conditions of low policy resources and highly autocratic political systems, targets are indeed more likely to respond with force if their economy is doing poorly. Similarly, Leeds and Davis (1997, 831) find that in their sample of 18 democracies, domestic political vulnerability appears to enhance deterrence. All three studies, however, employ the country as the unit of analysis and limit their sample to democracies. Clark (2003, 1031) appropriately focuses on leaders – e.g. American presidents – and finds that "high levels of [presidential] approval increase opportunities for U.S. use of force, although ... approval appears not to directly affect whether the United States actually uses force or not abroad ... " Clark (ibid., 1035), however, also finds ample room for presidents to manufacture crises if they so desire. If leaders can create crises when they need to, there may thus be relatively little other leaders can do to avoid leaders with diversionary incentives.

Finally, the psychological variant of the strategic interaction formulation of diversionary conflict posits an endogenous relationship between becoming a target and the loss of office. The generally mixed results about "rallying around the flag" discussed above weigh against this formulation. In another of our earlier articles (Chiozza and Goemans, 2004a) we provided a rigorous test of the strategic interaction variant of diversionary conflict. There we found that, as postulated, an increase in the probability of losing office indeed decreases the probability of becoming a target in an international conflict. However, and somewhat contrary to the theory, the risk of becoming a target did not significantly affect the probability of losing office.

Our evaluation of the competing theories of diversionary conflict revealed gaps in their theoretical scaffolding and, at best, mixed support. In the next two chapters, we present carefully crafted empirical tests of our re-conceptualization of the diversionary use of force.

2.3 Conclusions

In this chapter, we presented our new leader theory of international conflict. Our theory turns on the claim that leaders can lose power through two distinct processes. There exists a regular, institutionalized process which usually provides the leader a safe retirement; and there is a forcible, coercive process associated with death, imprisonment or exile. With this distinction in place, we amended the key assumption that leaders base their policies on how these affect their probability of staying in power (Downs, 1957; Bueno de Mesquita et al., 2003). In its place we propose that leaders base their policies not just on the probability, but the manner and consequences of losing office. We develop a simple theoretical argument, building on Fearon (2004), to explain why and when leaders should anticipate a forcible removal from office. In countries that lack the institutional protection to safeguard leaders after they lose office, a temporary shock in the leader's legitimacy or capabilities introduces a commitment problem. To buy off the strengthened opposition, the leader would like to make some concessions, but this deal is not credible, since the leader will revoke any concessions once he regains his strength. Since the clash between opposition and leader cannot be avoided through peaceful deals, this commitment problem results in coups, revolts, and insurgencies. We then analyzed how international conflict can solve this commitment problem by increasing the probability of victory against the leader's opponents, e.g. by elimination of the other player in the game, as well as by reversing the temporary shock. Our analysis led us to propose two new leader-level explanations for war: *fighting for survival* and *gambling for survival*. In addition, we presented a *peace through insecurity* mechanism whereby leaders who need fear only a regular removal from office have dis-incentives to initiate conflict.

In the next chapter we empirically scrutinize the core claims and predictions of our new theory of diversionary conflict: how international conflict affects the overall tenure of leaders – as in the traditional literature – as well as how conflict affects the manner of losing office, specifically the hazards of a regular and an irregular removal from office. Thus in Chapter 3 we examine the connection between the processes of removal from office and the leader's subsequent fate, as well as the following core claims:

- Challengers enjoy a lower hazard of a regular removal from office.
- Challengers enjoy a lower hazard of an irregular removal from office.
- Victory decreases the hazard of a regular removal from office.
- Victory decreases the hazard of an irregular removal from office.
- Defeat increases the hazard of an irregular removal from office.
- Defeat does not increase the hazard of a regular removal from office.

In that chapter, we bolster our claim that international conflict has not much to offer to leaders who face the prospect of a regular removal, but has much to offer to leaders who fear for their life and liberty. In Chapter 4, we focus on our central contribution, to examine how the risks of a forcible removal from office and the risks of a regular removal from office affect the probability of conflict initiation. We examine the following central claims:

- As the risk of a forcible removal from office increases the probability of conflict initiation also increases.
- As the risk of a regular removal from office increases the probability of conflict initiation decreases.

In Chapter 5, finally, we examine the history of Central America between 1840 and 1919 to historically trace the explanatory power of our proposed mechanisms.

3 | International conflict and the fate of leaders

3.1 Introduction

"I am reasonably sure of only three things today," *New York Times* columnist Anna Quindlen (1991) wrote on March 3, 1991, "that George Bush will be re-elected President in 1992; that if he chooses either Colin Powell or Norman Schwarzkopf as his running mate, he might win by the largest landslide in the history of the nation, and that we are incredibly skilled at war." These were reasonable claims that many at the time would have shared. In a military campaign that lasted 100 hours and gripped the attention of the American people in front of the television screen, the United States had liberated Kuwait and achieved a decisive victory against the Iraqi Army.

With the benefit of hindsight, we can say that of the three assertions made by Anna Quindlen (ibid.), the last one is undoubtedly true: Americans are indeed quite skilled at war. The second could have been true, but we will never know. The first one – the prediction that President George H. W. Bush was going to win re-election easily – however, turned out to be false. On election day, November 3, 1992, just twenty months after the victorious conclusion of the Gulf War, President Bush was defeated by Arkansas Governor Bill Clinton by a wide margin: 43% vs. 37% of the popular vote.

In that very same issue of *The New York Times* where Anna Quindlen liberally prophesied about US presidential politics, James E. Akins (1991), former US Ambassador to Saudi Arabia, made a very reasonable prediction about Saddam Hussein's fate. While dismissing any facile euphoria about the prospects for peace in the Middle East, Ambassador Akins was nonetheless very confident that Saddam Hussein would no longer be one of the political factors to be reckoned with in the Middle Eastern political landscape. "In fact," he wrote, "there is little reason to concern ourselves with Saddam. He has been defeated and humiliated and will soon be dead at the hands of his own people unless some unlikely country gives him refuge. And the martyrdom he has courted will elude him unless we or the Saudis bring him before a war crimes tribunal and execute him."[1] In the end, Saddam Hussein met the fate Ambassador Akins predicted: death at the hands of his own people. That occurred, however, on December 30, 2006, not in 1991. Saddam was to remain in power for twelve more years, until the United States, under the leadership of George W. Bush, toppled his regime in 2003, and a new democratically elected government, led by Prime Minister Nouri al-Maliki, was in power in Baghdad.

If we were ever in doubt that the business of prediction is a mine-field for experts of politics, these two examples would put those doubts to rest. But as we assess the different fates of the victorious and the defeated leader of the Gulf War of 1991, we can also notice a pattern that our theory of the costs and benefits of conflict would help us explain. As we argued in Chapter 2, international conflict generates fleeting and limited benefits for leaders ruling countries with well-established, non-violent, processes of leadership change, as was the case for US President Bush. For leaders of countries where the risk of a forcible removal is high, on the other hand, defeat in an international conflict makes that risk higher, as Saddam Hussein experienced from the Kurdish and Shi'a uprisings he mercilessly suppressed after retreating from Kuwait. International conflict, though, might still be a *gamble* worth pursuing if the alternative is no different: a high risk of forcible removal.

In this chapter, we place these two examples in a broader context. To understand how leaders could view international conflict as a rational strategy in light of their double goal of staying in power and safe-guarding their personal fates, we need to establish that (*a*) *regular* and *forcible* processes of leadership turnover are systematically associated with the post-tenure fate of leaders; and (*b*) that international conflict affects not just *whether* but also *how* leaders lose power. Specifically, we need to establish when and how international conflict affects the risks of a forcible removal from office separate from its effect on the risks of a regular removal from office and *vice versa*.[2]

---

[1] See also Mueller (2004, 124) for a reflection on these predictions.
[2] Although providing important insights, the limited but ongoing research into the causes (and consequences) of coups (O'Kane, 1983; Gupta, 1990; Londregan and Poole, 1990; Person and Tabellini, 1994; Alesina *et al.*, 1996;

Since we argue that leaders anticipate when and how they might lose office – and base their policy choices on this anticipation – we examine how international conflict alters the timing and the manner of leaders' removal under a broad range of economic and domestic political conditions that directly address the fundamental assumptions of our theory. Thus, we first distinguish political systems that can credibly commit to the safety of their leaders, e.g. democracies as Riker (1982) suggested, from political systems that cannot make such credible commitments, mixed regimes, and autocracies. Second, we compare leaders who face a high risk of a forcible removal from office with leaders under no such a threat. To do so, we split our data into two; one sub-sample contains leaders involved in civil war, the other sub-sample contains leaders at civil peace. Third, we explore a second potential dimension to differentiate systems that can credibly promise their leaders a safe retirement by splitting our sample by the levels of economic development. Finally, we seek to assess the effects of a temporary shock in the leader's capabilities and resources by splitting our sample into one sub-sample of leaders who experienced positive economic growth and one sub-sample of leaders who experienced economic recession.

In sum, in this chapter we assess the major building blocks of the theory developed in Chapter 2. We show that starting, winning or losing an international conflict have a different impact on regular vs. forcible processes of leadership change; and thus we show that international conflict entails different costs and benefits *for leaders* depending upon the manner in which they might lose power.

While we bracket the issue of the endogeneity of conflict initiation in this chapter, we tackle this head-on in Chapter 4, where we investigate the mechanisms for conflict initiation we derived from our theory: *peace-through-insecurity, fighting for survival*, and *gambling for survival*.[3]

Feng, 1997; Belkin and Schofer, 2003, 2005) – a subset of our cases of forcible removal from office – fails to examine whether the same factors that increase the risk of a coup also and similarly raise the risk of a regular removal from office. Our empirical analysis, therefore, not only covers a broader set of cases of forcible removal, but it also has broader theoretical implications for the study of leadership selection and turnover.

[3] For this analysis, as well as the analyses in the subsequent chapters, we use the new data on leaders we gathered for this book, "Introducing Archigos" (Goemans, Gleditsch and Chiozza, 2009). Our data set contains information

3.2 The manner and consequences of losing office

Leaders can lose power in two fundamental ways: in a regular and peaceful manner, which we call *regular* removal, or in an irregular and potentially violent manner, which we call *forcible* removal. Regular removals include elections, parliamentary votes of confidence, or hereditary successions. Forcible removals include coups, insurrections, or assassinations. In general, regular processes are prevalent. From 1919 until 2003, about two-thirds of the leaders in power lost office in a regular manner. Forcible removal is less common. Overall, more than a quarter of all leaders lost office in an irregular manner, which makes the danger of such an overthrow a real threat and not a remote possibility for leaders.[4] To be sure, as we see in Figure 3.1, some countries, particularly in Latin America, Central Africa, and Central Asia are systematically more prone to such forcible removals from office. Ecuador and Bolivia top the list with 19 and 17 instances of leaders who were forcibly removed, respectively. Leaders in Western European countries, in contrast, rarely lose office in a forcible manner.

Forcible removal might occur through several processes, involving different political forces and players, with and without foreign support. As we show in Table 3.1, of the 495 leaders who lost power in a forcible manner since 1919, the largest majority – 262, or 53% – were unseated in a coup executed by the military with no foreign support. Some 93 leaders owed their fate to some form of direct or indirect foreign intervention. But regardless of how it occurs, forcible removal is fundamentally different from a regular process of leadership change because it is systematically associated with severe punishment for leaders.

We distinguish four alternative fates for leaders who lose power. Overall, leaders might expect to remain free citizens who might keep a public profile or stay outside of politics, but with no threats to their own personal lives. Or leaders can be punished: they can be forced

not just about when, but also how the leader lost office, and about his post-exit fate up to one year after he lost office. The information on leaders' fate was collected independently of the manner of the leader's removal. We limited the scope of our analysis of the leader's post-tenure fate to one year in order to preclude the possibility that the leader's behavior after he lost office rather than his behavior in office provided the cause for any form of punishment.

[4] Leaders, of course, can also die while in office or step down because of ill-health, a third mode of leadership change, which plays only a marginal role in our argument, given that it is truly exogenous to any policy choice.

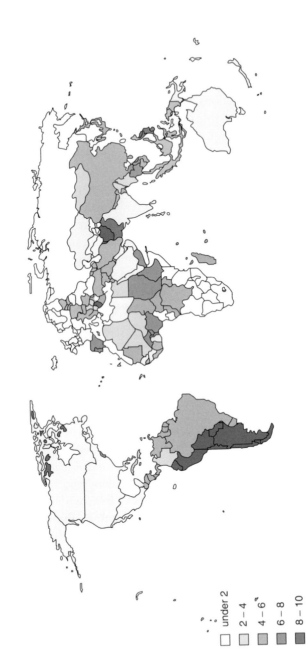

Figure 3.1: Number of forcible removals, 1919–2003

under 2

2 – 4

4 – 6

6 – 8

8 – 10

over 10

Table 3.1: *Forms of forcible removal*

	Foreign Support		
	With	Without	Total
Domestic popular protest	1	26	27
Domestic rebel forces	11	40	51
Domestic military actors	4	262	266
Other domestic government actors	4	40	44
Threat or use of foreign force	44		44
Assassination by unsupported individual		21	21
Other means or processes	29	13	42
Total	93	402	495

Table 3.2: *How leaders lose office and the consequences*

	OK	Exile	Jail	Killed	Total
Ill health	30	3	1	0	34
%	88.24	8.82	2.94	0	100
Regular	1380	70	33	2	1485
%	92.93	4.71	2.22	0.13	99.99
Forcible	97	198	112	82	489
%	19.84	40.49	22.9	16.77	100
Total	1507	271	146	84	2008

Note: Pearson χ^2 (6) = 1074.189, p-value < 0.001.

into *exile*; sent to *jail*; or *killed*.[5] Leaders can thus be *OK*, the label that we use, with irony, in Table 3.2. They would write books, run foundations, serve as opposition leaders, or simply retire. They might still risk having their freedoms curtailed, as General Pinochet learned when on October 17, 1998 – about ten years after stepping down as dictator of Chile – he was arrested while seeking medical treatment in Britain. But even considering scenarios like Pinochet's, the fate of leaders who are "ok" is very different from the fate of leaders who face punishment when they lose power.

[5] In our coding rules, exile includes refuge in a foreign embassy, since such an embassy is considered foreign soil; imprisonment includes house arrest.

There is undoubtedly a qualitative difference between the three forms of punishment of exile, imprisonment, and death. Compare, for example, the fate of Dr. Mohammad Najibullah, the fourth and last President of the Democratic Republic of Afghanistan, with the fate of Mohammed Zahir Shah, the last king of Afghanistan. After the fall of his regime in 1992, Najibullah remained in a UN compound in Kabul until 1996, when the capital fell to the Taliban. He was then captured, tortured, mutilated, shot and hung from a lamppost (Burns, 1996). Mohammed Zahir Shah, instead, was ousted in a coup orchestrated by former Prime Minister Mohammed Daoud Khan in 1973. He spent 29 years in exile in Rome, playing golf, chess and tending his garden (Gall, 2007), hardly a bad life despite suffering minor wounds in an assassination attempt in 1991 (Bearak, 2007). He even stood a chance of being reinstated as Afghanistan's head of state in 2002 when, after the fall of the Taliban regime, a new constitution for Afghanistan was negotiated at the *loya jirga*, the grand council, that in the end elected Hamid Karzai as president (Jones, 2009).

As the experience of Zahir Shah testifies, exile is not a punishment *per se*, unless other conditions would intervene, such as the confiscation of property. No less an authority than Thomas Hobbes (1996 [1651], 209) wrote that exile is "an escape, a public commandment to avoid punishment by flight" and, citing Cicero, "a refuge of men in danger."[6] What makes exile a form of punishment for ousted leaders, therefore, is not necessarily the hardship it might impose, but the fact that he and his followers must depend for their safety and possessions on the leader of the country where they are allowed to reside. Colonel Mengistu Haile Mariam, the former head of the military junta in Ethiopia, managed to escape to Zimbabwe after he was overthrown in 1991. In an interview, he suggested not only how much he missed Ethiopia, but also how he now was at the protective mercy of his hosts and feared for his life: "As you can see, in my day-to-day life I and my family lack nothing. Like any Ethiopian exile, I miss my country … I have many enemies. You know that they have tried to kill me before how … I fear for my life" (quoted in Baker (2004, 1492)). In 2003, Mugabe of Zimbabwe allegedly considered leaving office and going

---

[6] Hobbes (1996[1651], 208) lists exile as one of the human punishments, i.e. the punishments "inflicted by the commandment of man," which also include corporal punishment, pecuniary punishment, and ignominy.

into exile, but refused to do so because his safety could not be guaranteed. "Senior Zanu-PF party sources told a journalist that Mugabe 'wants to leave but his personal security fears, the fate of his family and property... are his main obstacles'" (ibid., 1487). As a consequence, even for the leaders who expect to be punished with exile, holding office becomes something more than their motivational drive and a source of privileges; it is the way to preserve their personal freedom and their lives.

What, then, is the relationship between the manner of losing office and the fate of leaders? In Table 3.2, we report a simple cross-tabulation to establish this point, which is central to our theory.[7] Although simple, this cross-tabulation produces a straightforward and powerful result. The manner of exit is strongly associated with the leader's subsequent fate in the period up to one year after losing office. Of the leaders who lost office in a regular manner, fully 93 percent retired safely from their office and only 7 percent suffered some form of punishment. Of the leaders who were removed in a forcible manner, however, only 20 percent suffered no punishment; 40 percent were exiled or fled the country in self-imposed exile, 23 percent were imprisoned for some time; and 17 percent were killed.

Even for the leaders who step down through regular processes, there exists no "bullet-proof" guarantee that their life and freedom will never be in danger. Still, only two leaders were killed within a year after losing power in a regular manner, Dogsomyn Bodoo of Mongolia and Bonifacio Ondó Edú of Equatorial Guinea. Both leaders ruled their countries through the processes that led to creation of independent nations. In highly unstable conditions, a resignation, for Bodoo, and an electoral defeat in elections certified as free and democratic by the United Nations, for Ondó Edú, were not sufficient to save their lives (Campos, 2003; Atwood, 2004). But even with these two exceptions, the findings in Table 3.2 firmly establish the association between how leaders lose power and their fate out of office.

---

[7] Post-exit fate is considered missing for 134 leaders who lost office as a result of natural death, 15 who lost power as a result of illness, and 3 who committed suicide in office. Post-exit fate is also missing for 5 leaders who lost office in a regular manner, and 1 who lost office in an irregular manner but died within six months after losing office. For 26 leaders, no information could be found on their post-exit fate; of these, 21 lost office in a regular manner, 4 lost office in an irregular manner, and 1 could not be determined.

Table 3.3: *The fate of leaders and conflict involvement*

	How many leaders	In power	Natural death	OK	Exile	Jail	Killed
No conflict	2069	8023	132	1242	230	124	73
%		81.67	1.34	12.64	2.34	1.26	0.74
Challengers	196	449	8	18	5	6	4
%		91.63	1.63	3.67	1.02	1.22	0.82
Targets	286	484	9	55	22	10	4
%		82.88	1.54	9.42	3.77	1.71	0.68
Inheritors	91	92	0	23	6	5	1
%		72.44	0	18.11	4.72	3.94	0.79

Note: Entries are the number of leaders every year given their conflict involvement and their fate.

3.2.1 International conflict and the fate of leaders

Before we test the hypotheses from our theory, we present two simple tables and discuss specific leaders and events to give the reader a deeper and richer understanding of the connections between international conflict and the fate of leaders out of office. We distinguish two possible sources of costs and benefits for leaders: (*a*) those that obtain from participation in conflict, which relate to the mechanism of *fighting for survival*; and (*b*) those that accrue as the result of the outcomes of conflict, which relate to the mechanisms of *peace through insecurity* and *gambling for survival*.

At any given time, as we show in Table 3.3, most leaders are in power and out of conflict. If removal occurs, it is mostly associated with a safe retirement for the leader. Only few experience some form of punishment. This result is analogous to the one we reported in Table 3.2, this time using a different unit of analysis – leaders-per-year rather than leaders *per se*. International conflict participation, however, changes the picture drastically.

A Challenger leader – a leader who started a conflict – will see his political prospects in power improve. Challengers rarely lost office when the conflict was still ongoing. If they did – an outcome that befell 41 out of 196 Challenger leaders (21%) – they were more likely to preserve their personal freedom than they were to experience some form of punishment. Of the 41 leaders who lost power when they were involved in a conflict they initiated, 18 (44%) managed to preserve their freedom, 15 (37%) suffered some form of punishment, and 8 (20%) died in office. As we quoted Hérault in Chapter 2, the decision to initiate a conflict creates political possibilities which are perhaps not available during peace. With the cover of an ongoing conflict, the leader can take steps to mute the opposition and disrupt potential coup plans by sending the conspirators to the front. This empirical pattern reflects our conjecture about leaders fighting for their survival.

Leaders who suffer an attack – the Targets – on the other hand, were less able to protect their political and personal fate. While most of the time a Target leader stayed in power when the conflict was ongoing as was the case for the Challengers, a larger number – 100 out of 286 (35%) – lost office. Of these 100 leaders, 55 were "ok" afterwards; 36 were punished, most commonly by sending them into exile, and 9 died in office. Finally, few leaders qualify as inheritors, that is, leaders who get into power while a conflict is still ongoing. Overall, these leaders experienced shorter periods of time while in conflict, as we would expect from leaders who gain the reins of power during a long protracted conflict with the explicit mandate to bring it to a conclusion. This obvious conjecture is reflected in the fact that the 91 "conflict-inheriting" leaders in our data accumulated only a total of 92 years in power when the conflict was still ongoing. When inheritors lost power, they were usually able to preserve their personal freedom (see Croco (2008)); still, 12 of them were punished. One, Inukai Tsuyoshi of Japan, was killed during a coup attempt carried out in 1932 by elements of the Japanese Imperial Navy in the power struggle between the civilian leadership and the armed forces as Japan had launched its imperial expansion in Manchuria.

From this simple analysis, we gather some preliminary evidence of the benefits of international conflict for leaders. In particular, the difference between the fates of leaders that initiated conflicts compared to those who suffered an attack gives support to the mechanism of fighting for survival, while adding yet another weak finding to the long list of inconclusive results for the alternative hypothesis of the in-group/out-group bias theory. Any benefit that might accrue to leaders does not follow involvement in international conflict *per se*, but primarily involvement in the conflicts that the leaders themselves *started*. Suffering an attack, therefore, poorly serves the purpose of undermining rebels and coup plotters.

Table 3.4: *The fate of leaders and the outcomes of conflict*

After	International crises					Wars				
	In power	Nat. death	OK	Punished	Total	In power	Nat. death	OK	Punished	Total
					Victory					
1 yr.	133	2	13	4	152	40	0	2	3	45
%	87.5	1.32	8.55	2.63	100	88.89	0	4.44	6.67	100
2 yrs.	110	5	17	6	138	44	2	1	0	47
%	79.71	3.62	12.32	4.35	100	93.62	4.26	2.13	0	100
3 yrs.	90	4	12	3	109	36	2	3	0	41
%	82.57	3.67	11.01	2.75	100	87.8	4.88	7.32	0	100
4 yrs.	73	4	10	3	90	32	1	2	1	36
%	81.11	4.44	11.11	3.33	100	88.89	2.78	5.56	2.78	100
					Defeat					
1 yr.	103	1	10	13	127	25	2	3	19	49
%	81.1	0.79	7.87	10.24	100	51.02	4.08	6.12	38.78	100
2 yrs.	79	3	13	14	109	18	2	4	1	25
%	72.48	2.75	11.93	12.84	100	72	8	16	4	100
3 yrs.	64	3	5	8	80	15	0	1	1	17
%	80	3.75	6.25	10	100	88.24	0	5.88	5.88	100

4 yrs.	49	1	8	5	63	12	0	0	2	14
%	77.78	1.59	12.7	7.94	100	85.71	0	0	14.29	100
					Draw					
1 yr.	168	3	14	4	189	49	2	4	0	55
%	88.89	1.59	7.41	2.12	100	89.09	3.64	7.27	0	100
2 yrs.	134	3	25	9	171	41	1	3	4	49
%	78.36	1.75	14.62	5.26	100	83.67	2.04	6.12	8.16	100
3 yrs.	110	4	10	5	129	32	0	3	2	37
%	85.27	3.1	7.75	3.88	100	86.49	0	8.11	5.41	100
4 yrs.	95	1	9	3	108	23	1	4	1	29
%	87.96	0.93	8.33	2.78	100	79.31	3.45	13.79	3.45	100

Note: Entries are the number and percentage of leaders experiencing a given fate given the outcome of conflict over time. See Table B.43 in the Appendix for the disaggregate data for the punishment fates.

The second aspect of conflict that affects leaders' fate is the outcome of conflict. In Table 3.4, we again show that leaders in general know how to weather the consequences of international conflict. Most of the time, leaders remain in power after the termination of conflict.[8] In general, about 80 percent of the leaders in power at the end of a conflict continued to remain in power afterwards, regardless of the outcome. The exception is the fate of leaders who lost a war. Of the leaders defeated in war, 25 (51%) remained in power, 24 (49%) lost power. Of these, 12 were sent into exile, 7 were jailed, 2 died a natural death, and only three preserved their freedom. Unsurprisingly, defeats in war led to higher rates of removal. More surprisingly, however, the negative consequences of a war defeat were short-lived. For the leaders who managed to survive the immediate aftermath of a war defeat, their survival chances improved. Only four leaders suffered punishment: King Abdullah Al-Hussein of Jordan and Benito Mussolini of Italy, who were executed in 1951 and 1945, respectively; Shukri al-Quwatli of Syria and King Farouk of Egypt, who were sent into exile in 1949 and in 1952, respectively.

Within a year of a defeat in an international crisis, 24 leaders lost power, 10 of them in an "ok" manner, 13 of them with punishment; still, 103 (81%) remained in power. A defeat in an international crisis short of war had only a limited impact on leaders' survival. However, losing an international crisis had longer lasting effects than losing a war. From two to four years after the unsuccessful conclusion of an international crisis, leaders continued to experience a risk of turnover analogous to the one they experienced within one year.[9] In sum, then, defeats decreased the ability of leaders to stay in power and preserve their freedom when out of power. Defeats, however, were not

[8] It might look puzzling that we list 40 leaders in power after 1 year of a victory in war and 44 leaders in power after 2 years of a victory in war. This depends on the fact that while our data covers the period from 1919 to 2003, we coded the delayed effect of outcomes that occurred in 1918. For example, the Australian Prime Minister, Billy Hughes, who was in power from October 27, 1915 until February 3, 1923, receives credit in 1919 – the first observation for Australia in our data – for the victorious outcome of World War I that accrued to him in 1918. We also report the table with the three punishment fates disaggregated in Table B.43.

[9] Two years after a defeat, 30 (28%) leaders lost power; three years after, the number slightly declined to 16 (20%) leaders; four years after, 14 (22%) leaders lost power.

necessarily a catastrophic event under two conditions: first, if leaders managed to avoid the escalation of a conflict to full-scale war; and second, in case of war, if they managed to stop domestic opponents from orchestrating a coup within a year of the conclusion of the war.

Victories and draws appear to have little effect. In general, leaders who could reach a victory or a draw apparently continued to remain in office at similar rates. Only a handful of leaders experienced removal with punishment. But before generalizing from these patterns, we should acknowledge that our crude first-cut description is not appropriate to sort out more complicated multivariate causal relations. For example, one of the leaders killed two years after the conclusion of a victorious crisis is US President John Fitzgerald Kennedy, who prevailed in the first Pathet Lao crisis in May of 1961. During his tenure, though, President Kennedy also reached a draw – in the Berlin Wall crisis – and was soundly defeated in the fiasco of the Bay of Pigs. Whether any of these events played any role in his assassination would be just a matter of historical speculation, or fodder for conspiracy theorists.

Kennedy's crisis record is hardly unusual. By the time of his violent death, Anastasio Somoza Debayle of Nicaragua had both victories and defeats on his record; Abdul Karim Kassem of Iraq and Yitzhak Rabin of Israel had a defeat and a draw; Liaquat Ali Khan of Pakistan had a draw and a victory. Rafael Trujillo of the Dominican Republic not only generated much hatred during his brutal rule, but also accumulated victories and defeats in international crises, which contributed to his violent removal. Trujillo's assassins, all former associates of his, were allegedly driven by a range of motivations, "patriotism, political ambition, and greed to revenge (Trujillo had ordered the execution of the brother of one of them, and the brother of another had been sentenced to a long prison term)" (Atkins and Wilson, 1998, 119). His failed attempt to assassinate Venezuelan President Rómulo Betancourt in June of 1960, however, was the straw that broke the camel of US support.[10] The United States joined the Organization of American States (OAS) in imposing economic and diplomatic sanctions against the Dominican Republic and cut off military aid, though

---

[10] A brief overview of the international crisis triggered by the attempt to assassinate Betancourt can be found in International Crisis Behavior Project (2007) at www.cidcm.umd.edu/icb/dataviewer/.

the extent of CIA involvement in the plot to kill Trujillo is obviously disputed.[11]

Only two leaders had a victory and no other crisis outcome on their records when they were assassinated: Inukai Tsuyoshi of Japan, who lost his life during a failed coup attempt in 1932 at the hands of radical elements in the Japanese Navy who saw Inukai as an obstacle to their expansionist goals; and Ngo Dinh Diem of the Republic of Vietnam, who was executed during the coup d'état orchestrated by Duong Van Minh with the consent of the United States in 1963. These leaders met their fate because of a combination of factors during periods of domestic and international crisis rather than any reason that can be specifically linked to the outcomes of an international confrontation short of war. The political benefits of a success in an international crisis, therefore, were no match against other forces conspiring to forcibly remove these leaders.

The cases of exile and imprisonment after victories and draws also have an idiosyncratic character. Eleftherios Venizelos of Greece went into exile to Paris in 1920 after the political and constitutional crisis that followed the death of King Alexander, who died of blood poisoning from a monkey bite.[12] Dimitrios Ioannides, also of Greece, was sent to jail after the war defeat in Cyprus in 1974. Obviously, the initial success in the overthrow of Archbishop Makarios in Cyprus did not matter much, given that it triggered a military intervention from Turkey, which then set into motion the downfall of the military junta of the colonels. The other leader who suffered imprisonment after a crisis success is Shehu Shagari of Nigeria, who lost power in a coup led

---

[11] According to Atkins and Wilson (1998, 119–20), "The Central Intelligence Agency (CIA) then encouraged, organized and planned the assassination, promising to provide automatic rifles." In a secret memorandum prepared in January 1975, Associate Deputy Attorney General James Wilderotter, however, portrays a more limited and indirect role: "With respect to Trujillo's assassination on May 30, 1960, the CIA had 'no active part;' but had a 'faint connection' with the groups that in fact did it." The Wilderotter memorandum was declassified in 2007 in conjunction with the release of the "Family Jewels" Report, which had been compiled at the request of CIA Director James R. Schlesinger to document illegal and inappropriate actions taken by the CIA from the 1950s until the 1970s. It can be accessed at the National Archives via www.gwu.edu/~nsarchiv/NSAEBB/NSAEBB222/family_jewels_wilderotter.pdf.

[12] Apparently, he was bitten in a delicate place on his body.

by General Muhammadu Buhari in 1983. Prevailing in a dispute with Chad in the spring and summer of 1983 was at best a minor palliative to reverse the impact of endemic corruption and economic decline on the decision to stage a coup.

In sum, Tables 3.3 and 3.4 suggest that the only sizeable effect of international conflict is the reduction in the risk of removal for the leaders who had started a conflict while this conflict was ongoing. Otherwise, the tenure costs and benefits appear very uncertain. Eighty-four leaders, that is 18 percent of leaders who lost a crisis, also lost power afterwards. Forty were punished in some manner. The effects of victories and draws were similar: 15 percent and 11 percent of the leaders who won a crisis or reached a draw lost power afterwards.

International conflict might very well be *costly* from the perspective of a state and its populace, but for leaders international conflict triggers political forces that make it more difficult to orchestrate a removal when the conflict is ongoing. When the conflict is over, its outcome factors as only one parameter in a larger array of political forces that combine to drive the probability and manner of losing office.

The findings in these tables, however, only serve to illustrate and describe some basic patterns in the data. While they offer *prima facie* evidence in support of the causal mechanisms in our leader theory of international conflict, they do not directly speak to the political effects of international conflict *compared to staying at peace*. To do so, we turn to statistical modeling in the next section.

3.3 Competing risks: regular and forcible removals

From our theoretical perspective, but also from the perspective of the leaders themselves, staying in power is only one component of what drives policy choices. The preservation of personal freedom and life when out of office is also a fundamental component of leaders' "utility functions." From this assumption, it follows that the analysis of the factors that affect leaders' time in office is not sufficient to explain leaders' decisions to start a conflict, important though it is (Bueno de Mesquita *et al.*, 2003; Chiozza and Goemans, 2004b). We also need to know what factors influence the *manner* of office removal, that is, not just whether a leader is likely to lose power, but also how a leader loses power. In our analysis, we concentrate on the effects of international conflict, both in terms of conflict participation and conflict outcomes.

Specifically, we test six (of the eight) hypotheses that summarize our theory in Chapter 2.

To answer these questions, we estimate what is known as a competing risks model (Diermeier and Stevenson, 1999; Box-Steffensmeier and Jones, 2004), which allows us to examine how a variable affects the timing of one type of office removal *separate* from its effect on the other type of office removal failure.[13] The competing risks model generates two sets of regressions coefficients: those pertaining to the hazard of regular removal and those pertaining to the hazard of forcible removal. In both cases, a positive regression coefficient indicates that, compared to a condition in which no conflict occurred, a given conflict variable *increases* the risk of office removal; a negative coefficient indicates that, compared to no conflict, a conflict variable *decreases* the risk of office removal. We report the coefficients and the 95 percent confidence intervals; confidence intervals that cross zero indicate that there is too much uncertainty in the empirical patterns to claim that a variable is consistently related to office removal.[14]

3.3.1 Testing the hypotheses

In Figure 3.2, we present the results from an encompassing investigation of international conflict for all the leaders in power over an

---

[13] We estimate competing risks Cox proportional hazard models with a frailty term, clustered at the country level. Tests for the existence of non-proportional hazards yield a non-significant finding both in the global test and in the coefficient tests. We report the full set of results, as well as a discussion of our method, in the Appendix. This approach requires that two fundamental assumptions are satisfied. First, as we posited in the theoretical framework developed in the previous chapter, the hazards of losing office for one manner of exit must be independent of the other potential modes of exit. While we leave further details of this approach to the Appendix of this chapter, we briefly note that appropriate statistical tests showed that, as required, the hazards of a regular and a forcible removal from office were indeed statistically independent of each other.

[14] It is important to remember, though, that the mechanisms we developed in Chapter 2 suggest that both the risk of losing office and the risk of conflict initiation could be endogenous. Our competing risks model in this chapter ignores such potential endogeneity. The statistical analysis in the next chapter directly addresses this issue and, thus, offers a second set of empirical tests of different elements of the main causal mechanisms of our theory of conflict onset. The analyses here lay the necessary foundations before we pursue more complicated statistical models.

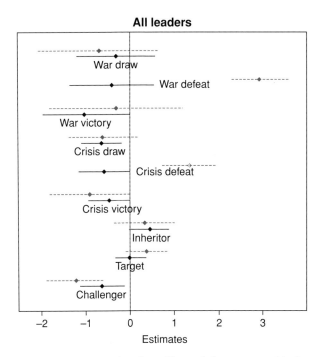

Figure 3.2: International conflict and the manner of losing office

Note: We report the coefficients and the 95% confidence intervals for the regression coefficients of a competing risks Cox proportional hazard model with a frailty term. The solid lines measure the coefficients for the risk of regular removal; the dotted lines measure the coefficients for the risk of forcible removal. Positive coefficients indicate an increase in the hazard of office removal; negative coefficients indicate a decrease in the hazard of office removal. These results can be found in Table B.44 in the Appendix.

80-year period. As we contended, the disaggregation of the different ways leaders can lose office produces striking results. In a nutshell, there are benefits from international conflict which accrue to leaders if they fight as Challengers. There are uncertain gains from victory. There are *serious* costs for leaders if they lose a war or a crisis. Strikingly, but consistent with our expectations, defeat in an international crisis reduces the risk of regular removal from office.

In more detail, Challengers on average enjoyed significantly lower risks of both a regular and a forcible removal from office, although the effect is both statistically and substantively stronger for the hazard of a forcible removal.[15] Contrary to the logic of rallying around the flag, where a foreign threat leads to in- or out-group bias and support for the leader, targets did not enjoy a significantly lower hazard of either a regular or a forcible removal from office. Our analysis shows that it is more difficult to unseat an incumbent after he started a conflict. The fact that leaders who started a conflict obtained political benefits gives support for the fighting for survival mechanism we outlined in the previous chapter.

The leaders who entered into office when a conflict was ongoing – the inheritors – were on average more likely to experience a regular removal than leaders who had remained at peace, while they were as likely to be forcibly removed as the leaders who did not fight. The office tenure of inheritors is thus shorter than that of the leaders who did not participate in conflict. What they gain, though, is a lower risk of a forcible removal. If a leader comes into office to bring a conflict to a conclusion, then he will not be able to obtain the political advantages of a Challenger, but at least he will be able to avoid the adverse consequences that might follow from a long and persistent conflict (Croco, 2008).

The remaining six coefficients in Figure 3.2 summarize the effects of conflict outcomes. Focusing first on victory, we see that victory in a crisis and victory in a war both reduced the hazards of either form of removal, although the large confidence intervals indicate that much uncertainty surrounds these estimates. Victory in a crisis decreased the hazard of both a forcible and regular removal from office; while the effect fails to reach the 5% level, it is significant at the 10% level.

Victory in war decreased the hazard of both a regular and a forcible removal from office. The effect of victory on a regular removal again barely misses the 5% level, but is significant at the 10% level. The effect of victory on a forcible removal fails to reach significance. For both the regular and forcible removals from office, the coefficients are offset by large standard errors, indicating the high levels of uncertainty about the political benefits of victory in war. Overall, it appears as if a leader who prevails in a crisis can reduce the prospects of a forcible removal, while victory in a war does not generate similar benefits, as Winston Churchill and George H. W. Bush would certainly attest.

---

[15] Recall that a leader who initiated a conflict is coded a Challenger for each year of the conflict. Similarly, a defending leader is a Target for each year of the conflict.

A victorious war, thus, seems to hold out the somewhat uncertain prospects of increased time in office (but see Chapter 4); it makes it more likely, though, that when leadership transition takes place, it will follow regular and non-violent processes. This pattern is consistent with the empirical fact that democracies have strong records of war victories (Reiter and Stam, 2002). If the victorious leaders are democratic for the most part, they gain at best some political benefit when they win a war, as indicated by a decreased hazard of regular removal; these benefits, however, are just one of many parameters democratic publics consider when they vote to re-elect the incumbents, which then would account for the uncertainty in this finding. As our *peace through insecurity* mechanism contends, leaders who are predominantly concerned about regular removals have relatively little to gain even from prevailing in international conflicts.

The apparently insignificant effect of victory in war on the hazard of a forcible removal from office also runs contrary to the *gambling for survival* mechanism proposed in the previous chapter. Before we reject this mechanism, however, we need to consider two potential explanations for this apparent insignificance. First, as found by Reiter and Stam III (1998), conflict initiation may significantly increase the probability of victory. As a result, the coefficient for challenging would be inflated while the coefficient for victory would be deflated. Second, victory could have an insignificant effect because of the endogeneity of conflict initiation. We explore these potential confounding factors in the next chapter.

When we examine the effects of defeat, our model reveals a striking pattern. As we claimed in the previous chapter, defeat had either a *decreasing* or an insignificant effect on the hazard of regular removal. Notably, and again confirming our argument, defeat in both crises and wars substantially increased the risk of a forcible removal. Before jumping to the conclusion that *even* in the case of defeat, an international crisis serves as a boon for the political career of a leader, we should explain again why we expected to find a *negative* coefficient on regular removals. The reason is that after a defeat a coercive removal becomes so likely that few leaders managed to avoid it.[16] While only 21

---

[16] Technically, the leaders who lost power by forcible removal are coded as "censored" in the model that predicts regular removal. Thus, the negative and significant coefficient (p-value = 0.054) on the crisis defeat variable is generated by the fact that many leaders left the sample as censored in the regular removal model.

percent of the leaders who did *not* lose an international crisis stepped out of office by forcible means, the percentage nearly doubled (39%) among the leaders who *did* lose an international crisis. If we look at the findings on the two manners of leadership turnover simultaneously, therefore, we see that a defeat triggered strong political dynamics that led to coercive and irregular losses of power for many leaders. The leaders who managed to prevent a forcible removal were of a special kind: tyrants and charismatic leaders like Kim Il-Sung, Marshal Tito, King Hussein of Jordan, or Fidel Castro. As we see in Table 3.5, all the leaders who were still in power fifteen years after a defeat in a crisis or a war were leaders that, for better or worse, made history for their countries.

These findings about defeat directly contradict the logic of the traditional *gambling for resurrection* argument (Richards *et al.*, 1993; Downs and Rocke, 1994) which assumes that the punishment of leaders is truncated at the mere loss of office. We find, to the contrary, that the punishment for defeat typically implies a forcible removal from office, with its associated unpleasant subsequent consequences for leaders. The punishment for war defeat is, therefore, *expanded* and not truncated. A leader who is about to lose power cannot view war just as a risky gamble whose potential negative consequence is the "mere" loss of office. A war that ends in defeat implies more than loss of office. It implies a high risk of *loss of life* or *liberty*.

Finally, we find that draws in crises reduced the hazard of regular removal, but did not have a statistically significant impact on the hazard of forcible removal. We also find that draws in war did not significantly affect either manner of losing office. When both sides to a conflict can claim they obtained something, either because they managed to reach a compromise or they fought and bargained to a stalemate, they were not any better or any worse off than a leader who stayed at peace.

If taken as a whole, the findings in Figure 3.2 show that, on average, the leaders who started a conflict and kept it to the level of low intensity of a crisis were able to benefit from more secure time in office, as long as they were not defeated. International conflict would seem to bring uncertain benefits, but can be quite costly in case of defeat for leaders who anticipate a forcible removal from office. These results, however, do not take into consideration the domestic political conditions in which conflict might make a difference, and as such, they can

Table 3.5: *Leaders in power after fifteen years of a defeat in a war or crisis*

Leader	Country	In power		Manner of exit
		from	to	
Biya	Cameroon	1982–11–06	2004–12–31	In power
Castro	Cuba	1959–01–02	2004–12–31	In power
Masaryk	Czechoslovakia	1918–10–28	1935–12–14	Ill health
Husak	Czechoslovakia	1968–08–28	1989–12–17	Regular
Mobutu	Dem. Rep. of the Congo	1965–11–25	1997–05–16	Forcible
Rafael Trujillo	Dominican Republic	1930–08–16	1961–05–30	Forcible
Rawlings	Ghana	1981–12–31	2001–01–07	Regular
Hussein Ibn Talal El-Hashim	Jordan	1952–08–11	1999–02–07	Natural death
Qaddafi	Libya	1969–09–01	2004–12–31	In power
Kim Il-Sung	North Korea	1948–09–09	1994–07–08	Natural death
Al-Assad H.	Syria	1971–02–22	2000–06–10	Natural death
Chiang Kai-shek	Taiwan	1950–03–01	1975–04–05	Natural death
Yahya	Yemen Arab Republic	1904–06–04	1948–02–17	Forcible
Tito	Yugoslavia	1945–03–06	1980–05–04	Natural death
Kaunda	Zambia	1964–10–24	1991–11–02	Regular

only serve as a broad baseline. Obviously, factors other than international conflict affect the fate of leaders (Goemans, 2008).[17] In the next section, we investigate which leaders, under which conditions, might find international conflict politically beneficial.

3.4 Under what conditions?

We analyze whether, compared to the general case we have analyzed so far, domestic political institutions, domestic unrest, economic development, and growth change the costs and benefits of international conflict for leaders' personal and political well-being.[18] These four different conditions address specific assumptions of our theory; i.e. the ability to commit to safeguard the fate of deposed leaders, which is related to the nature of domestic political institutions and the level of economic development of a country; the existence of a high risk of forcible removal, which we measure by the involvement in a civil war; and the role of unexpected shocks to a leader's capabilities and legitimacy, as they are captured in the disruption to the normal patterns of functioning of the economy that occurs during a recession.

3.4.1 Conflict and domestic political institutions

In the footsteps of Riker (1982), we argued in Chapter 2 that the development of domestic political institutions is closely tied with credible guarantees of the leader's post-tenure safety. These credible guarantees of safety are in turn closely related with how leaders lose office. Riker (ibid.) suggested that these guarantees were a hallmark of democracy. We would therefore expect that democratic leaders are significantly

---

[17] In a recent analysis, Goemans (2008) has presented an extensive model of the causes of office removal. For instance, a poor growth rate assuredly increases the hazard of a regular as well as an irregular removal from office.

[18] Rather than estimating an encompassing model with a long list of potential control variables, we "split the samples," that is, we evaluate the impact of conflict in a set of countries and leaders who meet a specific condition. Our approach complements the larger analysis presented in Goemans (2008). As is the case for the model in Figure 3.2, we estimate competing risks Cox proportional hazard models with a frailty term, clustered at the country level. We add a penalty term to the likelihood for the parameters associated with variables where no failure outcomes occur, i.e. the "empty cell" problem (Therneau and Grambsch, 2000, 120–4).

less likely to lose office in a forcible manner.[19] Therefore, we rely on regime type as a – noisy – indicator for political institutions that can or cannot credibly guarantee the leader's post-tenure safety. Autocracies and mixed regimes, then, are systems that lack such institutions and as such should be typically associated with the forcible process of leader removal. Presidential and parliamentary democracies should be systems that do provide credible guarantees and thus should be associated with regular removals from office.

If this classification captures our theoretical distinction, international conflict should have the effects postulated by our theory most strongly for leaders of autocracies and mixed regimes. These provide the weakest protections for leaders and thus tend to remove their leaders in a forcible manner. We would thus expect that for leaders of autocracies and mixed regimes, Challenging lowers their hazard of a forcible removal from office, while democratic leaders would gain less, if any, advantage from Challenging. The leaders that rule in autocratic and mixed regimes, in other words, would be the ones that gain the most from fighting for survival. For leaders of democracies, on the other hand, the combination of insecurity *in office* and security *out of office* makes staying at peace a preferable option for their political careers.

In Figure 3.3, we show that domestic political institutions do indeed significantly mediate how international conflict roles and outcomes affect the tenure of leaders. First, we find that international conflict presents significant risks and benefits for Autocratic leaders, especially with respect to the prospect of forcible removal. If they start a conflict, Autocrats can expect to strengthen their hold on power as long as a conflict they initiated is ongoing. Only one leader in our data, Ioannides of Greece, was removed from power regularly while still in the role of Challenger. If we consider that this event occurred during the final days of the Greek regime of the Colonels, we can conclude that autocratic

---

[19] This expectation is borne out in Goemans (2008), who found that leaders of parliamentary and presidential democracies enjoy a lower hazard of a forcible removal from office than do autocratic leaders and leaders of mixed regimes. The difference between presidential and autocratic leaders did not reach statistical significance. Leaders of parliamentary democracies were not significantly different from leaders of presidential democracies. See an "Additional" paper accompanying Goemans (2008), available at http://mail.rochester.edu/~hgoemans/research.htm.

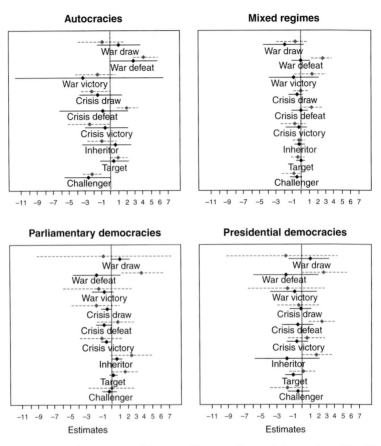

Figure 3.3: The manner of losing office: conflict and domestic political institutions

Note: We report the coefficients and the 95% confidence intervals for the regression coefficients of a competing risks Cox proportional hazard model with a frailty term. The solid lines measure the coefficients for the risk of regular removal; the dotted lines measure the coefficients for the risk of forcible removal. Positive coefficients indicate an increase in the hazard of office removal; negative coefficients indicate a decrease in the hazard of office removal. These results can be found in Tables B.45, B.46, B.47, and B.48 in the Appendix.

leaders have a substantial track record of avoiding regular removals as Challengers.

Analogously, only six autocratic Challenger leaders were forcibly removed from power. These leaders, who are listed in Table 3.6,

Table 3.6: *Autocratic challengers who suffered a forcible removal*

Leader	Country	In power from	to	Fate
Mullah Omar	Afghanistan	1996–09–27	2001–11–13	Unknown
Galtieri	Argentina	1981–12–12	1982–06–17	Jail
Hitler	Germany	1933–01–30	1945–04–30	Suicide
Mussolini	Italy	1922–10–30	1943–07–25	Killed
El-Atassi, N.	Syria	1966–02–25	1970–11–13	Jail
Amin	Uganda	1971–01–25	1979–04–11	Exile

Table 3.7: *Autocratic targets who suffered a forcible removal*

Leader	Country	In power from	to	Fate	Externally deposed?
Zogu	Albania	1925–01–10	1939–04–12	Exile	Yes
Schuschnigg	Austria	1934–07–30	1938–03–11	Jail	Yes
Sihanouk	Cambodia	1953–11–09	1970–03–18	Exile	No
Pol Pot	Cambodia	1975–04–11	1979–01–07	OK	Yes
Sampson	Cyprus	1974–07–16	1974–07–23	Jail	No
Dubcek	Czechoslovakia	1968–01–05	1968–08–20	Jail	Yes
Cedras	Haiti	1991–09–30	1994–10–14	Exile	Yes
Kun	Hungary	1919–03–21	1919–08–01	Exile	Yes
Nagy	Hungary	1956–10–25	1956–11–04	Jail	Yes
Saddam Hussein	Iraq	1979–07–16	2003–04–09	Jail	Yes
Jabir As-Sabah	Kuwait	1978–01–01	1990–08–02	Exile	Yes
Jonathan	Lesotho	1966–10–04	1986–01–20	Exile	No
Anastasio Somoza Debayle	Nicaragua	1967–05–01	1979–07–17	Killed	No
Noriega	Panama	1983–08–15	1990–01–03	Jail	Yes

however, owe their fate to the fact that were also on the losing side of the conflict in which they were involved. We also find that Autocratic leaders who were targeted in a conflict were more likely to suffer a forcible removal. Indeed, as we illustrate in Table 3.7, ten of the fourteen Target leaders who lost power in a forcible manner were deposed by a foreign country.

Once the conflict terminates, Autocratic leaders gained some benefits from Victories and Draws in crises, but incurred large tenure punishments from Defeats. The sign and size of the coefficients for Victories and Draws indicate that the chances to remain in power and to avoid a coercive removal from power improve. The large standard errors, however, show that the effects of Victory and Draws are relatively uncertain – most likely because few Autocrats manage to prevail in War and Crises (Gelpi and Griesdorf, 2001; Reiter and Stam, 2002). Moreover, to add uncertainty to this finding, the Autocrats who prevailed in war often ended up suffering major defeats as well, as was the case for King Hussein of Jordan, Nasser, Hitler, and Mussolini. Saddam Hussein is a perfect illustration of how short-lived the benefits of war can be for an authoritarian leader. He conquered Kuwait in 1990 allegedly dampening the risk of a coup, only to be defeated by a large international coalition a few months later. The defeat heightened the risk of an insurrection, which Saddam Hussein brutally repressed to reconsolidate his power.

Defeats were another matter. Losing a war increased the hazard of both forms of removal. The effects of losing a crisis were no less damaging. While the coefficient on crisis defeat is statistically insignificant, and negative, this estimate is due to the fact that the leaders who lost a crisis experienced a disproportionately high rate of forcible removals, which implies that few leaders remained at risk of a regular removal. Those who avoided a coercive removal from power remained in office for long spells – from three years in the case of Kruschev to fourteen and twenty-two years in the case of Nyerere and Husak, respectively – before losing power in a regular manner. Taken together, the results suggest that autocratic leaders might both *fight* and *gamble for survival*, although the latter mechanism appears most likely to work to the Autocrat's advantage as long as he can limit the conflict to a crisis.

For leaders of mixed regimes and of democratic regimes, we find only a few systematic patterns in the data. As postulated, Challenging leaders of mixed regimes lowered their risk of a forcible removal from office. The effect (just barely) fails to reach significance at the 5% level but is significant at the 10% level.[20] Thus, for leaders of mixed

---

[20] As we report in Table B.46 in the Appendix, the significance levels are 0.083 and 0.114, respectively in the case of forcible and regular removal.

regimes, international conflict initiation appears to bring relatively uncertain benefits. Moreover, victory does not reduce the probability of a forcible removal from office. Defeat, on the other hand, significantly increases the risk of a forcible removal, particularly if the conflict escalated to war. Given that we postulated mixed regimes would lack the institutions to protect leaders after they lose office, these results are disappointing for the *fighting for survival* mechanism, but not sufficient to outright reject it. Leaders of mixed regimes can still fight for survival, because Challengers do gain some reduced hazard of a forcible removal.

Leaders of democracies, in contrast, enjoy the safeguards after their retirement; they therefore need not fear a forcible removal from office and thus have little to gain from conflict initiation or victory. As expected, leaders of both presidential and parliamentary democracies do not appear to fight or gamble for survival: Challenging does not affect their hazard of either a forcible or regular removal from office, and neither does victory.

Very few other conflict variables achieved statistical significance: leaders of parliamentary democracies who were attacked face an increased hazard of forcible removal; inheritors in parliamentary democracies face an increased hazard of regular removal. These significant findings, though, reflect very specific conditions. Three of the four democratic prime ministers who lost power irregularly after an attack were the leaders defeated by Nazi Germany in the terrible year of 1940.[21] The cases of democratic prime ministers inheriting a conflict and losing power shortly afterwards were predominantly in the French Fourth Republic (nine cases) and in Spain during the Civil War (three cases).

It might seem puzzling to observe that in the case of democratic prime ministers a defeat in a crisis has a negative and significant coefficient on regular removal, and a non-significant coefficient on forcible removal. Recall, however, that we predicted in the previous chapter that defeat might actually lower the risk of a regular removal from office. Certainly, the fact that, of the twenty-one prime ministers who lost an international crisis, only two – Yitzhak Rabin of Israel in 1995

---

[21] The fourth leader was Sayyid Khalil of Sudan, who lost power in a bloodless coup in November of 1958 during a period of tensions with Nasser's Egypt. Specifically, Khalil was involved in a minor border dispute with Egypt in February of 1958.

and Omar Sharif of Pakistan in 1999 – lost power irregularly afterwards explains why there is no systematic relation between crisis defeat and forcible removal. Of the remaining leaders, fifteen lost power by regular means; one, Stauning of Denmark in 1940, died of natural causes in office two years later; one, Borden of Canada, retired because of ill-health in 1920; and another one, Simitis of Greece, was still in power at the end of 2003, the last year in our data set. Table 3.8 lists all the cases of defeated prime ministers, and the time elapsed from the crisis defeat to the loss of office.

3.4.2 Conflict and domestic political unrest

How does international conflict alter the timing and manner of losing power for leaders who face severe domestic political unrest in the form of a civil war?[22] If we take civil war as indicative of the absence of credible guarantees of the leader's safety and of a high risk of losing office in a forcible manner, this amounts to a most likely scenario for the *fighting for survival* mechanism. Therefore, we would expect Challenging to significantly decrease the risk of a forcible removal from office for a leader engaged in a civil war, while having no impact on the risk of regular removals. Importantly, though, this analysis also offers an additional contribution to the study of warfare, beside assessing one of the causal mechanisms of our theory. Given the pervasive spillover effects of domestic unrest into international conflict, as documented in Gleditsch, Salehyan and Schultz (2008), our empirical analysis also grounds the processes of externalization into the domestic political incentives of leaders who care about surviving politically *and* personally.

In Figure 3.4 we report the findings of the competing risks model for the leaders involved in a civil war.[23] We find that in general, international conflict – both in terms of roles and of outcomes – did not affect processes of regular leadership turnover. None of the conflict coefficients was large enough to be statistically discernible from a null

---

[22] Goemans (2008) found that, as one would expect, leaders who experienced a civil war were less likely to be removed from office in a regular manner. Interestingly, Goemans also found that for leaders caught in a civil war, the risks of a forcible removal increased over time.

[23] We report the findings for the leaders who enjoyed domestic political peace in Table B.50 in the Appendix.

Table 3.8: *Leaders of parliamentary democracies and crisis defeat*

Country	Leader	Year	Conflict	Adversary	Out of power
Belgium	van Zeeland	1936	Remilit. of Rhineland	Germany	1937–10–25
Belgium	Lefevre	1962	Katanga	Dem. Rep. of Congo	1965–07–27
Canada	Borden	1919	Russian Civil War	Russia	1920–06–10
Denmark	Stauning	1940	WWII	Germany	1940–04–09
France	Millerand	1920	Russian Civil War	Russia	1920–09–03
France	Sarraut	1936	Remilit. of Rhineland	Germany	1936–06–03
France	Chautemps	1938	Alexandretta	Turkey	1938–03–12
France	Daladier	1938	Alexandretta	Turkey	1940–03–21
France	Daladier	1939	Alexandretta	Turkey	1940–03–21
Germany	Adenauer	1961	Berlin Wall	DDR	1963–10–15
Greece	Simitis	1996	Aegean Sea	Turkey	2004–03–10
Israel	Ben Gurion	1949	Sinai Incursion	UK	1953–12–08
Israel	Ben Gurion	1956	Suez	USSR	1963–06–16
Israel	Begin	1981	Al-Biqa Missiles	Syria	1983–10–10
Israel	Rabin	1993	Operation Accountability	Lebanon	1995–11–04
Pakistan	Sharif	1999	Kashmir Kargil	India	1999–10–12
Turkey	Demirel	1976	Aegean Sea	Greece	1977–06–21
Turkey	Demirel	1992	Nagorny-Karabakh	Armenia	1993–05–16
United Kingdom	Lloyd-George	1919	Russian Civil War	Russia	1922–10–19
United Kingdom	Churchill	1940	Closure Burma Road	Japan	1945–07–27
United Kingdom	MacMillan	1961	Berlin Wall	DDR	1963–10–18

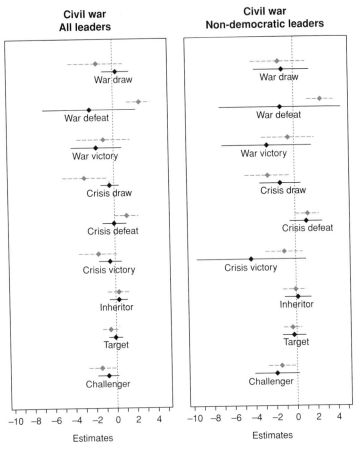

Figure 3.4: The manner of losing office: conflict and domestic political unrest

Note: we report the coefficients and the 95% confidence intervals for the regression coefficients of a competing risks Cox proportional hazard model with a frailty term. The solid lines measure the coefficients for the risk of regular removal; the dotted lines measure the coefficients for the risk of forcible removal. Positive coefficients indicate an increase in the hazard of office removal; negative coefficients indicate a decrease in the hazard of office removal. These results can be found in Tables B.49 and B.51 in the Appendix.

effect. Of the 327 leaders who stepped out of power while a civil war was ongoing, 129 (39%) suffered a forcible removal, while 181 (55%) left power in regular way, and 17 (5%) were still in power at the end of our period of analysis. More leaders, thus, left power in a regular

manner than otherwise. This result underscores the experience of countries like Britain, Israel, and India, that suffered serious domestic political unrest. For British, Israeli, and Indian leaders, a civil war was
certainly a political concern, a national tragedy, and occasionally a
threat to their lives. In these cases, however, the risk that the civil
war would imperil the foundations of regular processes of leadership
turnover was inconceivable. It is not surprising, therefore, that we
found no connections between civil war, international conflict, and
regular removal.

For leaders who would face removal with punishment, however,
international conflict opened up a window of opportunity for their
survival. Initiating an international conflict in the midst of a civil war
significantly reduced the hazard of a coercive leadership change. In
our sample, there were eleven leaders who lost power while they were
involved simultaneously in an international conflict they had started
and in a civil war; four were forcibly removed – Mullah Omar of
Afghanistan, Patrick Lumumba of the Democratic Republic of Congo,
Idi Amin of Uganda, and Al-Sallal of the Yemen Arab Republic; five
lost power regularly – Habibie of Indonesia, Golda Meir and Men-
achem Begin of Israel, Benazir Bhutto of Pakistan, and Namaliu of
Papua New Guinea; and two died a natural death in office – Neto of
Angola, and Eshkol of Israel. Most often, the leaders who initiated
a conflict during a civil war managed to avoid removal at a remarkable rate. Of the 55 leaders who took the risk of initiating a conflict
during a civil war, 44 were able to stay in power throughout the duration of the conflict. Under conditions of a civil war, fighting helped
survival.

Once the conflict was over, only defeats strongly affected the risk of
forcible removal. Of the ten leaders who lost a war when their countries
were undergoing major domestic unrest, only two – Ben Gurion and
Nehru – were not removed with force. Of the remaining eight, only
one, the Cambodian tyrant Pol Pot, avoided punishment after losing
office.[24]

If defeats were a nearly sure recipe for punishment, victories and
draws were not systematically associated with the fate of leaders. The

[24] The negative and insignificant coefficient on war defeat in the model predicting
regular removal is due to the fact that only one leader, Ben Gurion,
experienced such an outcome, seven years after the Suez debacle.

large negative signs indicated that victories and draws improved survival prospects; the large confidence intervals indicated the high degrees
of uncertainty associated with their effects. Among the ten war victors,
for example, we have democratic leaders like Margaret Thatcher and
Golda Meir who did not suffer punishment, on the one hand, and dictators like Mengistu Mariam of Ethiopia and Habre of Angola who were
sent to exile, on the other. Overall, then, as long as they avoided defeat,
the leaders who initiated an international conflict "bought" extra time
in office for themselves while the conflict was ongoing, and some risky
chances of making it fine at the end of it. If the alternative was a high
risk of punishment in the *absence* of an international conflict, we see
why leaders have personal political incentives to externalize conflict
during civil war.

When we distinguish between democratic and non-democratic (i.e.
both authoritarian and mixed regimes), we find that the personal and
political fates of the non-democratic leaders drove our results (right
panel of Figure 3.4). For democratic leaders, international conflict
during civil war did not have any discernible impact on their survival
as leaders.[25] After all, there were only thirteen democratic leaders who
suffered a forcible removal from power when their countries were
involved in a civil war. Of these leaders, *none* had either initiated a
conflict or suffered an attack; only one – Miaja of Spain – had suffered
a defeat in a war that he had "inherited" in 1939. The benefits and
costs of conflict during civil war only accrued to the non-democratic
leaders.

The results strongly suggest that non-democratic leaders involved
in a civil conflict *fight for survival*, since Challenging clearly reduced
their risk of a forcible removal from office. We suspect that leaders
involved in a civil war initiate an international conflict to deal, not
so much with their international enemies, as to deal with domestic
enemies. Operations to eliminate safe havens across the border can
significantly reduce a leader's risk of a forcible removal. As suggested
in Chapter 2, victory against a foreign leader and country does not
appear to be necessary to obtain the private benefits of conflict. We find
less evidence in favor of *gambling for survival*, since victory does not
appear to significantly affect either manner of losing office. However,

---

[25] The findings for the democratic leaders are reported in Table B.52 in the
Appendix.

as noted above, this might be the result of the endogeneity of conflict initiation or of the fact that initiation is significantly associated with victory.

3.4.3 Conflict and economic development

In Figure 3.5, we distinguish three levels of economic development: (*a*) poor countries; (*b*) middle-income countries; and (*c*) rich countries.[26] Building upon one of the most venerable research traditions in comparative politics (Lipset, 1959; Huntington, 1968; Przeworski *et al.*, 2000), we contend that relatively under-developed countries systematically lack the political institutions to guarantee political leaders their safety after they lose office, and thus should be most likely to exhibit the process of forcible removals from office.[27] If this conjecture is correct, we would expect conflict to have the biggest effect on the forcible removal from office among the poorer countries. In other words, Challenging should decrease the risk of a forcible removal from office among poor, but not among rich countries.

Both among poor and rich countries, international conflict does not have much to offer to leaders. Starting from the right panel, we find that defeat in war increased the risk of regular and irregular removals for leaders of wealthy countries, while neither victory nor a draw significantly affected leaders' survival. To have a sense of this pattern, we should note that seventeen leaders of wealthy countries achieved victories in war. All these leaders but one – Al-Assad of Syria – were democratic leaders – from Australia, Britain, Canada, France, Israel, New Zealand, and the United States. None of these leaders suffered a forcible removal; none suffered any form of punishment.

On the other hand, there were only five "rich losers." Of these, two were forcibly removed – General Galtieri of Argentina in 1982 and Kuwatli of Syria in 1949; two were removed regularly – Ioannides of

---

[26] We define economic development on the basis of the distribution of the GDP per capita (logged) of the countries in our sample. Poor countries are those in the bottom 20% of the distribution (below $990); middle-income countries are those between the 20th and the 80th percentile in the distribution; and rich countries are those in the top 80% of the distribution (above $6,180).

[27] Goemans (2008) did indeed find that countries with a higher GDP per capita are significantly less likely to experience a forcible removal from office.

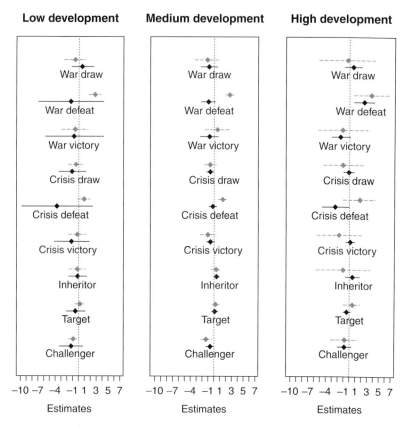

Figure 3.5: The manner of losing office: conflict and economic development

Note: We report the coefficients and the 95% confidence intervals for the regression coefficients of a competing risks Cox proportional hazard model with a frailty term. The solid lines measure the coefficients for the risk of regular removal; the dotted lines measure the coefficients for the risk of forcible removal. Positive coefficients indicate an increase in the hazard of office removal; negative coefficients indicate a decrease in the hazard of office removal. These results can be found in Tables B.53, B.54, and B.55 in the Appendix.

Greece in 1974 and Costa Gomes of Portugal in 1976; one died in office – Al-Assad of Syria in 2000, who also claimed a victory.

Analogously, we also find that international conflict was not a major determinant of leaders' fate in poor countries. Again, a war defeat significantly increased the hazard of forcible removal, while we estimated that a defeat in war had no effect on the hazard of regular removal. No leader in a poor country who suffered a defeat in war lost power in a regular manner. All the "poor losers" were forcibly removed, with the exception of the democratic leader of India, Nehru, who died in office. All the leaders forcibly removed, with the exception of Pol Pot, also suffered punishment: Zogu of Albania (1939), Mobutu of the Democratic Republic of Congo (1997), Farouk of Egypt (1952), Selassie of Ethiopia (1936), and Idi Amin of Uganda (1979) were sent to exile; Yahya Khan of Pakistan (1971) was imprisoned; and Yahya of the Yemen Arab Republic (1948) was killed.[28]

All the "action" in terms of conflict effects and leaders' survival takes place among the middle-income countries. There we find that defeats and initiation were significantly associated with leaders' fate, while victory and draw in crisis were close to statistical significance. To explore how the effects of economic development mix with those of regime type, we "split" the group of middle-income countries again, this time adding the distinction between democratic and non-democratic countries.

In Figure 3.6, we find that in countries that have reached medium levels of economic development, democratic leaders were rewarded with lower hazards of regular removal from office after victories in crises. Initiating a conflict, on the other hand, did not generate tenure benefits. For the democratic leaders in middle-income countries, conflict was a political resource when they could claim that a victory in the international arena was a sign of their superior competence. Unlike the leaders of non-democratic countries where the risk of a forcible removal is high, however, the leaders of middle-income democracies could not use international conflict to disrupt potential coup plotters by sending them to the front. The insignificant coefficient on the variable measuring whether a leader started the conflict underscores a specific aspect of the relationship between conflict and

---

[28] The negative and insignificant coefficient, therefore, indicates that all the possible regular removals were censored events. This coefficient can only be estimated by placing a penalty term for it in the likelihood. The fact that there are no failure events for the war defeat implies a monotone likelihood with infinite coefficient and standard error. The penalty term "shrinks" the coefficient towards zero (Therneau and Grambsch, 2000). For an example of this problem, also see Goemans (2000a), as well as the discussion in Section B.5 in the Appendix.

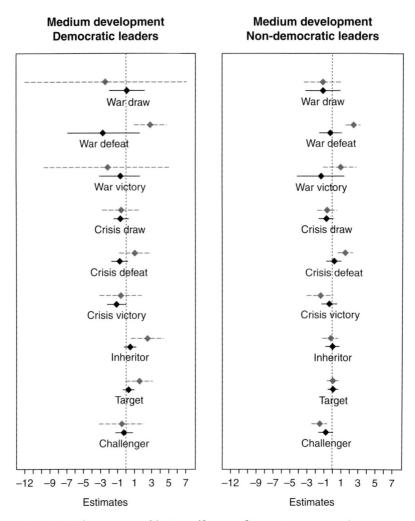

Figure 3.6: The manner of losing office: conflict, regime type and economic development

Note: We report the coefficients and the 95% confidence intervals for the regression coefficients of a competing risks Cox proportional hazard model with a frailty term. The solid lines measure the coefficients for the risk of regular removal; the dotted lines measure the coefficients for the risk of forcible removal. Positive coefficients indicate an increase in the hazard of office removal; negative coefficients indicate a decrease in the hazard of office removal. These results can be found in Tables B.56, and B.57 in the Appendix.

tenure in countries where the life and liberty of the leaders is hardly at risk.

International conflict, however, also entailed substantial risks for the leaders of middle-income democracies. When their countries were targeted in an international conflict, they experienced increased risk of forcible removal, a fate that befell six of them – Pierlot, de Geer, and Nygaardsvold at the hands of Nazi Germany in 1940; Archbishop Makarios of Cyprus in 1974, Shagari of Nigeria in 1983, and Bosch of the Dominican Republic in 1963. Tenure was also shorter and more likely to end in a forcible manner for the middle-income democratic leaders who "inherited" a conflict when they acceded to power. The leaders in question were predominantly the leaders of the French Fourth Republic between 1920 and 1949, and the leaders of Spain at the time of the Civil War.[29] Should a war end in defeat, the middle-income democratic leaders faced serious risks of forcible removal. A war defeat occurred to only six leaders; three were forcibly removed: Miaja of Spain, Pierlot of Belgium, and Nygaardsvold of Norway; of the remaining three, two were removed regularly – Ben Gurion of Israel and Briand of France; one, Masaryk of Czechoslovakia, retired because of ill-health in 1935, more than 15 years after suffering a war defeat against Hungary.[30]

In the right panel of Figure 3.6, we also find that international conflict substantially affected leaders' fate in middle-income non-democratic countries. This time, however, initiating a conflict rather than winning mattered. Challengers were significantly less likely to suffer a regular removal, and with slightly weaker statistical significance, to experience a forcible removal. Conflict outcomes, on the other hand, were mostly ineffectual, with the exception of losing. In the case of regimes where coups were not just a distant prospect, leaders were able to maneuver their domestic opponents by initiating a conflict, and thus secure for themselves reduced chances of a forcible removal. As before, these findings indicate support for the *fighting for survival* mechanism, but not for *gambling for survival*.

---

[29] We already identified these leaders when we discussed the fate of prime ministers in parliamentary democracies.

[30] The paucity of cases of democratic leaders losing a war generates the negative and highly insignificant coefficient in the model predicting regular removals.

3.4.4 Conflict and economic growth

The final set of conditions we investigate is the state of the economy. We concentrate on the most dire situation, negative economic growth. This scenario should arguably come closest to capturing a temporary shock in the leader's legitimacy and capabilities. As the literature on civil war has extensively documented, coups and domestic political unrest become more likely when the economy suddenly declines (Londregan and Poole, 1990; Collier and Hoeffler, 2004), which in turn should make conflict initiation most attractive for leaders who now anticipate a forcible removal from office. As a result, we expect Challenging to pay for leaders experiencing negative economic growth and less, if at all, for leaders experiencing positive growth.

The presence of severe economic recession affected about one-third of the observations in our data, an outcome common enough to make the analysis relevant. Overall, the findings in Figure 3.7 are not that different from those we just discussed for non-democratic leaders of middle-income countries. When the economy tanked, the leaders who started a conflict saw their survival chances improve. Similarly, the outcomes of conflict, with the exception of defeat, were not systematically related to the fate of leaders. For comparison, we also report the results we obtained when we estimated our competing risks model on the leaders who were in power when the economy was experiencing positive growth. In general, we did not find any new or relevant patterns under such a broad condition as positive economic growth. Sudden "jumps" in the economy, steady slow progress, and double-digit growth are all different conditions that are lumped together in the blanket category of positive growth.

A disproportionate number (76%) of the observations in the sample of countries experiencing severe economic recession were non-democratic, either authoritarian or mixed regimes. We, therefore, disentangle some of the forces that change the effects of international conflict on leaders during good and bad economic times by focusing on non-democratic leaders and on leaders of middle-income countries.

In the top part of Figure 3.8, we show that for non-democratic leaders, international conflict provided a risky but beneficial strategy for their survival when the economy was in bad condition, but not when it was in good shape. Only the coefficient measuring the impact of

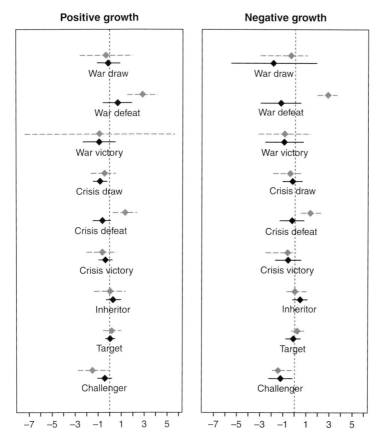

Figure 3.7: The manner of losing office: conflict and economic growth

Note: We report the coefficients and the 95% confidence intervals for the regression coefficients of a competing risks Cox proportional hazard model with a frailty term. The solid lines measure the coefficients for the risk of regular removal; the dotted lines measure the coefficients for the risk of forcible removal. Positive coefficients indicate an increase in the hazard of office removal; negative coefficients indicate a decrease in the hazard of office removal. These results can be found in Tables B.58, and B.59 in the Appendix.

war defeat on forcible removal was statistically discernible from zero when a country was experiencing positive growth. All the other coefficients were close to zero, or had very large standard errors. Leaders who managed to keep the economy growing did not find it necessary or helpful to resort to international conflict to bolster their prospects

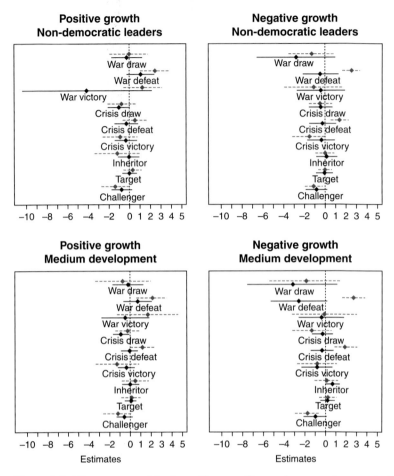

Figure 3.8: The manner of losing office: conflict and economic growth for middle-income and non-democratic leaders

Note: We report the coefficients and the 95% confidence intervals for the regression coefficients of a competing risks Cox proportional hazard model with a frailty term. The solid lines measure the coefficients for the risk of regular removal; the dotted lines measure the coefficients for the risk of forcible removal. Positive coefficients indicate an increase in the hazard of office removal; negative coefficients indicate a decrease in the hazard of office removal. These results can be found in Tables B.60, B.61, B.62, and B.63 in the Appendix.

in office. When the economy was in dire straits, however, starting a conflict provided the opportunity to postpone a forcible removal. Certainly, the leaders who made that decision took a risk. If their gamble ended in defeat, they would expose themselves to heightened risks of forcible removal. But if the risk of being thrown out of office violently, with its associated risk of punishment, was already high, international conflict paid off.

A similar pattern emerges in the bottom part of Figure 3.8 where we investigate how international conflict and economic conditions interacted in the group of middle-income countries. Again when the economy was good, the leaders of middle-income countries did not find their fate in office systematically affected by international conflict. When the economy was doing poorly, however, starting a conflict reduced the hazards of both regular and forcible removals.

Overall, there were fifty-six leaders of middle-income countries that started a conflict when the economy was in a recession. Only six of these lost power when they were involved in the conflict they started. All the others pushed the day of their political reckoning further away in time. The leaders who lost power included the leaders of the Axis countries: Hitler, who committed suicide, Mussolini, and Tojo.

If negative economic growth represents a temporary shock to the leader's capabilities and legitimacy, we would expect leaders of countries that cannot credibly guarantee their safety after losing office to gain from conflict initiation. Accordingly, leaders of non-democracies or medium levels of development should gain a lower hazard of a forcible removal from office. Leaders of developed or democratic countries, in contrast, should have little reason to fear a forcible removal from office and therefore have little to gain from conflict initiation. These patterns are confirmed in the data, and indicate support for our *fighting for survival* mechanism. The results provide only very tentative support for *gambling for survival*, since victories in crises hold out only uncertain benefits.

3.4.5 Summary

What do all these findings amount to? Our analyses probed into the costs and benefits of conflict for leaders that face different risks of forcible and regular removal. The differences in the chances of either type of removal might be due to structural conditions, such as economic and political institutions that do not guarantee safe retirements, or to specific events unfolding in their countries, such as domestic political unrest or economic recession. In either set of circumstances, we documented how leaders who are afraid of losing power through forcible means stand to benefit from initiating conflicts, as long as they manage to avoid defeat in the end. Winning, on the other hand, generates too uncertain benefits to motivate leaders.

Specifically, both Autocratic and Mixed regimes lack the provisions that can effectively guarantee leaders their safety after losing office. As a result, leaders in these systems are likely to lose office in a forcible manner and have the most to gain from the initiation from conflict. As expected, we found that Challenging autocratic leaders lowers their risk of a forcible removal from office, although Challenging brought only relatively uncertain benefits to leaders of mixed regimes.

The converse relation also applies. When leaders are reasonably confident about their lives and freedom out of office, as is the case for leaders in Democracies, they would have little to benefit from initiating conflict. Indeed, democratic leaders did not lower their already low risk of a forcible removal, nor did they postpone their regular removal by resorting to international conflict. Given that leaders in Democracies do not have much to gain from conflict even when they win, we can infer that they would prefer resorting to conflict when they are fairly secure in power, as our *peace through insecurity* mechanism suggests.

Not just the structural features of political and social institutions, but also temporary "shocks," such as domestic political unrest and economic recessions, can alter the risk of forcible removal for leaders. Following this logic, we would expect that leaders in a civil war gain from Challenging, a pattern that was confirmed in the data. Similarly, if negative economic growth constitutes a plausible temporary shock to the leader's legitimacy and capabilities, our theory suggests that leaders experiencing such negative economic growth – particularly, leaders of non-democracies – should significantly lower their risk of a forcible removal from office. The data again supported this conjecture.

3.5 Conclusions

Our theory of conflict initiation establishes a relationship between the risk and the manner of losing office and the decision to initiate an international conflict. Leaders who face no risk of forcible removal might decide to start a conflict when they are secure in office and their removal is an unlikely event. Leaders who are at risk of a forcible removal, on the other hand, are more likely to initiate a conflict when the prospects of removal with punishment are high. Security in *and* out of office affects conflict onset differently, on the basis of two distinct processes of leadership turnover.

These propositions, which we call *peace through insecurity* and *fighting* and *gambling for survival*, are premised on the fact that international conflict entails specific political costs and benefits for political leaders. For secure leaders, international conflict is at best a risky prospect that generates political costs for uncertain benefits. For leaders who see grim prospects for their lives and well-being once out of office, international conflict again holds out risky gains.

In this chapter, we provided an assessment of the six hypotheses that serve as the foundation for our argument. We found that (*a*) initiating international conflicts reduces the risk of both regular and forcible removals; (*b*) victory in crises or wars in general brings very uncertain (statistically insignificant) benefits on the two manners of losing office, with the exception of victory in crises short of war, which reduces the risk of forcible removal; and (*c*) defeat in crises and wars makes forcible removals more likely, while it has no significant impact on regular removals. Overall, the result suggested support for our *fighting for survival* mechanism, whereby conflict initiation – Challenging – pays more-or-less independent of the outcome. Surprisingly, we found that victory paid only occasionally, and its effect was associated with a fair amount of uncertainty, while defeat increased the risk of forcible removals. These results, therefore, appear to weigh against the *gambling for survival* mechanism, which requires that conflict can pay.

In their entirety, these results reformulate the claims about conflict initiation and political survival now predominant in what we would call the standard theory (Reiter and Stam, 2002). Initiation does not help survival, because it gives leaders the ability to start conflicts that they are more likely to win; rather, it helps the political *and* personal survival of leaders because it helps solve their *domestic* political problems, i.e. their hold on power *and* the dynamics of their succession. In this light, the apparently disparate cases of (*a*) Anwar Sadat, who started the War of Attrition and the Yom Kippur War and lost, but improved his political standing at home; (*b*) Mao Ze Dong, who intervened in the Korean War for a stalemated outcome internationally and a disruption of the networks of potential coup plotters domestically; and (*c*) Idi Amin, who launched an attack against Tanzania to settle scores against his own army, can all be subsumed under our leaders theory of conflict. The apparently paradoxical fate of Saddam Hussein and George H. W. Bush after the first Gulf War, a fate that, as we saw, so extensively challenged the predictive abilities of regional experts and political commentators (Akins, 1991; Quindlen, 1991), can also be subsumed into the larger pattern explained by our theory.

To fully probe our mechanisms of conflict initiation, *fighting for survival*, *gambling for survival*, and *peace through insecurity*, in the next chapter we explicitly model the endogeneity of both the risk of conflict initiation and the risk of losing office in a regular, as well as the risk of losing office in a forcible manner.

4 | The fate of leaders and incentives to fight

4.1 Introduction

On April 2, 1982, the Argentinian armed forces invaded and occupied the Falklands Islands, a small archipelago 250 nautical miles off the coast of Argentina. The islands were, and still are, sovereign territory of Great Britain, one of the many territorial legacies of the British maritime empire. Argentinians call the islands Malvinas and claim them – in the words of their Constitution – as "integral part of the National territory [whose] recovery and the full exercise of sovereignty (...) are a permanent and unrelinquished goal of the Argentine people."[1] The attack occurred at a time when Argentina had been undergoing a period of economic decline and domestic strife, with mounting inflation, repeated economic contractions and mass unrest (Dabat and Lorenzano, 1984; Pion-Berlin, 1985; Oakes, 2006; Fravel, 2010). Only three days before the invasion, on March 30, fifteen thousand people took to the streets to demonstrate against the ruling military junta under the slogans of "Peace, Bread, and Work", and "The Military Dictatorship Is Near Its End" (Dabat and Lorenzano, 1984, 75; Fravel, 2010, 321).

The coincidence of economic decline, domestic unrest, and war has led many scholars to conclude that the Argentinian attack on the Falklands constitutes an instance of diversionary war theory (Dabat and Lorenzano, 1984; Lebow, 1985; Oakes, 2006), a venerable theory with a contradictory record (Levy, 1989; Miller, 1995; Gelpi, 1997; Oneal and Tir, 2006). The theory claims that leaders go to war to shore-up domestic support by focusing the public's attention away from

---

[1] These are the words in the First Temporary Provision in the Argentinian Constitution, which can be accessed at www.argentina.gov.ar/argentina/portal/documentos/constitucion_ingles.pdf.

domestic political troubles; what Richard Ned Lebow (1981, 66) calls "the time-honored technique of attempting to offset discontent at home by diplomatic success abroad."

But even in this case, the evidence for diversionary war is limited and questionable. How can it be diversionary war, asks Taylor Fravel (2010, 325), when the domestic support that followed the invasion came as a surprise for the leaders of the Argentinian junta? If it were an instance of diversionary war, popular support should have been what they were counting on, not an unexpected outcome. Moreover, not all the people cheering for regained sovereignty of the Argentinian irredenta were also cheering for the junta. As David Pion-Berlin (1985, 71) points out:

> The estimated 250,000 people that crowded in front of the presidential palace on April 6 to back the Malvinas operation, also shouted their disapproval of the regime itself. In fact, organized labor and the multiparty coalition made it clear to the president that they would press for swift restoration of their social and political freedoms at war's end. Consequently the war had not altered the agenda of the opposition nor drawn them into Galtieri's "movement."

While the central expectations from diversionary war theory fail to match the empirical record, it might still be the case that domestic political concerns played a role in the decision to invade the Falklands Islands (Levy and Vakili, 1992). As a leader who had come to power through a coup, General Leopoldo Galtieri, Commander-in-Chief of the Army and leader of the military junta, should have been well aware both of divisions within Argentina's armed forces and of how his tenure could terminate as the result of a coup by other members of the armed forces. Rather than the opposition in the labor movement and the political forces organized under the multiparty coalition the *Multipartidaria*, General Galtieri might have been worried about his fellow generals, who were restive and divided (Pion-Berlin, 1985; Levy and Vakili, 1992). At a time of social unrest and political uncertainty, the invasion of the Falklands was a unifying mission for an institution that was lacking a sense of purpose and mission, and allegedly the quid-pro-quo that earned General Galtieri the support for his rule from the navy commander, Admiral Jorge I. Anaya (Hastings and Jenkins, 1983, 46; Pion-Berlin, 1985, 70; Cardoso,

Kirschbaum and van der Kooy, 1987, 1–23 and 72; Thornton, 1998, 74).[2]

Even in this most favorable case for diversionary war theory, we find signs of the causal mechanism we proposed. We argued that leaders fight when they face domestic unrest or potential rebellions and plots that expose them to the risk of a forcible removal from power. As King Henry IV told his son and heir, the future Henry V, on his deathbed in Shakespeare's play,[3]

> Yet, though thou stand'st more sure than I could do,
> Thou art not firm enough, since griefs are green;
> And all my friends, which thou must make thy friends,
> Have but their stings and teeth newly ta'en out;
> By whose fell working I was first advanced
> And by whose power I well might lodge a fear
> To be again displaced: which to avoid,
> I cut them off; and had a purpose now
> To lead out many to the Holy Land,
> Lest rest and lying still might make them look
> Too near unto my state. Therefore, my Harry,
> Be it thy course to busy giddy minds
> With foreign quarrels; that action, hence borne out,
> May waste the memory of the former days.

---

[2] As an illustration of the sources cited above, Pion-Berlin (1985, 70) writes that: "Under strong prodding from navy commander Almirante Jorge I. Anaya, who had backed the new government on condition that they break the deadlock over the Malvinas, the junta decided, on January 6, to go ahead with an invasion." Analogously, Cardoso, Kirschbaum and van der Kooy (1987, 72) write that: "But Anaya, however, had agreed to support Galtieri's access to the Casa Rosada, only in return for the green light on the Falklands. Any futher postponement would finish this pact, bringing with it, sooner or later, deep dissension in the heart of the military regime." To this, Levy and Vakili (1992, 140, fn. 32) add, "Galtieri might have needed Anaya's backing not simply to assume the presidency but also to maintain his position as commander-in-chief." This version of the events, however, is disputed among historians. Amy Oakes (2006, 446–7) writes that: "In this same vein, it was rumored that Galtieri promised Anaya that he would invade the Falklands if the admiral backed his bid for the presidency. There is, however, no consensus regarding whether such a deal was ever made."

[3] These lines come from Act 4, Scene V of *King Henry IV* Part 2, which is available at www.online-literature.com/shakespeare/henryIV2/16/.

When peace – "rest and lying still" – makes potential *domestic* rivals too keen on unseating the ruler, that is the time to start a war, in Henry IV's words, "to lead out many to the Holy Land." The reason, and causal mechanism, is not to distract the public, as diversionary war theory maintains, but to engage potential contenders for power in foreign lands and thus disrupt any plots to remove the leader from power.

Conversely, in countries where leadership succession takes place through regular (peaceful) channels, conflict initiation is too risky an endeavor to bolster a shaky hold on office. As a consequence, leaders who govern with the expectation that they will be replaced peacefully have few incentives to initiate a conflict when their rule is about to end. Rather, it is politically more prudent for them to initiate conflict when the prospects of being replaced in office are low. This finding thus turns the venerable proposition of diversionary war theory on its head: in the case of regular institutionalized channels of leadership turnover, peace – not war – follows from office insecurity. Diversionary leaders still do exist – these are the leaders who are ready to initiate a conflict to postpone or avert a forcible removal, and thus preserve their lives or liberty.

In this chapter, we present a direct empirical test of the central proposition of our theory of conflict onset. We show that the leaders at risk of suffering a forcible removal from power are *more* likely to initiate military conflict than the leaders who are either safe in office or at risk of losing office in a regular manner. We also show that the leaders who face the prospect of losing power through the regular channels in their countries are less likely to initiate military conflict than leaders who are safe in office. As the theory of diversionary war maintains, leaders' hold on power affects their decisions to initiate international conflict. But unlike the diversionary war argument, it is the manner of leadership succession that makes a difference, not just the desire to stay in power. Our empirical findings identify two specific conditions that link leaders' hold on power to international conflict. Conflict follows from domestic political *insecurity* when loss of power puts the personal freedom and the lives of leaders in jeopardy. When the loss of power does *not* entail direct personal consequences for the leaders, however, domestic political insecurity leads to *peace*.

The analysis in this chapter starts with a description of how we obtain an empirical estimate of the risk to lose power in either a regular or forcible manner. We use statistical modeling to assess when and how leaders are at risk of losing office from their historical experience. Our approach takes a comprehensive view of the institutional, societal, and individual factors that affect leaders' tenure rather than focusing specifically on economic conditions or domestic unrest. Consistent with the analysis we pursued in our 2003 article in the *Journal of Conflict Resolution*, we also evaluate how the endogenous risk of international conflict initiation in turn affects the tenure of leaders. In other words, we allow for rallying around the flag or other potential simultaneous relations to affect the probability of losing office depending on the risk of an international conflict initiation. We innovate our previous analysis by assessing how the two manners of losing office affect leaders' propensity to initiate a conflict.[4]

4.2 Measuring the risk of losing of office

In 1991, in the immediate aftermath of his military defeat in the Gulf War, President Saddam Hussein of Iraq faced a serious threat to his rule. With the encouragement of US President George H. W. Bush (1991), who urged Iraqis to take the fate of their country into their own hands and force Saddam Hussein out of power, rebellions erupted in the Kurdish areas in the North and in the Shi'a regions in the South.[5] The rebellions rapidly spread; but when the rebels started to move towards the capital Baghdad, support from the coalition forces

---

[4] In the previous chapter we examined conflict initiation as an independent variable; in this chapter conflict initiation functions as an (endogenous) independent variable as well as a dependent variable. However, we discuss initiation from a rather different perspective here, which merits brief discussion to avoid confusion. In Chapter 3 we sought to isolate the effects of conflict initiation on the hazard and manner of losing office. To that end, we focused on Challengers, and coded leaders who initiated a conflict as Challengers *for each year of the conflict*. In this chapter, initiation is a dummy variable, coded as 1 when the leader initiated a conflict in a particular year and 0 otherwise. The endogenous variable of the risk of conflict initiation thus measures the risk of conflict initiation in a given year.

[5] As President Bush (1991) stated, "But there's another way for the bloodshed to stop, and that is for the Iraqi military and the Iraqi people to take matters into their own hands to force Saddam Hussein the dictator to step aside and to comply with the UN and then rejoin the family of peace-loving nations. We have no argument with the people of Iraq. Our differences are with Iraq's brutal dictator."

that had just expelled Saddam's army from Kuwait failed to materialize. Saddam reacted swiftly and brutally and reaffirmed his hold on power.[6] Our statistical model of leadership turnover captures these events and estimates that Saddam Hussein faced a very high probability of forcible removal, nearly 85 percent, the second highest probability for all the leaders in power from 1919 until 2003. Only the long-forgotten Gyula Peidl of Hungary, the last leader of the short-lived Hungarian Soviet Republic, faced a higher risk of forcible removal in 1919 (94%). And indeed, as predicted, Peidl was forcibly removed in a coup, and sent into exile.

When Saddam Hussein's hold on power was in peril, other leaders safely slept in their beds, with no risk of ever facing a forcible removal. For example, Saddam's nemesis, US President George W. Bush, faced a 0.002 (1 out of 500) probability of forcible removal. President Bush certainly faced higher risks of regular removal. In 2003, for example, our statistical model estimates that President Bush faced a 6 percent probability of regular removal, the fifth-lowest probability of regular removal for any US president since Woodrow Wilson. From a constitutional viewpoint, that probability was zero, given that 2003 was not an electoral year in the United States. Our estimate, therefore, counts not as measure of what is going to happen *per se*, but rather as a measure of how confident a democratic leader is about his security in office and his likelihood to be re-elected in the next electoral cycle.[7]

These estimates present a few examples of what we can measure with our statistical model – a simultaneous-equation probit regression model – which predicts whether a leader is going to suffer office removal, by regular or forcible means, in a given year. In our analysis, we are not privy to any classified information that would constantly track the fluctuations in a leader's security in office. As the King in Italo Calvino's (1988) short story, leaders are always listening to the rumors that might portend the end of their rule.[8] We definitely are not in a

---

[6] For a brief overview of these events see Malanczuk (1991); Makiya (1993); Brownlee (2002) as well as the Frontline report at www.pbs.org/frontlineworld/stories/iraq501/events_uprising.html.

[7] This argument is analogous to the argument that presidential approval ratings in US politics serve as a functional surrogate of a monthly confidence vote from the electorate, and therefore become a form of political capital that affects US presidents' ability to lead and govern (Marra, Ostrom and Simon, 1990).

[8] The short story is entitled "Un Re in Ascolto" ("A King Listens").

position to gather that kind of information, nor is anyone working in our discipline, political science. It is beyond the means of our science, for example, to relate the recurrent crises in the Korean peninsula, from the threats to launch long-range missiles or to resume the operations of the nuclear plant at Yongbyon or the (alleged) attack to the South Korean patrol boat *Cheonan*, to any real or imagined weakening in the control of Kim Jong-Il, the North Korean leader, though those connections are routinely made in the press (Oliver, 2010). Nonetheless, using statistical analysis and publicly available information, we can obtain an assessment of how the prospects of leadership change vary between leaders in different countries and vary over time for a given leader.

To do so, we rely upon a series of systematic indicators about the state of the economy, domestic political institutions, domestic conditions, and the personal characteristics of the leader himself, from his age to his previous experience in power. These indicators offer an encompassing picture of the systematic determinants of leadership turnover. Specifically, we evaluate the extent to which we are able to predict whether a leader was removed from power using the following indicators:[9]

- *domestic political institutions*: (*a*) regime type, distinguishing between autocracies, mixed regimes, parliamentary democracies, and presidential democracies;
- *domestic political conditions*: (*a*) involvement in a civil war; (*b*) whether the current leader entered into power by regular (constitutional) means or not, discounted by time; (*c*) days elapsed since the previous election (logged);

[9] We present a detailed description of how we measured these variables in the Appendix. As often the case with political science data, our data set is affected by the presence of missing values on some of the variables, which leads to the loss of valuable information and potentially biases estimates and inferences. Following Schafer's (1997) approach, we impute the missing values using data augmentation under a multivariate normal model based on all the explanatory variables as well as the dependent variables. We run five parallel chains of 500 steps each, and we set the starting values for each chain by using the EM estimates of the model parameters computed on a bootstrap sample a quarter of the size of the whole data set (Allison, 2002, 38, fn. 11). We then run our analysis on five data sets with the missing values filled through multiple imputation. We present the model for the missing data in more detail in Appendix B.

- *state of the economy*: (*a*) level of GDP per capita (logged); (*b*) economic growth; (*c*) levels of trade openness and their growth; (*d*) size of the population;
- *leader's features*: (*a*) age; (*b*) number of days in office; and (*c*) previous experiences in office; (*d*) conflict record, distinguishing whether the leader achieved victories, defeats or draws in international crises and wars (discounted by time);
- *country's international political context*: (*a*) major power status; (*b*) military mobilization; (*c*) number of borders; (*d*) whether the country was targeted in an international crisis or war in a given year; (*e*) involvement in an ongoing international crisis or war; and (*f*) number of days since the last crisis initiation.

Our model generates a parameter, the regression coefficient, for each of these indicators. We measure how economic growth or victory in war, for example, affect the risk of regular and forcible removal, net of all the other factors. As we would expect, we find that democratic leaders faced higher risks of regular removal, and lower risks of forcible removal, compared to leaders of authoritarian and mixed regimes. Similarly, our model documents how defeats in war put office tenure in jeopardy. The results from the regression coefficients are important, as they replicate the findings we presented in Chapter 3.[10] What is more important, however, is that our statistical model generates a reasonable measure of the underlying propensities of losing office by regular or forcible means for a leader every year of his tenure. By reasonable, we mean that our model passes several tests of goodness-of-fit for non-linear regression models like our probit regression model.[11] We can,

---

[10] We present the regression results in detail in Appendix C.

[11] We primarily rely on McKelvey and Zavoina's pseudo–R^2, the measure of fit that most closely approximates the R^2 of linear regression models (Hagle and Mitchell, 1992) and also least vulnerable to changes in the proportion of 1s in the sample (Windmeijer, 1995, 112). As we report in Table C.2 in the Appendix, our models yield a measure of the McKelvey and Zavoina statistics well above the 0.1 threshold that is conventionally used to discriminate between weak and valid measures (Bollen, Guilkey and Mroz, 1995, 119; Bound, Jaeger and Baker, 1995, 444). In Table C.2 we also report several alternative measures of goodness-of-fit: Efron's, McFadden's, Cragg-Uhler's likelihood ratio-based pseudo–R^2 measures; Hosmer and Lemeshow's χ^2 measure; the area under the ROC curve; and the percentage of events correctly predict while fixing the probability threshold to identify an event at 0.5. All

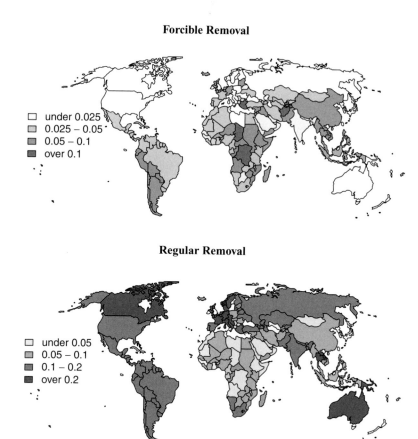

Forcible Removal

under 0.025
0.025 – 0.05
0.05 – 0.1
over 0.1

Regular Removal

under 0.05
0.05 – 0.1
0.1 – 0.2
over 0.2

Figure 4.1: Average probability of forcible and regular removal, 1919–2003

therefore, have confidence that our measures capture the fluctuations in the underlying propensities to lose office by either forcible or regular means.

We can have a better sense of how our model operates from Figure 4.1, where we plot the average probability of losing power that leaders faced over the entire time period in our dataset. The probabilities have low ranges in general. After all, we mostly observe

these measure indicate that our models generate values that are closely related to the observed measures, and therefore can serve as proxies for our key theoretical concepts.

leaders in office, given that for any leader who loses power a new leader comes in. The maximum probability is 0.33 for the risk of regular removal, a record obtained by France as a consequence of the high turnover rates in the Fourth Republic; and 0.16 for the risk of forcible removal, a record obtained by Tajikistan, a country that experienced a period of high political instability after gaining independence in 1991, before Emomalii Rahmon engineered a series of constitutional reforms that allowed him to run repeatedly for office and consolidate his power. Figure 4.1 gives an overview of four different political environments for the leaders. There are parts of the world where stable political processes of leadership change has been the common practice – the countries in the darker shades. There are parts of the world where forcible removal has been a serious risk – the countries in the darkest shades. But if we look at Libya or North Korea in Figure 4.1, we notice that on average the probability of leadership turnover was low both in the case of forcible removal and in the case of regular removal. These are two examples of countries where leaders have been protected from any forms of removal, have persevered in office year after year, and will mostly likely succumb in old age when illness and death will have the final say.

Notably, our measures of forcible and regular removal do not just evaluate differences in political environments across countries, but also *over time*. There are moments in the political career of a leader when the risk of removal is high, as we explored in Chapter 3. In Figure 4.2, we illustrate how our model assessed security in office over time for the leaders of four countries: Great Britain, Chile, the Democratic Republic of Congo, and Indonesia.

Britain, as a consolidated democracy, experienced only minimal risks of forcible removal for its leaders. Throughout the 85 years covered in our data set, British leaders never found themselves in a situation in which they faced serious prospects of forcible removal. Occasional threats to their lives certainly occurred. On October 12, 1984, for example, Prime Minister Thatcher narrowly escaped an assassination attempt when the Irish Republican Army bombed the hotel where the Conservative Party was holding a conference. These threats, real though they were, never undermined the constitutional fabric of Britain, and the usual processes of leadership change through elections and party politics.

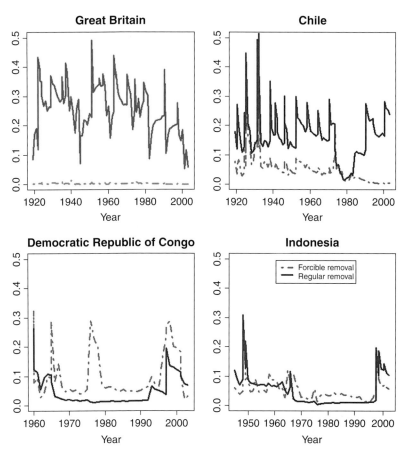

Figure 4.2: Probability of forcible and regular removal from office in four countries

The estimates for Chilean leaders show that regular removal was the common process of leadership change for the most part of Chile's history. The large fluctuation in the probability of regular removal until the 1970s indicates a country that experienced a certain degree of political instability, but not major threats to its normal political processes of leadership change. Interestingly, our model captures the change in political conditions that occurred when General Pinochet gained power in a violent coup in 1973. During the darker years of Pinochet's rule, from the mid-1970s until the mid-1980s, both the probability of regular and forcible removal were very low, which indicates the degree of control and oppression imposed by the dictatorship. As the political system started to open up in the late 1980s, the probability of regular removal started to increase again, but not the probability of forcible removal, which seems to have become a matter of the "past" in Chilean politics.

In the bottom part of Figure 4.2, we show two countries that have been ruled by a single authoritarian leader for a long period of time. Consistently with our intuition that time in office is not synonymous with security in office, our model is able to distinguish a secure hold on power from a long spell in office. For example, our model shows that in the Democratic Republic of Congo, the threat of violent removal has been a staple feature of its political processes. For most of the period since gaining independence in 1960, the leaders of the Democratic Republic of Congo faced higher risks of forcible removal than of regular removal. That was the case during the more than 30-year rule of Mobutu Sese Seko, and it continued to be the case during the rule of Laurent Kabila and Joseph Kabila, who entered into power in 1997 and 2001, respectively. The graph for Indonesia shows how a leader, Suharto, was able to consolidate his power, minimizing both the risk of regular and forcible removal, during his 32 years in power from 1966 until 1998. In his case, time in office went hand-in-hand with security in power. In the end, Suharto's rule terminated in the exceptional circumstances of the deep economic crisis triggered by the Asian financial crisis of 1997, when he decided to step down after his attempt to run for re-election in 1998 was met with mass demonstrations and popular protests.

To sum up, from the point of view of statistical fit and the point of view of historical accuracy, our statistical model generates a measure of the risk of regular and forcible removal that can serve as a valid proxy for the theoretical concepts in our theory. Along the same lines, the statistical model allows us to generate a measure of the risk of a conflict initiation. Armed with these measures, we now turn to evaluate our propositions about conflict onset.

4.3 A statistical test of our theory of conflict initiation

In Chapter 2 we presented three basic mechanisms to explain conflict initiation. *Peace through insecurity* proposes that as the risk of a regular loss of office increases, the probability of conflict initiation

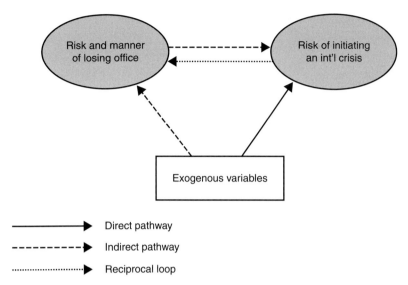

Figure 4.3: A graphical representation of direct and indirect effects

decreases. The other two mechanisms focus on the risk of a forcible removal from office. *Gambling for survival* proposes that leaders initiate conflict as the risk of a forcible removal from office increases because victory reduces that risk. *Fighting for survival* proposes that leaders initiate conflict when the risk of a forcible removal increases because fighting itself decreases the risk of a forcible removal from office. The traditional literature on diversionary war – in particular, the psychological variant – argues that the risk of an international conflict, in turn, can crucially affect a leader's probability of losing office. To not rule out *by fiat* such potential competing explanations, we estimate a fully reciprocal model, as presented in Figure 4.3. We test this model with a simultaneous-equation probit model similar to the model we estimated in Chiozza and Goemans (2003).[12] We make

---

[12] We coded our conflict onset variable using the international crisis events Gelpi and Griesdorf (2001) coded on the basis of the International Crisis Behavior (ICB) dataset (Brecher and Wilkenfeld, 1997). We updated the Gelpi and Griesdorf series using version 7 of the ICB data International Crisis Behavior Project (2007). In our data, we list 342 instances in which a leader triggered an international crisis between 1919 and 2003 (Brecher and Wilkenfeld, 1997, 4–5).

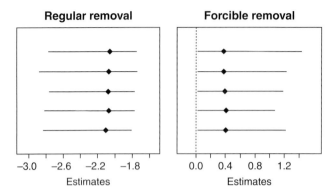

Figure 4.4: Coefficients for the risks of losing office on conflict intiation

Note: We report the coefficients and the 95% (bootstrapped) bias-corrected confidence intervals for the regression coefficients of a simultaneous equation probit model with three endogenous regressors. The solid lines measure the coefficients for the risk of regular removal; the dotted lines measure the coefficients for the risk of forcible removal. Positive coefficients indicate an increase in the risk of office removal increases the probability of conflict onset; negative coefficients indicate an increase decreases the probability of conflict onset. The models are based upon five data sets with missing values estimated through multiple imputation. These results can be found in Tables C.3, C.6, C.9, C.12, and C.15 in the Appendix.

sure that the statistical relationships are not due to chance using boot-strapping, a computer-intensive technique that generates more conservative estimates of the degree of certainty associated with statistical parameters.[13]

In Figure 4.4 we present the main findings of this chapter.[14] In a nutshell, the positive and significant coefficient for the risk of forcible removal shows that leaders could *fight for survival* or *gamble for survival*; the negative and significant coefficient for the risk of regular removal shows that peace becomes more likely *through insecurity.*

---

[13] We drew 1,000 samples with replacement from the system of equations in our model. We report bias-corrected confidence intervals, as they offer the most "conservative" assessment of the null hypothesis, i.e. the assessment most likely to report in favor of the null hypothesis against the hypotheses derived from our theory. We explain our modeling approach in Appendix C.

[14] Figure 4.4 reports five coefficients and their 95% confidence intervals, one per data set with multiple imputation of missing values (as described in fn. 9 on page 97).

The statistical evidence summarized in our model is consistent with the predictions of our theory about the private costs and benefits of conflict for political leaders.

Concretely, the probabilities of conflict involvement that these coefficients generate are also of substantial magnitude. For example, if we take a leader in a parliamentary democracy who is "average" on all dimensions, with stable institutions and a low risk of forcible removal, we observe that, on average, the probability of starting a crisis *declines* from about 1.1% to basically zero (0.005%) when the probability of losing office in a *regular* manner increases from a 1-in-10 chance to 3-in-10 chance. For a leader of a mixed regime who is again "average" on all dimensions, facing a low risk of regular removal, the probability of starting a crisis *increases* from about 8.1% to 13.6% when the probability of losing office in a *forcible* manner increases from a 1-in-10 chance to 3-in-10 chance.

As we showed earlier in our discussion of the measures for the regular and forcible removal from power, a 1-in-10 and a 3-in-10 probability of removal are high values that rarely occur. In Table 4.1, therefore, we report a broader set of comparisons to convey the substantive impact of our theoretical propositions, while distinguishing across different regime types. Specifically, we assess how the probability of conflict onset changes as the risk of regular and forcible removal takes on representative values we empirically observe in our dataset. The low, median, and high risk of removal are the observed values that occur at the 25th, 50th, and 75th percentile of the distribution of the risk of removal, respectively. These values, as we should expect, are different across regime types. For example, leaders of mixed regimes faced higher risks of forcible removal than leaders of democracies; conversely, leaders of democracies systematically faced higher chances of regular removal than leaders of autocracies. We directly account for these differences in the calculation of probabilities in Table 4.1 to offer a more realistic assessment of our claims.

When we look at the probabilities of conflict onset under more realistic scenarios, we have a better appreciation of the importance of the manner and consequences of leadership turnover. Not only do the risk of regular and forcible removal substantially alter the risk of crisis initiation, but note also that it takes a small shift towards more regular and peaceful processes of leadership turnover to reduce the occurrence of international crises.

Table 4.1: *Estimated probabilities of crisis onset*

		Risk of regular removal		
	Overall effects	Low	Median	High
Autocracy	.80	4.11	1.06	.39
Mixed regime	.72	1.52	.60	.20
Parliamentary democracy	.24	.77	.32	.08
Presidential democracy	.66	.27	.10	.03
		Risk of forcible removal		
	Overall effects	Low	Median	High
Autocracy	.80	6.88	7.87	9.11
Mixed regime	.72	5.38	6.23	7.39
Parliamentary democracy	.24	2.08	2.58	3.13
Presidential democracy	.66	.68	.80	.98

Note: Overall effects are computed from the reduced-form equations. Low, median, and high risks of regular and forcible removal are set to the 25th, 50th, and 75th percentiles empirically observed in our data for each regime type, respectively. All remaining explanatory variables are set at their median values.

4.3.1 The risk of conflict initiation

We first examined whether and how the risk and manner of losing office affects the probability of conflict initiation. We now reverse the causal arrow to examine the effect of the risk of conflict initiation on the probability of a regular and forcible removal from office. Figure 4.5 shows the results. In a twist on the traditional psychological variant of diversionary war, an increase in the risk of conflict initiation significantly reduces the probability of a regular, but not of an irregular removal from office. Thus, there may indeed exist some rallying around the flag, but these results suggest that citizens (voters) only rally around leaders safely embedded in the regular process of leadership turnover. Somewhat surprisingly, perhaps, an increase in the risk of conflict initiation also increases the risk of a forcible removal. This result suggests that leaders do not seem to be systematically able to profit from an impending conflict to send potential opponents to the front to fight and die. The Father Brown

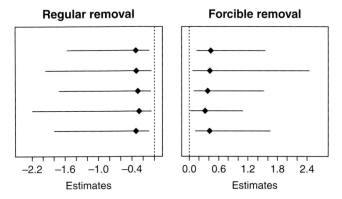

Figure 4.5: Coefficients for the risks of conflict initiation on the manner of losing office

Note: We report the coefficients and the 95% (bootstrapped) bias-corrected confidence intervals for the regression coefficients of a simultaneous equation probit model with three endogenous regressors. The solid lines measure the coefficients for the risk of regular removal; the dotted lines measure the coefficients for the risk of forcible removal. Positive coefficients indicate an increase in the risk of office removal increases the probability of conflict onset; negative coefficients indicate an increase decreases the probability of conflict onset. The models are based upon five data sets with missing values estimated through multiple imputation. These results can be found in Tables C.4, C.7, C.10, C.13, and C.16 and in Tables C.5, C.8, C.11, C.14, and C.17, respectively, in the Appendix.

story, whereby a leader takes advantage of a crisis to fight for survival, seems to be outweighed by other dynamics.[15] Note, though, that the results in Figure 4.5 in no way contradict the *fighting for survival* mechanism in a broader sense, because they capture only one narrow variant. It is not so much the threat or risk of conflict initiation, but rather actual conflict that allows a leader to rotate the troops of his domestic enemies to different commanders, as Chairman Mao skillfully did (Tullock, 1987). As we will see below, the risk of conflict initiation increases the risk of a forcible removal from office because it opens the door to defeat, with all its devastating consequences.

---

[15] The Father Brown story is discussed in Chapter 2.

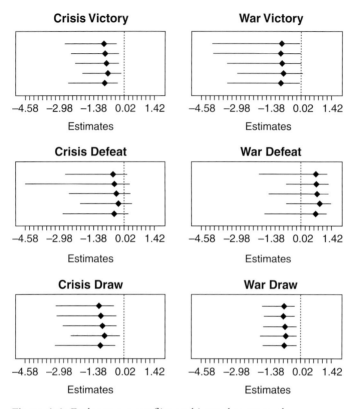

Figure 4.6: Endogenous conflict and irregular removal

Note: We report the coefficients and the 95% confidence intervals for the regression coefficients of a simultaneous-equation probit model, on five imputed data sets. These results can be found in Tables C.5, C.8, C.11, C.14, and C.17 in the Appendix.

4.3.2 Conflict outcomes

Finally, we examine how controlling for the endogenous risk of conflict initiation affects the probability and manner of losing office. Recall we suggested in Chapter 3 that initiation might systematically increase the probability of victory and thereby affect the coefficients for the outcome of conflict. In Figure 4.6 we report how international conflict affects the probability of a forcible removal from office, once we control for the endogenous risk of conflict initiation.

Figure 4.6 allows us to tease out more precisely how the outcome of conflict affects the probability of a forcible removal from office. In the previous chapter, we found that Victory in a crisis appeared to decrease the risk of a forcible removal, but just barely failed to reach significance at the 5% level.[16] We postulated that this (marginal) insignificance might be the result of the fact initiation increases the probability of Victory, and that the true effect of Victory would therefore be masked by the Challenger variable. The results in Figure 4.6 suggest this is indeed the case. Once we isolate and control for the effect of initiation, we find that Victory in a crisis does significantly decrease the probability of a forcible removal from office, as posited by our *gambling for survival* mechanism. Victory in war also seems to decrease the risk of a forcible removal from office, but fails to reach significance at the 5% level.[17] Note, moreover, that defeat no longer significantly increases the probability of a forcible removal from office. This latter pattern we would expect to hold if *compared to staying at peace* leaders estimated that by initiating conflict they would not significantly increase their risk of a forcible removal from office, even as the result of victory. In other words, the results suggest that if indeed leaders with a high risk of a forcible removal from office initiate conflict, they can rationally choose to do so because their punishment is truncated. Even the worst case outcome of an international conflict does not significantly worsen their prospects for survival.

Figure 4.6 delivers one final striking result. A draw in an international conflict, be it a crisis or a war, significantly decreases the risk of a forcible removal from office. A distinguishing feature of our *fighting for survival* mechanism is that it does not require a victory against the international opponent to yield private benefits for the leader. Indeed, the international opponent is not the real target of such "international" conflicts; rather, the real target is the domestic political opposition. A leader who obtains a draw against the international opponent can lower his risk of a forcible removal from office if, in the process of

---

[16] As we report in Table B.44 in Appendix B, the significance level for Crisis Victory in the hazard-model predicting forcible removal is 0.051.

[17] As we report in Tables C.20, C.23, C.26, C.29, and C.32 in Appendix C, in four out of the five imputed data sets, the coefficient on War victory in the forcible removal model is significant at the 10% level.

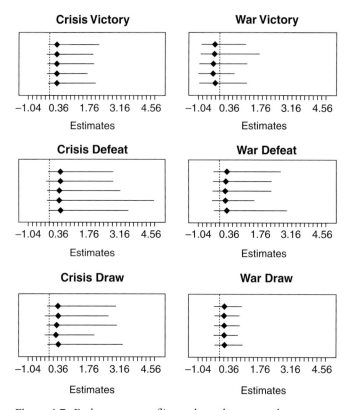

Figure 4.7: Endogenous conflict and regular removal

Note: We report the coefficients and the 95% confidence intervals for the regression coefficients of a simultaneous-equation probit model, on five imputed data sets. These results can be found in Tables C.4, C.7, C.10, C.13, and C.16 in the Appendix.

fighting an international enemy, he secures a decisive victory against his domestic enemies.

Once we control for the endogenous initiation of international conflict, defeat does not increase the risk of a forcible removal from office. Yet victories and draws decrease such a risk of a forcible removal from office. These results show that leaders at risk of a forcible removal from office can rationally *fight* as well as *gamble for survival*.

To complete our analysis, Figure 4.7 reports the effects of conflict on the probability of a regular removal, controlling for the endogenous risk of conflict initiation. None of the coefficients, we see, comes even close to significance. In other words, neither the conflict role nor the outcome of an international conflict is significantly associated with the probability of a regular removal from office. To be sure, defeat increases the risk of a regular removal, but the effect is not significant.

At first blush, these results might seem surprising, but they become less so once we consider they emerge from a model that controls for the endogenous risk of conflict initiation. Recall that leaders who find themselves safely ensconced in the regular process of leader removal have little to gain from victory, but could suffer much as a result of defeat. Since these incentives structure their decisions, such leaders initiate conflict only if they are secure in office, to have a safety cushion, as it were, in case of defeat.

4.3.3 An overview of the findings from the statistical model

What other findings does our model – the simultaneous-equation probit regression model – yield, beyond the key result showing that the dynamics of leadership succession have a direct bearing on the likelihood of conflict initiation? In this section, we present an overview of all the findings with regard to (*a*) regime type; (*b*) state of the economy; (*c*) the country's international political context. As is the case in all simultaneous-equation models, we need to assess two sets of results: those that pertain to the so-called reduced-form equation and those that pertain to the so-called structural equation. Both are important because both shed empirical light on different aspects of the dynamics modeled. The reduced-form estimates yield a measure of the long-run effects of the exogenous variables, whereas the structural coefficients assess the net effects of the explanatory variables controlling for the effect induced by the endogenous regressors (in our case, the two variables measuring the risk of regular and forcible removal, respectively).

Single-equation regressions that include exogenous variables which may affect a leader's time in office – i.e. the typical models in the quantitative literature on conflict initiation, as well as in the models we reported in Chapter 3 – can only measure the *overall* effect of an exogenous variable on international conflict. However, as we illustrated in Figure 4.3, an exogenous variable may affect conflict initiation through two pathways: indirectly, through its effect on the probability of losing office by either forcible or regular means, as well as directly net of its effect on the two distinct probabilities of losing office. It is crucial to recognize that an exogenous variable may therefore have differing, even opposite, direct and indirect effects on international conflict. Hence, by failing to model endogeneity – i.e. the reciprocal relationship between the risk and manner of losing office, on the one hand, and the risk of initiation of a conflict, on the other hand – the typical models in the conflict processes literature could present a misleading picture and even fail to find a real and significant relationship between that variable and international conflict. It is also important to recognize that the reciprocal loop involves two distinct processes, the ones related to regular removal and the ones related to forcible removal. The long-run effects (summarized in the reduced-form equations), therefore, are a summary aggregation of these two effects. With this in mind, we can now turn to the results.[18]

Regime type

We start with the results about domestic political institutions, one of the most studied relationships in conflict processes research in the last twenty years (Russett, 1993; Ray, 1995; Gleditsch and Hegre, 1997). First, recall that we examine four regime types: autocracies, mixed regimes, parliamentary democracies, and presidential democracies, where autocratic regimes serve as the excluded baseline category. A careful examination of the effects of the regime-type variables shows how the leaders of the four regime types are affected by tenure considerations in their decisions to initiate international conflict.

Recall that our simultaneous-equation probit model estimates two sets of equations. In the first set of equations – the reduced-form equations – we estimate three separate regressions. One of these has conflict initiation as the dependent variable, the other two have the regular and the forcible removal from office as their dependent variable. These regressions then allow us to create instruments for the risk of conflict initiation, the risk of a regular and the risk of a forcible removal from office, which we include in the structural equation.

In the reduced-form equation, we find that, on average, the leaders of mixed regimes and presidential democracies are about as likely to initiate conflict as leaders of autocratic regimes, whereas leaders

---

[18] We report the full set of results and coefficients for all the models in section C.4 of Appendix C.

of parliamentary democracies were significantly less likely to initiate than autocrats. In the structural equation, however, we find that both in democracies and mixed regimes the propensity to initiate conflict is greater than that attributed to authoritarian leaders. These differences between the results from the structural and the reduced-form equations must be attributed to the effect of controlling for the endogenous risk of losing office by either regular or forcible means.

To understand this apparent discrepancy, we must turn to the findings in the two equations that predict the probability of losing office, those very equations that generated our empirical measures of the risk of losing office. In those models, we find that democratic leaders are significantly more likely to lose office by regular means than autocrats. Thus, both in parliamentary and presidential systems, democratic leaders have a higher probability of losing office through regular processes of leadership succession; and the higher the probability of losing office by regular means, the lower the probability of conflict initiation. In addition, again both in parliamentary and presidential systems, democratic leaders are less likely to experience forcible removal than leaders of autocracies and mixed regimes. This second effect further reduces the propensity of leaders of parliamentary democracies to resort to crisis initiation to protect their life and liberty, as our theoretical arguments led us to expect. Why this effect does not also obtain for leaders of presidential democracies remains a puzzle, though we might conjecture that, as we have shown in Chapters 2 and 3, democratic leaders, in particular prime ministers, have not much to gain and plenty to lose from that course of action.

In the case of leaders of mixed regimes, our findings identify two divergent tendencies. On the one hand, compared with autocrats, their relatively higher probability of losing office by regular processes constrains their decisions to initiate a conflict. On the other hand, leaders of mixed regimes face higher risks of forcible removal than leaders ruling in any other institutional settings, which makes them more prone to fight for their survival by initiating an international crisis. These two countervailing effects "average" out to make leaders of mixed regimes overall about as likely to initiate conflict as leaders of autocracies. The impact of the different chances of removal for leaders in different regime types generates the patterns we present in Table 4.1.

In sum, these findings suggest that the overall relative peacefulness of democratic leaders should be attributed to their (relatively) higher probability of losing office by regular means and their (relatively) lower probability of losing office by forcible means. Thus, the main mechanism through which democratic institutions constrain leaders' propensity to start a crisis is the institutionalized mechanism of leadership succession through peaceful and constitutional elections. As we argued in Chapter 2, this finding substantiates our claim when it comes to the decision to start an international crisis, the manner in which leaders are selected, replaced, and treated when in retirement forms the fundamental political distinction that differentiates countries. The public's ability to control their officials through repeated elections creates strong incentives for democratic leaders to avoid military adventures in the international arena and complements the informational advantages attributed to democracy (Schultz, 2001a). Furthermore, our results suggest that the contradictory findings on the possible existence of a monadic democratic peace might be the result of the extent to which different researchers included or omitted control variables that affect the leader's manner of losing office.

State of the economy
We next shift our attention to the impact of the variables that measure a country's domestic economic features. We find that the conflict onset is (*a*) more likely to occur in countries that have larger economies; (*b*) but less likely to occur during periods of economic growth; (*c*) and also less likely to occur in countries with open economies. Change in levels of economic openness and the size of the market, as measured by population size, have no direct effect on crisis initiation. Net of the effects that the state of the economy has on leaders' positions in power, economic growth and trade openness inhibit the incentives to start an international crisis.

In the reduced-form equation, however, we find that, with the exception of population size, which is positively correlated with conflict onset, the variables measuring the state of the economy do not reach statistical significance. In its long-run effects, therefore, the state of the economy is a poor predictor of whether a leader would decide to initiate an international crisis. On the one hand, when the economy grows, for example, an international conflict would disrupt business transactions or undermine the expectations of stable returns to investments, which would then account for the lower propensity to initiate a conflict we measured in the structural equations. At the same time, however, economic growth makes a leader more secure in power. When the economy grows, leaders are less likely to experience forcible or regular removal from office.

If we combine these results, our empirical investigation offers a new perspective on the relationship between economic conditions and conflict. Unlike the conventional theory of diversionary war that posits a linear relationship between the economy and conflict – to simplify, a bad economy makes conflict more likely; a good economy makes conflict less likely – our approach disentangles two countervailing (nonlinear) tendencies. In good economic times, leaders have the incentive to maintain the stability that favors investments and makes business flourish, and thus avoid international crisis; at the same time, in good economic times, leaders can find the political conditions to initiate an international crisis out of choice, rather than necessity, under the belief that should things go poorly, their security in office would serve as an insurance guarantee against loss of power or even loss of life or liberty.

In sum, our empirical analysis documents how economic conditions operate *both* independently of leaders *and* through leaders. On the one hand, when we say *independently* of leaders, we mean that there exist economic conditions that make conflict more or less costly, and thus a preferable course of action, *for a country*. On the other hand, when we say *through* leaders, we mean that the same economic conditions create a political context that directly affects *the leader* by altering his risk of facing regular or forcible removal. As economic conditions change, a leader can find himself in a position to absorb the potential costs of conflict without endangering his power or personal survival. From this perspective, then, conflict can ensue because of, rather than despite, a favorable status of the economy. Again, to reiterate our point, our leader approach distinguishing the effects of the likelihood and manner of leadership succession recasts the theory of diversionary war in a new direction.

International political context

The variables measuring the international political context turn out to be strong predictors of crisis initiation, and our results are consistent with previous results reported in the literature (Diehl, 1985; Bremer, 1992; Beck, Katz and Tucker, 1998; Bennett and Stam, 2004). Conflict onset is more likely to occur in countries that have major power status and in countries with many borders, which are potentially more exposed to the risk of conflicting claims and interests. We also replicate the conventional finding about decreasing likelihood of conflict associated with the passing of time since the last onset. We do not find, however, a correlation between the levels of military mobilization and conflict onset. As countries increase the size of their armed forces, they are as likely to defuse a potential conflict as they are to trigger one.

4.4 Conclusions

The claim that leaders care about staying in power is a common refrain among disillusioned citizens, and a powerful assumption for scholars (Downs, 1957; Bueno de Mesquita *et al.*, 2003). Our theory accepts this basic premise about politics, but extends it to embrace the consequences of losing office. We argue that there is more than the "simple" goal to stay in power for a leader. Their fate out of office is also of paramount importance; it is for many leaders the proverbial question of life and death.

In this chapter, we have presented statistical evidence in support of our leader theory of conflict onset. As leaders assess their risks of being removed from office by regular (peaceful) or irregular means, they view the onset of international conflict in a different light. An international crisis is a risk of uncertain rewards to be pursued when secure in power, for the leaders who govern stable countries with regular institutionalized processes of leadership succession. An international crisis, instead, is a palatable option for the leaders that face the prospect of a forcible removal. Through fighting, those leaders can interrupt the forces that conspire against their rule, and thus save their lives and liberty. In a large sample of all the leaders in power for about 85 years, from 1919 to 2003, our statistical model has shown that leaders fight when they are secure in power if facing a the prospect of a regular removal; leaders fight when they are at risk of losing power if facing the prospect of a forcible removal. Our statistical models provided support for the *peace through insecurity*, as well as the *gambling* and some versions of the *fighting for survival* mechanisms we developed in Chapter 2. In the next chapter, we continue our empirical investigation of our leader theory of conflict onset with a case-study analysis of conflict processes in Central America.

5 | Case studies: Central America 1840–1918

5.1 Introduction

In the previous two chapters, we used quantitative methods to assess both how leaders lose office and how the manner of losing office affects the probability of conflict initiation. We found, as hypothesized, that the risk of an irregular removal does indeed significantly increase the probability of conflict initiation. As suggested in Chapter 2, however, the risk of an irregular removal can lead to war through several distinct pathways. Although the statistical tests in the previous chapters demonstrated correlation of the risk of an irregular removal from office and conflict initiation, we would not want to claim that these tests establish causation. Much less are we able to disentangle the various pathways through which an expected irregular removal from office would motivate leaders to initiate international conflict. In other words, these tests do not suffice to assess the power of our proposed causal mechanisms, especially because we suggested the fear of an irregular loss of office can increase the probability of conflict initiation through various pathways.

In the previous chapter we used the data to direct us to some prominent examples where the risk of an irregular removal from office should have most affected the probability of conflict initiation. Given, however, that these cases came from a sample which in the aggregate found strong support for our central hypotheses, we would like to examine our claims out of sample. That is, we would like to examine the plausibility, and specific pathways of our claims, outside of the domain of our statistical sample. Given that *Archigos* contains information on leaders from 1875 until 2004 and our statistical sample spans only 1919–2003, a straightforward solution suggests itself. The countries that experienced the most irregular exits from office (and/or the most leaders punished after losing office) should merit detailed historical examination, since in these countries leaders should have a significantly

117

higher than average expectation of an irregular removal from office. Once we scrutinize the period 1875–1918, three basic regions stand out as particularly prone to irregular removals from office: Hispaniola, e.g. Haiti and the Dominican Republic, with over 30 irregular exits from office between 1875 and 1918; Central America – Guatemala, El Salvador, Nicaragua, Honduras, and Costa Rica – with about 20 irregular exits from office; and Ecuador and Peru, with similarly about 20 irregular exits from office.

In this chapter we focus on the history of Central America between 1840 and 1919. We chose to focus on the cases of Central America because they span more countries and a longer period of time. More importantly, there exists a good historiography on these countries for that period, much of it built on the contemporary works by Montúfar (1887). There exists much less, indeed very little, contemporary historiography for Haiti and the Dominican Republic. This is undoubtedly due to the fact that the Haitian archives have in succession been torched, blown up, stolen, and again torched. The existing literature on relations between Haiti and the Dominican Republic, however, indicates the presence of patterns of conflict very similar to those we found in Central America (Welles, 1928; Craige, 1934; Rodman, 1964; Fagg, 1965; Logan, 1968; Plummer, 1988; Heinl and Heinl, 1996; Matibag, 2003).

5.2 Central America

We begin with some brief historical background on Central America. The area composed of the current states of Guatemala, El Salvador, Honduras, Nicaragua, and Costa Rica declared its independence from Spain, peacefully, on September 1, 1821 (Rodriguez, 1965, 54) only to be annexed to Emperor Iturbide's Mexican Empire the very next year.[1] After the collapse of Iturbide's Empire in 1823, representatives of all provinces gathered in a Congress and established the United Provinces of Central America, which in 1824 became the Federal Republic of Central America.

The decision to form a federal government was intended to allow the states maximum authority over their internal affairs, while gaining

---

[1] To avoid annexation by Mexico, San Salvador unsuccessfully sought membership of the United States of America in 1822 (Hall and Brignoli, 2003).

Table 5.1: *Conflicts during the Union (1824–42)*

State	Battles	Killed	Leaders
Guatemala	51	2291	18
El Salvador	40	2546	23
Honduras	27	682	20
Nicaragua	17	1203	18
Costa Rica	5	144	11
Los Altos	3	222	7

Note: Los Altos existed for only two years.

advantages of scale in foreign policy, defense, and international trade (Hall and Brignoli, 2003, 172). However, some very deep regional and ideological differences quickly produced a series of civil wars in 1827–28, 1832–33, and in 1837–39, leading to the dissolution of the union. Table 5.1 from Karnes (1961, 94)[2] shows how endemic conflict was in this period. While the numbers of killed may seem small, given that less than 1.2 million people lived in the five states in 1824, this represents 0.6% of their total population killed in these skirmishes and battles. (With the current US population, that would amount to more than 1.8 million US citizens killed.)

At the root of these civil wars and of enduring significance to all countries in the region for the next 80 years was an intense political competition within each of the separate states (with the exception of Costa Rica) as well as across them between Conservatives (or *serviles*) and Liberals (or *fiebres*). To be sure, these were not well-defined ideologies, and individual leaders sometimes switched their ideological leanings for purely instrumental reasons, but the difference between Conservatives and Liberals was real and enduring. In a nutshell, whereas Conservatives:

emphasized the maintenance of law and order, the continuation of traditional ways of life (particularly in the countryside), and the preservation of the Hispanic Catholic culture, . . . the Liberals favored economic

---

[2] Karnes (1961, 94) cites Marure (1895, 141 and 154) and notes, "Marure admitted that he erred on the conservative side when he was in doubt" on the accuracy of the numbers.

liberalization and free trade, the abolition of privilege and protection, promotion of foreign immigration, and restrictions on the Catholic Church.
(Hall and Brignoli, 2003, 171) (See also Cruz (2002, 162–3).)

Not surprisingly, with friendly communities of exiles across the respective borders, conflicts between Conservatives and Liberals often did not remain confined within each state. Ideological opponents instead sought and often found ideological allies in the other republics. As Scheina (2003, 250) succinctly puts it: "Conservatives in one country made common cause with those in another; no less could be said for the Liberals." As a result, revolutions and civil wars quickly became internationalized. (For some examples, see Scheina (ibid., 253) and Bancroft (1887, 256).)

It was, indeed, a Conservative revolt against the Liberal leader of the union, Francisco Morazán, which led to the demise of the federation and the emergence of the five independent states.[3] Morazán's liberal policies, both financial and religious (i.e. against the Catholic Church), were fiercely contested by the local Conservatives, when a dreadful cholera epidemic swept the region, further undermining Morazán's legitimacy. Local priests were quick to blame the Liberal regime's anticlerical measures and accused doctors of trying to poison the poor peasants. As a result, the tide turned against Morazán. In May 1838 the Federal Congress allowed the states to go their separate ways and a subsequent motion to dissolve the Federation failed by only one vote. On July 7, 1838, finally, "Congress declared the states to be the 'sovereign, free and independent bodies'" (Woodward, 1993, 88–9).[4] Conservative-led Nicaragua was the first to formally choose secession on April 30, 1838; six months later, November 5 and 15, the Conservative leadership in Honduras and Costa Rica followed

---

[3] Technically, six states became independent. Los Altos, claimed independence on February 2, 1838, and was recognized as such by the Federal Congress on June 5, 1838 (Woodward, 1993, 114). However, Los Altos was quickly re-absorbed into Guatemala by Carrera. Notably, Los Altos had allied with Morazán and the Liberals (ibid., 113). Los Altos was defeated and reincorporated by Carrera on January 27, 1840 (ibid., 117–18).

[4] When to precisely date the demise of the Central American Union is debatable. We date the effective independence of the Central American states to Carrera's decisive defeat of Morazán in March 1840. Despite many subsequent attempts to re-form the union, these attempts have always faltered on the rocks of the self-interest of various leaders.

suit, and another six months later, on April 13, 1839, Guatemala's Conservatives effectively joined the secessionist movement (Rodriguez, 1964, 150, 160, 177–8). Loyal to the union remained only El Salvador, and even that loyalty was doubtful, and Los Altos, whose only hope for autonomy and survival rested with the union. The secessionist states, in particular Honduras under Francisco Ferrera, prepared to use force against their Liberal foe Morazán to unambiguously assert their independence. For the next two years, Central America was in a state of chaos, with Conservative forces from Honduras, Nicaragua, and Costa Rica fighting the Liberal forces of El Salvador under Morazán and José Trinidad Cabañas (who was to play a prominent role in the region in years to come (Woodward, 1993, 96–7)).[5]

After Morazán's term as Federal President expired in February 1839, he had himself elected as head of state of El Salvador. He intended to use El Salvador as a base to preserve, or rather, re-establish, the union and his own power in the region, which he had dominated since 1830 (ibid., 95; Hall and Brignoli, 2003, 175). He faced, however, a formidable opponent in Rafael Carrera, an Indian leader from Guatemala, who had been co-opted by the Guatemalan Conservatives.[6] By October 1838 it had become clear, as Woodward (1993, 93) notes, "that the future of the federation rested on Morazán's success against Carrera." After Carrera attacked and conquered Los Altos on January 24, 1840, Morazán had no choice but to go to war with Guatemala. Like the *caudillos* who dominated Central America and Latin America in the nineteenth century, Morazán had a very personal stake in the union's – and his own – survival. As the British diplomat in Central America, Frederick Chatfield, pointed out at the time, Morazán was motivated less by ideology than by a desire to maintain his power and prevent his overthrow. Chatfield concluded in May 1839 that "Morazán and his friends, have always been averse to the meeting of a convention [to change the constitution of the Federation], from a suspicion that under a new order of things they will be unable to monopolize the power which they have so

[5] It could be argued that this conflict and Honduras and Nicaragua's pre-emption fits our theory, since Ferrera and the Nicaraguan leaders sought to prevent their overthrow by Morazán (Woodward, 1993, 95, 110–11). However, this conflict qualifies better as a struggle for independence than international conflict. The dynamic in this case, however, recurs again and again, as we shall see below.
[6] Historians rarely fail to mention that Carrera once had been a muleteer.

long exercised, without profit to the public" (Rodriguez, 1964, 179, emphasis removed). While Morazán scored some early victories, he was finally and conclusively defeated by Carrera in Guatemala City on March 19, 1840, forcing Morazán to flee into exile.[7]

That Guatemala played a decisive role in the emergence of the new order befitted her status as the most powerful of the Central American states. According to a survey of 1824, Guatemala was by far the most populous of the five states with about 660,580 inhabitants, more than the other states combined. By 1880, Guatemala's population had grown to about 1,225,000, and by 1921 to slightly more than 2 million (Cardoso, 1991, 39, Table 1) (for slightly different population numbers and measurements at different years, see Scheina (2003, 491, fn. 7)). Guatemala's population and power gave its leaders a powerbase that was hard to match for the leaders of the other states. As a result, Guatemalan leaders such as Rafael Carrera, Justo Rufino Barrios, and Manuel Estrada Cabrera loom large in the history of Cental America between 1840 and 1918. Table 5.2 lists all Guatemalan leaders in that period, their dates and manners of entering and losing office, as well as their post-exit fate.[8] We note that while Mariano Rivera Paz was the nominal leader of Guatemala until about 1844, it was clear from March 19, 1840 on, after his defeat of Morazán, that Rafael Carrera was the effective ruler of Guatemala.[9] It was Rivera Paz, nonetheless, who declared Guatemala absolutely sovereign and independent of the federal union on April 17, 1839. Carrera, however, had the honor of presiding over Guatemala when it declared itself an independent republic on March 21, 1847.[10] Justo Rufino Barrios, who ruled Guatemala

---

[7] Morazán had reason to flee Carrera's wrath. In 1838 Morazán captured and ordered shot Carrera's father-in-law, whose head then was fried in a bucket of oil, placed on a pole and displayed on the corner of his house as a warning (Woodward, 1993, 85).

[8] Details on these leaders and sources on which we base our codings are available at mail.rochester.edu/~hgoemas/data in the codebook/case description file for *Archigos*.

[9] Woodward (1993, 121, see also 124, 125) notes that as a result of Carrera's victory on 19 March, "Carrera was now undisputed master of Guatemala. Rivera Paz exercised power only at Carrera's pleasure and at time was clearly uncomfortable in the position.... Passports without Carrera's endorsement were worthless." A similar discrepancy between official and effective leader occurred in the 1870s with Granados and Barrios.

[10] The new Republic of Guatemala was recognized by Honduras and Costa Rica. On the European side, Bremen, as member of the Hanseatic League, and Great Britain quickly followed.

Table 5.2: *Guatemala*

Name	Start	End	Entry	Exit	Fate
Mariano Rivera Paz	13/04/1839	19/03/1840	Irregular	Irregular	OK
Rafael Carrera	10/03/1840	16/08/1848	Irregular	Regular	Exile
Juan Antonio Martínez	16/08/1848	28/11/1848	Regular	Regular	OK?
José Bernardo Escobar	28/11/1848	01/01/1849	Regular	Regular	OK?
Mariano Paredes	03/01/1849	03/08/1849	Regular	Irregular	OK?
Rafael Carrera	03/08/1849	14/04/1865	Irregular	Died in Office	Natural Death
Vicente Cerna	14/04/1865	29/06/1871	Regular	Irregular	Exile
Miguel García Granados	29/06/1871	04/06/1873	Irregular	Regular	OK
Justo Rufino Barrios	04/06/1873	23/06/1882	Regular	Regular	OK
José Maria Orontes	23/06/1882	05/01/1883	Regular	Regular	OK?
Justo Rufino Barrios	05/01/1883	06/04/1885	Regular	Died in Office	Killed on the battlefield
Manuel Lisandro Barillas	06/04/1885	15/03/1892	Regular	Regular	OK
José Maria Reina Barrios	15/03/1892	08/02/1898	Regular	Died in Office	Assassinated
Manuel Estrada Cabrera	08/02/1898	15/04/1920	Regular	Irregular	Imprisoned

Note: For some leaders their post-tenure fate, while most likely OK, could not be definitely established. Those have a question mark after their fate.

Table 5.3: *El Salvador*

Name	Start	End	Entry	Exit	Fate
Francisco Malespín	20/09/1840	22/02/1845	Irregular	Irregular	Exile
Joaquín Eufracio Guzmán	22/02/1845	01/02/1846	Irregular	Regular	OK?
Eugenio Aguilar	21/02/1846	01/02/1848	Regular	Regular	OK
Doroteo Vasconcelos	07/02/1848	01/03/1851	Regular	Irregular	OK
J. F. Quiroz	01/03/1851	03/05/1851	Regular	Regular	OK?
Francisco Dueñas	13/05/1851	01/02/1854	Regular	Regular	OK
José María de San Martín	15/02/1854	01/02/1856	Regular	Regular	OK?
Rafael Campo	12/02/1856	01/02/1858	Regular	Regular	OK?
Miguel Santín de Castillo	15/02/1858	24/06/1858	Regular	Irregular	OK
Gerardo Barrios	24/06/1858	25/10/1863	Irregular	Deposed by Guatemala	Exile
Francisco Dueñas	26/10/1863	10/04/1871	Foreign Imposed	Irregular	Imprisoned
Santiago González	10/04/1871	25/04/1876	Irregular	Deposed by Guatemala	Exile
Rafael Zaldivar	25/04/1876	14/05/1885	Irregular	Irregular	Exile

Name					
Fernando Figueroa	15/05/1885	22/05/1885	Regular	Irregular	OK?
Francisco Menéndez	22/05/1885	22/06/1890	Irregular	Heart attack during coup	Died
Carlos Ezeta	22/06/1890	10/06/1894	Irregular	Irregular	Exile
Rafael Gutiérrez	10/06/1894	14/11/1898	Irregular	Irregular	Exile
Tomás Regalado	14/11/1898	13/07/1903	Irregular	Died in office	Killed on the battlefield
Pedro José Escalón	13/07/1906	28/02/1907	Regular	Regular	OK
Fernando Figueroa	01/03/1907	28/02/1911	Regular	Regular	OK
Manuel Enrique Araujo	01/03/1911	09/02/1913	Regular	Died in office	Assassinated
Carlos Meléndez	11/02/1913	15/08/1914	Regular	Regular	OK
Alfonso Quiñónes Molina	29/08/1914	28/02/1915	Regular	Regular	OK
Carlos Meléndez	01/03/1915	21/12/1918	Regular	Ill Health	Dies in 1919

from 1873 to 1885, promulgated a new constitution of the republic in 1879. This constitution stipulated a presidential term of six years (Burgess, 1926, 184).

Surprisingly, perhaps, for its small geographic size, El Salvador in 1824 was the second most populous Central American state with 212,553 inhabitants, growing to about 703,000 in 1892, and doubling to 1,459,000 in 1930 (Cardoso, 1991, 39, Table 1). In the late 1830s, El Salvador became the hub of the Federal Union when the Federal capital was moved to San Salvador, and subsequently a relatively large Federal district was carved out around San Salvador (Hall and Brignoli, 2003, 174). After Morazán's defeat, on January 30, 1841, the El Salvadoran Congress declared El Salvador an independent republic. Table 5.3 lists all El Salvadoran leaders, their date and manner of entry and exit, as well as their post-tenure fate between 1840 and 1919.[11] Notably, although officially presidents, Norberto Ramirez (20/09/1840–07/01/1841), Juan Lindo (07/01/1841–01/02/1842), José Escolástico (01/02/1842–12/04/1842 and again 19/07/1842–26/09/1842), Dionisio Villacorte (30/06/1842–19/07/1842), Juan José Guzmán 14/04/1842–01/02/1844), and Fermín Palacios (01/02/1844–07/02/1844) are omitted from the table, as the real and effective leader at this time was Francisco Malespín. After Carrera defeated Morazán, he installed Malespín as *Commandante armas* and thereby made him arbiter and the effective leader of El Salvador (Woodward, 1993, 121, 131). While El Salvador had its share of long-lived dictatorships, a new constitution promulgated by General Menéndez on August 13, 1886 mandated that presidents could serve one term and could not be re-elected until after four years had lapsed. A look at the leaders after 1886 in Table 5.3 suggests that subsequent leaders upheld this aspect of the constitution. The picture is misleading, however, as between 1914 and 1927 one family basically controlled the presidency, as Carlos Meléndez, his brother Jorge Meléndez, and their brother-in-law, Alfonso Quiñones Molina, handed power back and forth.

---

[11] As before, details on these leaders and sources on which we base our codings are available at mail.rochester.edu/~hgoemas/data in the codebook/case description file for *Archigos*.

In 1824, Nicaragua was the third most populous state on the isthmus with 207,269 inhabitants. Since then, of all Central American states, Nicaragua has experienced the lowest population growth. By 1875 its population grew to only 373,000, and in the next 45 years did not even double, rising to about 638,000 in 1920. When Nicaragua seceded from the union, it wrote a constitution for separate government which was adopted in November 1838. Under this constitution, which remained in force for about a quarter century, Nicaragua adopted a bicameral legislature and allotted its leader – the "supreme director" – a two-year term. Table 5.4 lists Nicaragua's leaders between 1838 and 1920. The list begins in 1838, not with a *Director*, but with the Liberal *caudillo*, Casto Fonseca, who was the effective ruler (Bancroft, 1887, 196–9; Gámez, 1889, 559; Diaz Lacayo, 1996, 36–7). The first president chosen under the new constitution, Pablo Buitrago, set up a dual system of government which recognized a civilian leader and a military leader (ibid., 38). This system remained more-or-less in place until the ascension of Fruto Chamorro. For this period, two main military leaders of Nicaragua stand out. The first was Casto Fonseca, "a drunkard, ignorant, and the most brutal tyrant Nicaragua ever had" (Bancroft, 1887, 196, fn. 31). The second was José Trinidad Muñoz who, temporarily in Salvadoran employ, took Fonseca's place in 1844 after he and Malespín defeated Fonseca. The system changed under Chamorro, under whose directorship, on February 24, 1854, the constituent assembly finally adopted the title of *República de Nicaragua* for the state and assigned the title of president to the executive (ibid., 257).

More than the other states, Nicaragua suffered from an intense conflict between not only political parties and factions but also cities, typically associated with one or the other faction. Thus, while León was considered a bastion of Liberals, so was Granada the citadel of Conservatives (Parker, 1964, 223). This struggle produced in Nicaragua "one of the most prolonged periods of anarchy in Latin America" (Hall and Brignoli, 2003, 172), overcome only after Nicaragua – and the whole of Central America, for that matter – had defeated the filibustering expedition of William Walker in the late 1850s. With the ascension of Gúzman in 1867, whom Martínez had apparently, but mistakenly, thought would be a useful puppet, Nicaragua entered a 22-year period of political stability and regular transfers of power.

Table 5.4: *Nicaragua*

Name	Start	End	Entry	Exit	Fate
Casto Fonseca	30/04/1838	16/12/1844	Irregular	Defeated by El Salvador	Executed
Trinidad Muñoz	16/12/1844	20/01/1845	Irregular	Regular	OK
Blas Antonio Sáenz	20/01/1845	04/04/1845	Regular	Regular	OK?
José León Sandoval	04/04/1845	12/03/1847	Regular	Regular	Natural death 19/10/1847
Miguel Ramón Morales	12/03/1847	06/04/1847	Regular	Regular	OK?
José Guerrero	06/04/1847	01/01/1849	Regular	Regular/Ill Health?	OK
Toribio Terán	01/01/1849	08/03/1949	Regular	Regular?	OK
Benito Rosales	08/03/1849	01/04/1849	Regular?	Regular?	OK?
Norberto Ramírez	01/04/1849	01/04/1851	Regular	Regular	OK
José Laureano Pineda	05/05/1851	04/08/1851	Regular	Irregular	Imprisoned
Trinidad Muñoz	04/08/1851	11/11/1851	Irregular	Irregular	Exiled
José Laureano Pineda	11/11/1851	01/04/1853	Irregular	Regular	OK
Fruto Chamorro	01/04/1853	12/03/1855	Regular	Dies in Office	Natural death
José Maria Estrada	12/03/1855	25/10/1855	Regular	Regular	Killed in battle
Patricio Rivas	25/10/1855	09/06/1856	Regular	Irregular	OK
William Walker	09/06/1856	14/01/1857	Irregular	Irregular	Exile; executed in 1860
Consultative Council	20/01/1857	24/06/1857	Irregular	Regular	OK
Gobierno Binario	24/06/1857	15/11/1857	Irregular	Regular	OK
Tomás Martínez	15/11/1857	01/03/1867	Regular	Regular	OK
Fernando Guzmán	01/03/1867	01/03/1871	Regular	Regular	OK
Vicente Quadra	01/03/1871	01/03/1875	Regular	Regular	OK

Pedro Joaquín Chamorro	01/03/1875	01/03/1879	Regular	Regular	OK
Joaquín Zavala	01/03/1879	01/03/1883	Regular	Regular	OK
Adán Cárdenas	01/03/1883	01/03/1887	Regular	Regular	OK
Evaristo Carazo	01/03/1887	01/08/1889	Regular	Died in office	Natural death
Roberto Sacasa Sarria	01/08/1889	01/06/1893	Regular	Irregular	Exile
José Santos Zelaya	31/07/1893	16/12/1909	Irregular	Irregular (US pressure)	Exile
José Madriz	16/12/1909	20/08/1910	Regular	Irregular (US pressure)	Exile
José Dolores Estrada	20/08/1910	29/08/1910	Irregular	Irregular	OK?
Juan José Estrada	29/08/1910	09/05/1911	Irregular	Irregular	Exile
Adolfo Diaz	09/05/1911	31/12/1916	Regular	Regular	OK
Emiliano Chamorro Vargas	01/01/1917	31/12/1920	Irregular	Regular	OK

In 1824, the census reported that Honduras was the second-least populous of the Central American states, with 137,069 inhabitants. Since then, however, Honduras has experienced a robust growth in population to 307,000 in 1881 and 553,000 in 1910, becoming larger than Nicaragua, in terms of population, by 1930 (Cardoso, 1991, 39, Table 1). Table 5.5 lists Honduran leaders between 1839 and 1919, the dates and manner of gaining and losing office as well as their post-tenure fate. The period before Ferrera took power was basically one of chaos and unclear effective leadership. Ferrera, however, applied a firm and conservative hand. Although the constitution forbid him to run for a third consecutive term in 1844, he remained the effective leader with the official president, Coronado Chavez, as his puppet (Bancroft, 1887, 311-12).

In 1824, Costa Rica was by far the least populated, with only 70,000 inhabitants. Its population increased to about 182,000 in 1883, and grew to 489,000 by 1927 (Cardoso, 1991, 39, Table 1). Costa Rica declared itself an independent republic on August 31, 1848 and was the first Central American state to be recognized as an independent nation by Spain, on May 10, 1850. After a period of chaos with the one-year leadership of "dictator-for-life" Braulio Carrillo and the return to Central America of Francisco Morazán, a new constitution in 1847 created a presidency with a six-year term. The president's term was halved to three years in the constitution of 1859 and extended to four years in the constitution of 1871. Although this latter constitution, promulgated by Tomás Guardia, did not allow a sitting president to stand for re-election, Guardia managed to remain the effective leader. While obeying the letter of the law he nevertheless remained the effective leader of Costa Rica until his death in 1882 (Parker, 1964, 260-1). Table 5.6 lists Costa Rica's leaders.

In the nineteenth century, Central American states offered little or no institutionalized protection for their politicians and leaders. Defeated opponents could not safely retire. As US Envoy John Lloyd Stephens concluded, "a political opponent is a robber, an assassin; it is praise to admit that he is not a bloodthirsty cutthroat. . . . *Defeated partisans are shot, banished, run away*, or get a moral lockjaw, and never dare express their opinions before one of the party" (quoted in Woodward (1993, 143, emphasis added)). To avoid such harsh personal punishments, adherents of the party currently not in power would often flee across the border, particularly if that country was currently ruled by a

Table 5.5: *Honduras*

Name	Start	End	Entry	Exit	Fate
Francisco Zelaya y Ayes	21/09/1839	31/12/1840	Regular?	Regular?	OK?
Francisco Ferrera	01/01/1841	12/02/1847	Regular	Regular	Exile
Juan Lindo	12/02/1847	01/02/1852	Regular	Regular	OK
Francisco Gomez Y Argüelles	01/02/1852	01/03/1852	Regular	Regular	OK
Trinidad Cabañas	01/03/1852	06/10/1856	Regular	Irregular	Exile
José Santiago Bueso	18/10/1855	08/11/1855	Regular	Regular	?
Francisco de Aguilar	08/11/1855	17/02/1856	Regular	Regular	OK
José Santos Guardiola	17/02/1856	11/01/1862	Regular	Died in office	Assassinated
José Francisco Montes	11/01/1862	04/02/1962	Regular	Regular	OK
Victoriano Castellanos	04/02/1862	04/12/1862	Regular	Ill Health	Natural death
José Francisco Montes	04/12/1862	21/06/1863	Regular	Irregular	Imprisoned?
José María Medina	21/06/1863	26/07/1872	Irregular	Irregular	Imprisoned
Céleo Arias	26/07/1872	13/01/1874	Foreign Imposition	Irregular	Imprisoned
Ponciano Leiva	13/01/1874	08/06/1876	Irregular	Irregular	Exile
Marco Aurelio Soto	27/08/1876	19/10/1883	Regular?	Regular	Exile
Council of Ministers	19/10/1883	30/11/1883	Regular	Regular	
Luis Bográn	30/11/1883	30/11/1891	Regular	Regular	Exile?
Ponciano Leiva	30/11/1891	09/02/1893	Regular	Irregular?	Exile?
Rosendo Agüero	09/02/1893	18/04/1893	Regular	Regular?	OK
Domingo Vásquez	18/04/1893	22/02/1894	Irregular	Irregular	Exile

(cont.)

Table 5.5: (*cont.*)

Name	Start	End	Entry	Exit	Fate
Policarpo Bonilla	22/02/1894	01/02/1899	Irregular	Regular	OK
Terencio Sierra	01/02/1899	30/01/1903	Regular	Irregular	Exile
Manuel Bonilla	01/02/1903	11/04/1907	Irregular	Irregular	Exile
Miguel Dávila	18/04/1907	28/03/1911	Foreign Imposition	Irregular	Exile
Francisco Bertrand	28/02/1911	02/02/1912	Regular	Regular	OK
Manuel Bonilla	02/02/1912	20/03/1913	Regular	Died in office	Natural death
Francisco Bertrand	20/03/1913	28/07/1915	Regular	Regular	OK
Alberto Membreño	28/07/1915	01/02/1916	Regular	Regular	OK
Francisco Bertrand	01/02/1916	09/09/1919	Regular	Irregular	Exile

Table 5.6: *Costa Rica*

Name	Start	End	Entry	Exit	Fate
Braulio Carrillo	27/05/1838	12/04/1842	Irregular	Irregular	Exiled, murdered in 1845
Francisco Morazán	12/04/1842	11/09/1842	Irregular	Irregular	Executed
Antonio Pinto	11/09/1842	23/09/1842	Irregular	Regular	OK
José María Alfaro	23/09/1842	28/11/1844	Regular	Regular	OK
Francisco María Oreamuno	29/11/1844	17/12/1844	Regular	Regular	OK
Rafael Moya	17/12/1844	30/04/1845	Regular	Regular	OK
José Rafael Gallegos	01/05/1845	07/06/1846	Regular	Irregular	OK
José María Alfaro	07/06/1846	08/05/1847	Irregular	Regular	Exile
José María Castro Madriz	08/05/1847	16/11/1849	Regular	Regular	OK?
Juan Rafael Mora	24/11/1849	14/08/1859	Regular?	Irregular	Exiled; Killed 30/09/1860
José Maria Montealegre	14/08/1859	07/05/1863	Regular	Regular	OK?
Jesús Jiménez	07/05/1863	08/05/1866	Regular	Regular	OK
José María Castro Madriz	08/05/1866	01/11/1868	Regular	Irregular	OK?
Jesús Jiménez	01/11/1868	27/04/1870	Regular	Irregular	Imprisoned
Tomás Guardia	27/04/1870	20/06/1872	Irregular	Regular	OK
José A. Pinto	20/06/1872	26/01/1872	Regular	Regular	OK
Tomás Guardia	26/01/1873	06/07/1882	Regular	Died in office	Natural death
Saturnino Lizano Gutiérrez	06/07/1882	20/07/1882	Regular	Regular	OK?
Prospero Fernandez Oreamuno	20/07/1882	12/03/1885	Regular	Died in office	Natural death
Bernardo Soto Alfaro	12/03/1885	01/05/1889	Regular	Regular	OK
Ascensión Esquivel Ibarra	01/05/1889	01/09/1889?	Regular	Regular	OK

(*cont.*)

Table 5.6: (cont.)

Name	Start	End	Entry	Exit	Fate
Bernardo Soto Alfaro	01/09/1889?	07/11/1889	Regular	Irregular	Exile
Carlos Duran Cartín	07/11/1889	08/05/1890	Irregular	Regular	OK?
José Joaquín Rodríguez	08/05/1890	08/05/1894	Regular	Regular	OK?
Rafael Yglesias Castro	08/05/1894	08/05/1902	Regular	Regular	OK
Ascensión Esquivel Ibarra	08/05/1902	08/05/1906	Regular	Regular	OK
Cleto González Víquez	08/05/1906	08/05/1910	Regular	Regular	OK
Ricardo Jiménez Oreamuno	08/05/1910	08/05/1914	Regular	Regular	OK?
Alfredo González Flores	08/05/1914	27/01/1917	Irregular	Irregular	Exile
Federico Tinoco Granados	27/01/1917	13/08/1919	Irregular	Irregular	Exile

leader sympathetic to their ideology. In these Central American states, thus, leaders worried almost constantly about coups, rebellions and revolts. As Tables 5.2–5.6 show, Central American leaders had good reasons to fear irregular removals: about forty percent (50 out of 129) of leader-spells in office were terminated as a result of the threat or use of force. The threat or use of force – the forcible process of terminating a leader's rule – thus played an important role in Central American politics between 1840 and 1919. As we argued in Chapter 2, this process was closely linked with the absence of post-tenure protection for leaders. About thirty five percent (45 out of 129) of all removals from office ended in significant personal punishment for the leaders involved. As we will see below, in many instances international conflict allowed leaders to postpone the day of reckoning.

With this background sketch of some of the driving forces and personalities of Central America in the nineteenth century, we are in a position to discuss how we plan to test our theory.

5.2.1 Empirical strategy

In Chapter 2 we argued that leaders have incentives to initiate international conflict when they face a high risk of a forcible removal from office. More precisely, we argued that an exogenous shock to the relative power of the leader and his potential challengers raises the threat of coups and domestic revolts because the leader cannot credibly commit to share power. If the exogenous shock introduces what may be only a temporary shift in favor of the opposition, the leader will want to renege on any promises he has made to stay in office when the tide turns in his favor once again. Leaders in such systems can then rationally choose to initiate international conflict, because this offers at least the opportunity to readjust the balance of power with their domestic opponents, or pre-empt civil war.

To test our theory we would of course, ideally, like to identify exogenous shocks in the balance of power between leaders and potential challengers, or at least identify *ex ante* when a leader faced a high risk of an irregular removal from office, and then trace whether and how this influenced the leader's decision whether to engage in international conflict. To rigorously trace all potential shocks or factors that affect the risk of an irregular removal from office for all five Central American countries between 1840 and 1918 would seem an impossible task.

The fundamental problem is that we simply do not have enough, and detailed enough, historical sources to reliably trace such shocks. A broad variety of factors, up to and including cholera epidemics and failed crops might play an important role in the domestic balance of power, but are simply impossible to reliably trace for the entire period.

However, the brief historical sketch above suggests an indicator to measure the risk of an irregular removal and of exogenous shocks in the balance of power between the leader and his potential challengers. As Scheina (2003, 250–1) and many others noted, the competition between Conservatives and Liberals transcended borders. On the one hand, if the leaders of the Central American states all adhered to the same ideology – as some eagerly sought and achieved for limited periods of time – exiles and emigrés would be unlikely to find fertile ground abroad to organize revolutions and revolts. On the other hand, if the leaders of two states belonged to opposing parties, a defeated party in one state could and often would find shelter and support to regroup in the other state. Thus, we would expect that Central American leaders faced a higher risk of an irregular removal from office when one leader is Conservative and his neighbor(s) Liberal. An exogenous shock to the domestic (and international) balance of power occurred when a previously ideologically aligned neighbor switches its ideology, as the result of the rise of a new leader or a fundamental realignment of the leader's policies. For example, in late 1848 both Guatemala and its neighbor El Salvador were ruled by Liberal leaders. In 1849, however, the Conservative Rafael Carrera returned to power in Guatemala. As a result, Salvadoran Conservative opponents to Salvadoran Liberal President Vasconcelos were strengthened, because they gained a safe place to organize, as well as material support from Conservative Guatemala. Moreover, Salvadoran Liberals could no longer rely on support from Guatemala. Carrera's return to power, thus, constitutes an exogenous shock to the relative power of Salvadoran Conservatives and Liberals in favor of the Salvadoran Conservatives.

To assess how the risk of an irregular removal affects international conflict, we need information on instances of international conflict. The Correlates of War project (Sarkees, 2000) with its criterion of 1,000 battle-deaths, identifies 4 major wars between 1840 and 1918: the 1876 war between Guatemala and El Salvador; the 1885 war between Guatemala and El Salvador; the 1906 war between Guatemala, Honduras and El Salvador; and, finally, the 1907 war between Honduras,

El Salvador, and Nicaragua.[12] However, as noted above, the small populations of Central America supported only relatively small armed forces. Typically, the national leader was supported by several lesser *caudillos* and their followers, both for support and manpower.[13] The national leader could sometimes also rely on a small number of mercenaries, many if not most of them from North America, but most of the soldiers were pressed into service. As a Nicaraguan recruiter wrote to his superior, "I send you forty volunteers. Please return the ropes" (quoted in Scheina (2003, 251)). Under these conditions, it seems misguided to focus only on international conflicts with 1,000 battle-deaths.[14] Instead, we classify instances when the armed forces of one country – often, if not almost always, personally led by the leader – cross the border or where a leader issued an explicit declaration of war as *wars*. Instances when (irregular) forces "with the support" of one country invade another country or when diplomatic relations are broken off and there exists a threat of the use of force count as *international crises*.

5.2.2 Ideology and international conflict in Central America

Surprisingly, perhaps, as far as we know only one book in English comprehensively examines international armed conflict in and across Central America in this period.[15] In his terrific two volumes on Latin American wars since 1791, Scheina (2003, vol. I, Ch. 22) devotes about 11 pages to provide thumbnail sketches of international conflicts "among *caudillos* of Central America, 1844–1907." In contrast to the 4 wars identified by the Correlates of War project, Scheina (ibid.) identifies about 20 wars and international crises in this period. A careful reading of the relevant history, in particular, Bancroft (1887) and

---

[12] Remarkably, the COW project omits the *National War* that pitted Guatemala, El Salvador, Honduras, and Costa Rica against Nicaragua between 1855 and 1857. The war certainly produced enough battlefield casualties, but might have been omitted because Nicaragua was led by an American filibuster, William Walker.

[13] Defeat in an international conflict often, but not always, meant that the local *caudillos* would withdraw their support for the national leader, leading to his fall.

[14] Moreover, battle-deaths are notoriously difficult to assess for this period.

[15] For a comprehensive Spanish-language monograph focusing on international conflicts involving El Salvador, see Bustamante Maceo (1951).

Bustamante Maceo (1951), suggests that Scheina (2003) omitted some conflicts – in particular, some conflicts before 1844 and the Guerra Nacional of 1855–57 that pitted Nicaragua – led by the American William Walker – against Guatemala, El Salvador, Honduras, and Costa Rica, as well as conflicts with states outside Central America which, admittedly, also bear little relevance for our enterprise.

In Tables 5.7 through 5.11 we list the major leaders of each country, their ideological allegiance, as well as the first year of an international conflict. A leader identified in SMALL CAPS belonged to the Conservative party, a leader identified in *italics* belonged to the Liberal party. A few leaders are listed in regular script, and were more-or-less independent and not strongly identified with one ideology or the other. In the international conflict column, capital letters indicate the initiation of a war, regular size letters indicate the initiation of a crisis; the country that initiated the conflict is listed first.

As shall become clearer in the analysis to follow, the tables show that if a new leader with a different ideology came to power, this often relatively quickly led to an international conflict. In other words, if Conservative leaders ruled four out of five countries, but one of those leaders was replaced by a Liberal leader, this would change the balance of power between Conservatives and Liberals in those other countries and often lead to war. The marked decline in international conflict after the mid-1870s is the direct result of that fact that Liberalism had triumphed and Guatemala, El Salvador, Honduras, and Costa Rica were, with few exceptions, continuously ruled by strong Liberal leaders, while Nicaragua was led by moderate Conservatives and, after 1893, also by Liberal leaders.

For more detailed analysis, we partition the period between 1840 and 1918 into three distinct eras: Birth Pangs of Independence, 1840–48, Conservatism Ascendant, 1849–71, and the Return of Liberalism, 1872–1918. The first two periods correspond roughly to Rafael Carrera's reign as leader of Guatemala, while the era of Liberalism begins with Justo Rufino Barrios' rise in Guatemala, and continues with the rule of his nephew, José Reina Barrios, and continues to 1919 with Manuel Estrada Cabrera's presidency of Guatemala. While many other non-Guatemalan leaders played a very important regional role, it is probably fair to say that none managed to obtain a position of power and regional control similar to Nicaragua's José Santos Zelaya between 1893 and 1909.

Table 5.7: *The era of Carrera and Conservative preponderance – I*

Year	Guatemala	El Salvador	Honduras	Nicaragua	Costa Rica	Conflict
1840	M. RIVERA PAZ R. CARRERA	F. Morazán J. A. Cañas F. MALESPÍN	J.F. Zelaya	C. Fonseca	B. Carrillo	ES/G; H/ES; uk/n ES/G; H,N/ES
1841			F. FERRERA			uk/n
1842					B. Carrillo F. Morazán J.M. Alfaro	g,es,h,n/cr; mex/g
1843						g/es
1844						G/ES
				C. Fonseca		ES,H/N
1845		F. MALESPÍN J.E. Guzmán J.E. Guzmán E. AGUILAR		T. MUÑOZ J.L. SANDOVAL 	J.M. Alfaro J.R. Gallegos J.R. Gallegos J.M. ALFARO	H/ES
1846						
1847			F. FERRERA J. LINDO	J.L. SANDOVAL J. Guerrero	J.M. ALFARO J. M. Castro	
1848	R. CARRERA J.A. Martínez B. Escobar	E. AGUILAR D. Vasconcelos				uk/n g/es

(cont.)

Table 5.7: (*cont.*)

Year	Guatemala	El Salvador	Honduras	Nicaragua	Costa Rica	Conflict
1849	Mariano Paredes			*J. Guerrero*	*J.M. Castro*	uk/h
	R. CARRERA			*N. Ramirez*	J.R. Mora	uk/n
1850						uk/es; uk/h
						ES, H, N/G
1851		*D. Vasconcelos*		*N. Ramirez*		
		F. DUEÑAS		L. PINEDA		
1852			J. LINDO			
			F. Gomez			
			T.Cabañas			
1853				L. PINEDA		G/H
				F. CHAMORRO		h/es

Note: CONSERVATIVES, *Liberals.* For the conflicts, capital letters indicate a WAR, otherwise crisis.

Table 5.8: *The era of Carrera and Conservative preponderance – II*

Year	Guatemala	El Salvador	Honduras	Nicaragua	Costa Rica	Conflict
1854	R. CARRERA	F. DUEÑAS	T. *Cabañas*	F. CHAMORRO	J. R. Mora	H/N; n/cr
1855		J.M. SAN MARTÍN		F. CHAMORRO		
				J. M. ESTRADA		
				W. Walker (Lib)		
1856		J.M. SAN MARTÍN	T. *Cabañas*			CR,ES,G,H/N
		R. CAMPO	S. GUARDIOLA			
1857				W. Walker (Lib)		CR/N
				T. MARTINEZ		
1858		R. CAMPO				
		M. SANTÍN				
		G. *Barrios*				
1859					J. R. Mora	
					J.M. Montealegre	
1860						
1861						
1862			S. GUARDIOLA			
			V. *Castellanos*			
1863		G. *Barrios*	J.F. *Montes*		*J.M. Montealegre*	G,N/ES,H
		F. DUEÑAS	J.M. MEDINA		J. *Jimenez*	
1864						

(cont.)

Table 5.8: (*cont.*)

Year	Guatemala	El Salvador	Honduras	Nicaragua	Costa Rica	Conflict
1865	R. CARRERA					es,h,g,n/cr
	V. CERNA					
1866					*J. Jimenez*	
					J.M. Castro	
1867				T. MARTINEZ		
				F. GUZMÁN		
1868					*J.M. Castro*	
					J. Jimenez	

Note: CONSERVATIVES, *Liberals*. For the conflicts, capital letters indicate a WAR, otherwise crisis.

Table 5.9: *The era of Justo Rufino Barrios and Liberal preponderance*

Year	Guatemala	El Salvador	Honduras	Nicaragua	Costa Rica	Conflict
1869	V. CERNA	F. DUEÑAS	J.M. MEDINA	F. GUZMÁN	J. Jimenez	
1870					J. Jimenez	
					T. Guardia	
1871	V. CERNA	F. DUEÑAS		F. GUZMÁN		ES/H
	M. García	S. González		V. QUADRA		
	Granados					
1872			J.M. MEDINA			H/ES, G
			C. Arias			
1873	M. García					G,ES/H
	Granados					
	J. Rufino Barrios					
1874			C. Arias			
			P. Leiva			
1875				V. QUADRA		
				P. CHAMORRO		n/cr
1876		S. González	P. Leiva			G/H
		R. Zaldívar	M. Aurelio Soto			G/ES; germany/n
1877						
1878						
1879				P. CHAMORRO		
				J. ZAVALA		

(*cont.*)

Table 5.9: (*cont.*)

Year	Guatemala	El Salvador	Honduras	Nicaragua	Costa Rica	Conflict
1880						
1881						
1882					*T. Guardia*	
					P. Fernandez	
1883			*M. Aurelio Soto*	J. ZAVALA		
			L. Bográn	A. CÁRDENAS		
1884						
1885	*J. Rufino Barrios*	*R. Zaldívar*			*P. Fernandez*	G,H/ES,N,CR
	M.L. Barillas	*F. Menéndez*			*B. Soto Alfaro*	

Note: CONSERVATIVES, *Liberals*, Ponciano Leiva was a non-partisan independent. For the conflicts, capital letters indicate a WAR, otherwise crisis.

Table 5.10: *Zelaya, Estrada Cabrera and the era of Liberal dominance – I*

Year	Guatemala	El Salvador	Honduras	Nicaragua	Costa Rica	Conflict
1886	*M.L. Barillas*	*F. Menéndez*	*L. Bogran*	A. CÁRDENAS	*B. Soto Alfaro*	
1887				A. CÁRDENAS		
1888				E. CARAZO		
1889		*F. Menéndez*		E. CARAZO R. SACASA	*B. Soto Alfaro* *C. Duran Cartin*	
1890		*C. Ezeta*			*C. Duran Cartin*	
1891			*L. Bogran* P. Leiva		J.J. RODRIGUEZ	G,H/ES
1892	*M.L. Barillas* *J. Reina Barrios*					
1893			P. Leiva D. VÁSQUEZ	R. SACASA		N/H
1894		*C. Ezeta* *R.A. Gutierrez*	D. VÁSQUEZ P. Bonilla	J.S. Zelaya	J.J. RODRIGUEZ R. YGLESIAS	n/uk
1895						
1896						
1897						
1898	*J. Reina Barrios* *M. Estrada Cabrera*	*R.A. Gutierrez* *T. Regalado*				es/n,h
1899						

(*cont.*)

Table 5.10: (*cont.*)

Year	Guatemala	El Salvador	Honduras	Nicaragua	Costa Rica	Conflict
1900			*P. Bonilla* *T. Sierra*			
1901						
1902					R. YGLESIAS *A. Esquivel*	
1903		*T. Regalado*	*T. Sierra* M. BONILLA			

Note: CONSERVATIVES, *Liberals*. For the conflicts, capital letters indicate a WAR, otherwise crisis.

Table 5.11: *Zelaya, Estrada Cabrera and the era of Liberal dominance – II*

Year	Guatemala	El Salvador	Honduras	Nicaragua	Costa Rica	Conflict
1905	M. Estrada Cabrera	P.J. Escalon	M. BONILLA	J.S. Zelaya	A. Esquivel	
1906		T. Regalado			A. Esquivel	ES/G
		P.J. Escalon				
1907		P.J. Escalon	M. BONILLA		C. Gonzalez Viquez	n/es; g/mexico
		F. Figueroa	M.D. Dávila			N/ES,H
1908						n/es
1909				J. S. Zelaya		n,g/es,h
				J. Madriz		
1910				J. Madriz	C. Gonzalez Viquez	
				J. Madriz	R. Jimenez	
				J.J. Estrada		
				J.J. Estrada		
				A. DIAZ		
1911		F. Figueroa	M.D. Dávila			
		E. Araujo	F. Bertrand			
1912						
1913		E. Araujo	F. Bertrand			
		C. Menendez	M. BONILLA			
1914		C. Menendez	M. BONILLA		R. Jimenez	
		A. Quinones	F. Bertrand		A. Gonzalez Flores	
1915		A. Quinones				
		C. Menendez				
1916				A. DIAZ		
				E. CHAMORRO		
1917			F. Bertrand		A. Gonzalez Flores	
			R. Lopez Gutierrez		F. Tinoco	
1918						cr/n

Note: CONSERVATIVES, *Liberals*. Nicaraguan leaders after Zelaya all fundamentally depended on the US for support. Ideological orientation played a much less significant role. For the conflicts, capital letters indicate a WAR, otherwise crisis.

5.3 Birth pangs of independence 1840–48

The civil wars between the states and ideological factions which erupted in 1837 finally brought about the *de facto* end of the union in mid-March 1840, when Carrera decisively defeated Morazán in Guatemala City. While Morazán was forced to flee Central America, the forces of Liberalism remained relatively strong. The *morazánistas* or *coquimbos* continued to promote the closely associated causes of Liberalism and union.[16] The Conservative leaders in Guatemala (Carrera), El Salvador (Malespín), Honduras (Ferrera), and Nicaragua (Rivas, Buitrago) therefore had to deal with continuous but relatively low levels of threat against their position and person.[17] We skip a discussion of the wars of 1840 because they formed an integral part of the struggle for independence and therefore constitute more of a civil war than a series of international wars (for details on these struggles, see Bustamante Maceo (1951, 35–8)).

5.3.1 The return of Morazán

The first major exogenous shock to the new system came in 1842 when Morazán, the strong man of the Liberals, returned. In the summer of 1841, Great Britain used its navy to start a conflict with Nicaragua over the independence of the Mosquito Coast and the Mosquito King (see Bancroft (1887, 248–53) and Rodriguez (1964) for details about British diplomacy in this time).[18] Outraged and worried about further British encroachments, the Nicaraguan *Director*, Pablo Buitrago,

---

[16] It should be noted, though, that for many Liberals, promoting the cause of union mainly served to obtain broad support in other states for their attempts to gain control in their own state (Rodriguez, 1965, 80).

[17] Bustamante Maceo (1951, 39) mentions an international conflict between Honduras and Nicaragua against the Liberals in El Salvador in January 1840. The heading of this brief section, however, "Events in Honduras 1840–1841" suggests that this conflict might have dragged into 1841, but no evidence could be found to substantiate such an end date.

[18] Another international conflict with states outside of Central America narrowly speaking occurred in August 1842, when "four hundred Mexican troops ... occupied the Tonalá region of Soconusco, long claimed by Guatemala" (Woodward, 1993, 154). This conflict would fester for another thirty years. It deserves note that international support also reflected ideological preferences. Whereas Great Britain tended to support "Conservatives," the United States of America tended to favor "Liberals."

called upon Morazán, then residing in Peru, to protect Central America from the British (Bustamante Maceo, 1951, 39). Morazán jumped at the opportunity and returned to Central America in February 1842, landing first at La Union, El Salvador. With fresh recruits and the company of important generals such as Gerardo Barrios and Trinidad Cabañas, Morazán then set sail for Costa Rica, where he landed on April 7, 1842 with about 500 men. Morazán quickly overthrew "dictator-for-life" Braulio Carrillo, when the government forces sent to meet him instead defected to his colors.[19] Morazán then immediately introduced harsh measures to raise the necessary resources to prepare for a military campaign to restore the union (Bancroft, 1887, 215–25).

The unexpected return of Morazán presented a clear and imminent threat to the Conservative leaders in the other states. Morazán had proven himself an able general, and capable leader of men. Many in the region still hoped the union would be restored, and as a result Morazán could count on the support of Liberals and unionists. With Morazán in power in Costa Rica, moreover, Liberals in the other states would be both strengthened and emboldened. Morazán's dream of restoring the union, as well as his support for Liberals in the other states, thus constituted a direct threat to the leaders in the other countries. As our theory would predict, an international crisis broke out almost immediately.

We consider Guatemala the initiator in this crisis because Guatemala was the first to suspend diplomatic relations with Costa Rica (the other states quickly followed suit).[20] In October 1842 Guatemala, El Salvador, Nicaragua, and Honduras concluded treaties of mutual defense (Bustamante Maceo, 1951, 39–40; Hall and Brignoli, 2003, 182). A war was prevented only because by the time of this pact, unbeknownst to the Conservative leaders, Morazán was already dead. On September 11, 1842 Costa Ricans rose against Morazán, largely because of his heavy-handed effort to collect enough money to raise,

---

[19] Carrillo obtained free passage out of the country for him and his family, personally guaranteed by Morazán. He settled in Salvador, where he was murdered in 1845 by a personal enemy (Bancroft, 1887, 217, fn. 10; Calvo, 1890, 277).

[20] As in several other cases, it does not really matter in this crisis who is coded as the initiator. Each leader feared a forcible overthrow, with its associated punishment, and initiation would have been intended to prevent such a fate.

arm, and equip troops. Behind the scenes, Guatemala's Carrera also worked to promote a revolution in Costa Rica. When the insurrection struck, Morazán was quickly defeated. Although promised his life in return for his surrender, Morazán was executed on 15 September.

5.3.2 Malespín and the Liberal exiles in Nicaragua

With this crisis averted, the Conservative leaders remained in a relatively precarious position, with the lurking threat of a Liberal resurgence. At first Malespín of El Salvador had cooperated with Carrera to overthrow Morazán and remove the unionist threat. Subsequently, however, Carrera received steadily more information that suggested Malespín would no longer play the role of obedient puppet (Woodward, 1993, 157). Malespín's shift towards the Liberals constitutes the first exogenous shock for this period; his switch back to a staunchly pro-Carrera and Conservative position constitutes a second shock. Malespín's overthrow and the rise of the Liberal Guzmán in El Salvador constitutes a third shock. As expected, each quickly induced an international war.

At the heart of the international conflicts to come, as so often, lay the issue of refugees and exiles. To Carrera's dismay, Malespín proved willing to "grant asylum to the remnants of Morazán's forces against the protests of Guatemala and Honduras" (Bustamante Maceo, 1951, 287). In addition, Malespín showed a new and marked inclination to listen to Salvadoran Liberals.[21] Finally, Malespín had developed good relations with the Nicaraguan Liberal regime, signing in July 1842 a new pact of confederation with Nicaragua which significantly strengthened the Liberals' hands (Diaz Lacayo, 1996, 36–7). Moreover, Liberals from other countries found safe haven in León, from which they agitated for the overthrow of the region's Conservative leaders.

Carrera now became deeply worried about a renewed Liberal offensive against Guatemala and his leadership (Woodward, 1993, 157).[22]

---

[21] Malespín's temporary tilt toward the Liberals is well documented, see for example Woodward (1993, 185).
[22] The historical record very strongly suggests that Carrera may have cared about the fate of his fellow Indians and the role of the Catholic Church. At the end of the day, however, Carrera was no true believer in any ideology and simply

In early June of 1843, therefore, Carrera declared war on El Salvador. In his declaration of war, Carrera explicitly phrased the threat in terms of the continued success of the Conservative revolution (Bustamante Maceo, 1951, 40). Two weeks later, in response Malespín called Salvadorans to arms, warning that Carrera was prepared to invade soon, and might well be supported by Ferrera from Honduras. As for Carrera's accusations regarding the Liberal exiles residing in El Salvador, Malespín declared: "Giving asylum to many unfortunate people who had repeatedly defended the homeland...can never be grounds for a just war" (ibid., 41).

Under the threat of an attack by both Guatemala and a resurgent Conservative Honduras, Malespín and the Nicaraguan Liberal leaders (Casto Fonseca, and *Directors* Manuel Pérez and Emiliano Madrid) on August 16, 1843 committed to a pact to overthrow the Conservative President Ferrera of Honduras. The plan apparently was to first replace Ferrera with the Liberal General Trinidad Cabañas, and then march upon Guatemala City. The invasion would be led by Francisco Malespín and the Nicaraguan general Manuel Quijano (Rodriguez, 1964, 263). By the summer of 1843, a fully-fledged war appeared ready to break out at any moment, but neither Bancroft (1887) nor Bustamante Maceo (1951) records any battles or skirmishes involving the armed forces from Guatemala and El Salvador in 1843, and we therefore consider this only a crisis.

Carrera, instead, chose a less risky and indirect approach to try to deal with Malespín and the Liberal threat. He backed the former Liberal Federal President Manuel José Arce, now turned Conservative, in an invasion attempt in May 1844 to overthrow Malespín.[23] Scheina (2003, 252, emphasis added) records that "Arce invaded El Salvador from Guatemala *at the head of an army that included Guatemalans (possibly filibusters) and penetrated ten miles*, as far Atiquizaya" (Bancroft 1887, 190; Gámez 1889, 501). However, Arce's forces were defeated by Malespín at Coatepeque and the victorious 4,000 Salvadoran army pursued Arce's fleeing forces back into Guatemala, reaching

---

strategically and tactically chose alliances which kept him in power (Woodward, 1993, 189).

[23] Aware of Arce's preparations and Guatemala's support, Malespín had broken off diplomatic relations with Guatemala on April 26, 1844 (Gámez, 1889, 501).

all the way to Jutiapa, about 75 miles south-east of Guatemala City, by May 20, 1844 (Bustamante Maceo, 1951, 42; Scheina, 2003, 252). In reaction, Carrera marshalled his troops and marched against the invading army. Malespín and Carrera, however, managed to avoid an all-out war between Guatemala and El Salvador when they agreed to the Treaty of Quezada of August 1844. Perhaps because of the nego-tiations with Carrera, perhaps because of a renewed appreciation of the Conservative cause or the danger posed to his position by Liberals, history does not record the reason, but in the treaty Malespín lays the blame for the troubles in El Salvador and Honduras squarely at the feet of Liberals residing in León, Nicaragua (Bancroft, 1887, 190–3).

When the *morazanista* generals – also known as *coquimbos*, e.g. unionist and Liberal generals who returned from Morazán's doomed expedition in Costa Rica – realized that Malespín would not fight to overthrow Carrera, they plotted a revolution. On September 5, 1844 General Trinidad Cabañas launched an insurrection against Malespín. The revolt was relatively easily quashed and Cabañas fled to Nicaragua, whose Liberal President Pérez offered him protection. Meanwhile, in Honduras Liberals also attempted and failed to over-throw President Ferrera. As had Malespín, Ferrera blamed his troubles squarely on exiles given protection and support in Liberal Nicaragua (Bancroft, 1887, 195; Gámez, 1889, 509–10; Bustamante Maceo, 1951, 42).

The Liberals' betrayal did not sit well with Malespín. Throwing his lot now firmly with the Conservatives, Carrera in Guatemala and Ferrera in Honduras, Malespín entered into a treaty with Honduras and demanded the Nicaraguan government extradite Cabañas. When *Director* Pérez refused, Malespín and Ferrera of Honduras declared war on Nicaragua (ibid.). Well aware of the looming danger, how-ever, Nicaragua moved first and struck Honduras on October 23, 1844 with a 1,000-strong army at Nacaome; the invasion was beaten back (Bancroft, 1887, 194–5). In reply, two armies invaded Nicaragua, and on 26 November besieged León. The first army, from Salvador, was led by the Nicaraguan, General Trinidad Muñoz. The second, Honduran, army was led by General José Santos Guardiola. In Nicaragua, mean-while, Emiliano Madrid became *Director* when Pérez abdicated; he held out for 59 days against the combined Salvadoran and Honduran armies. On January 24, 1845 the Plaza of León finally fell. Amidst atrocities committed by Malespín's forces, *Director* Madrid died in battle. Casto Fonseca fled but was captured, court-martialed, and executed. Cabañas, however, as well as his fellow Liberal Gerardo Barrios, managed to escape. Both would fight another day.

As a result of Malespín's poor performance on the battlefield and the atrocities committed, but mostly as a result of continued Liberal agitation back home in El Salvador, on February 22, 1845 a Liberal revolution promoted by Cabañas and Barrios ousted Malespín and replaced him with his Vice-President, Joaquín Eufracio Guzmán. Another round of international conflict ensued as Malespín's Conservative Honduran allies sent General Santos Guardiola in early June 1845 to invade El Salvador to restore Malespín (Bustamante Maceo, 1951, 43; Scheina, 2003, 252–3).[24] After tough fighting during the summer, the Hondurans had lost about 600 men (out of a population of less than 300,000) and most of their supplies. Both sides now were willing to conclude a treaty which re-established peace, notably containing one provision which forbade Malespín to set foot in El Salvador (Bancroft, 1887, 202–6).[25]

Although these conflicts were clearly related, we can distinguish four distinct international conflicts in Central America between 1843 and 1846. The first, a crisis, occurred when Guatemala and El Salvador declared war on each other in 1843, but managed to avoid armed confrontations. The second again pitted Guatemala against El Salvador and became a fully-fledged war when first Guatemalan troops marched with Arce to invade El Salvador, and then Salvadoran troops pursued Arce's troops deep into Guatemala. The third conflict, when El Salvador and Honduras both fought Nicaragua, qualifies as a full-scale war, since the armed forces of all three countries engaged in full-scale warfare and invasion. In the fourth conflict, in 1845, Honduran forces invaded El Salvador to restore Malespín. While it might

[24] Bancroft (1887, 204) notes that Ferrera "was using all possible means to exasperate [El Salvador] into committing acts of hostility against [Honduras], so that Carrera might have an opportunity to take a hand in the game." Guzmán, however, somehow managed to conclude a treaty of peace, amity, and alliance with Guatemala.

[25] Malespín died one year later, on November 25, 1846, in an attempt to regain power in El Salvador (Bustamante Maceo, 1951, 43). Woodward (1993, 185) suggests that peace was preserved between El Salvador and Guatemala at this point because of a "liberal slant" of Carrera's government at this time. This seems an exaggeration.

be considered somewhat tricky to specify the initiator in each of these conflicts, this turns out to be irrelevant for our purposes. The growing power and influence of the Liberals at León and their protection of Liberal exiles from the other countries threatened the Conservative leaders elsewhere. Malespín's apparent shift to the Liberals, whose increasingly assertive behavior Malespín himself attributed to the Liberals in Nicaragua, led Carrera to declare war on El Salvador in 1843 and to support with Guatemalan troops Arce's invasion in 1844. Later in 1844, Malespín and Ferrera combined forces and declared war on Nicaragua to once-and-for-all deal with the Liberal exiles in León. Another exogenous shock, the overthrow of Malespín in El Salvador by Liberal forces, then provoked the Honduran president, Ferrera, into an invasion to restore Malespín.

Each of these four conflicts started because exiles found a safe haven and launching pad abroad to prepare an invasion to overthrow the leader. Leaders, therefore, reasonably surmised an increased risk of their forcible overthrow. In each case, moreover, an international conflict, specifically, an attack across the border, offered the opportunity to derail the exiles' plans and strike a pre-emptive blow before the opposition was fully organized. Alternatively, a pursuit of rebels across the border offered the opportunity to deal them a crippling blow before they could reform. These international conflicts stem from leaders' attempts to pre-empt revolts, revolutions, and civil war. The historical scholarship indicates no ideological sympathies, indeed, nothing but naked self-preservation as the reason why these leaders went to war (Bancroft, 1887; Montúfar, 1887; Bustamante Maceo, 1951; Woodward, 1993).

5.3.3 The fall of Carrera

The years between 1846 and 1848 continued in a state of precarious peace. In 1846 Malespín tried to regain his position in El Salvador by invading from Honduras, but he was quickly defeated and killed (Bancroft, 1887, 293). To underline the failure of attempts to re-establish union and his opposition to such attempts, on March 21, 1847 Carrera declared Guatemala's "absolute independence" and promised elections for the next year. At the celebratory gala he toasted: "To the Republic of Guatemala, may it always find such loyal and dedicated defenders, as I feel myself to be!" (quoted in Woodward (1993, 187)). Others, however, were less convinced of Carrera's dedication and merit. As Woodward (ibid., 182) notes, in 1847 continuing into 1848 Guatemala experienced continued instability as a result of both natural disasters and rebellions: "Armed bands roamed certain regions, assaulting farms and towns, killing those who resisted their demands for money, food, horses and supplies. [In addition], [t]he public treasure was robbed on occasion. Carrera's own montaña district was the scene of much of this trouble, and it could not be blamed entirely on intrigue from neighboring El Salvador and Honduras." In October 1847 a major and spontaneous uprising, the Revolt of the Lucios, began in the east and quickly spread. A few Liberals joined this effort, but only in January 1848.

Two shocks affected international relations in Central America, the first brought conflict, the second brought peace. The first shock came about when in early February 1848 the Liberal Doroteo Vasconcelos took over power in El Salvador, providing to Guatemala's Liberals once more a safe haven and staging area for attacks against Carrera's regime. In reaction, El Salvador "was twice invaded by troops of Guatemala in pursuit of insurgents, against which Vasconcelos remonstrated, and satisfaction was given and accepted with good grace" (Bancroft, 1887, 295). One might have expected a bigger war, but Carrera had his hands full with the rebellion in the montaña and in eastern Guatemala.

From early 1848 on, Carrera was almost continuously in the field to crush the rebellion, but as soon as he put out the fire in one region it exploded elsewhere. It appeared the rebellion could not be contained. By the spring of 1848, Carrera's attempts to squash the rebellion by force, both inside Guatemala and by raids across the border in El Salvador, had utterly failed. Since force had failed to turn the tide, Carrera now re-scheduled elections for early July.[26] In what Woodward (1993, 200) calls a "remarkably honest" election, the Liberal opposition emerged victorious. True to his word, Carrera honored the election results and gave up power to the newly elected Assembly on August 16, 1848. But he was not foolish enough to trust the good will of his former enemies. As he had notified the new Assembly, two days

---

[26] Elections had first been scheduled for January, but then cancelled. Subsequently, Carrrera scheduled elections for 15 August before he moved them up to the first ten days of July (Woodward, 1993, 190–204).

after handing over power he retired to his ranch in Chiapas across the border in Mexico, under an armed escort (ibid., 203–4).[27]

Carrera thus left office in a regular manner, after an honest election. As Woodward (ibid., 201) suggests, "[t]he unfavorable military situation was undoubtedly a more important reason for Carrera's willingness to step down than the election results." In other words, Carrera probably calculated that he could not defeat the rebellion and thus faced a rather high probability of a forcible removal, and an unpleasant personal fate. A war with Guatemala's neighbors, in this instance, could do little to salvage his prospects. Even though the Liberal Doroteo Vasconcelos had taken power in El Salvador in February 1848, Liberal exiles counted for very little in what appears to have been a fast-spreading grassroots rebellion. The election, and his ranch in Chiapas, gave Carrera a relatively easy way out. He claimed that his days in the public service for Guatemala were over, but he may have shrewdly foreseen that the Liberal regime would not be able to defeat the rebellion either. If he could wait it out until the Liberals proved themselves unable to restore order, he might be offered another chance (ibid., 190–229).

Carrera's fall ironically enough constituted a shock which produced a relatively short spell of Liberal dominance. Juan Antonio Martínez and José Bernardo Escobar in Guatemala, Doroteo Vasconcelos (a former ally of Morazán) in El Salvador, and José Guerrero in Nicaragua, these four Liberal leaders ruled the biggest states of Central America. In Honduras, the moderate Juan Lindo ruled. With such an ideological alignment, we would expect little trouble from exiled Conservatives, who would be unlikely to find support, and thus little cause for international conflict. The short period of this Liberal alignment indeed witnessed no major international conflicts in Central America.[28]

5.4 Conservatism ascendant 1849–71

The five states of Central America had weathered the birth pangs of independence and the prospects for continued independence against

---

[27] He liquidated his assets in Guatemala as soon as he could to avoid confiscation by the Guatemalan government (Woodward, 1993, 216).

[28] For the confrontational British diplomacy by Frederick Chatfield, see Bancroft (1887, 317) and Rodriguez (1964, 1965, 89).

unionist pipe dreams looked good. However, after 1849 new threats to independence emerged. Carrera would come to dominate the scene and an invasion by Yankee filibusters threatened to turn Central America into one English-speaking slave state, perhaps to be annexed to the United States of America.

5.4.1 The return of Carrera

Just two weeks short of a year after he left office, Carrera returned triumphantly to again lead Guatemala (for details on the interlude, see Woodward (1993, 213–25)). The Liberals had indeed failed to establish order, a task which once again befell Carrera. Carrera's return to power constituted a major shock to the prospects of the other Liberal leaders in the region and it would not take long before war broke out. As usual, rivalling leaders supported their rival's exiles; the threatened leader than pre-empted a civil war or revolution by invading his neighbor to defeat the exiles before they were ready to strike.

With the Liberals' failures, Carrera could initially afford to focus largely on the internal revolt in the east. However, the "center" states – El Salvador, Honduras, and Nicaragua – began talks to re-establish union, a prospect strictly against Guatemalan – e.g. Carrera's – and British interests; at least, against British interests as perceived by its infamous consul, Frederick Chatfield. Chatfield attempted some gunboat diplomacy against El Salvador and Honduras to dissuade all this unionist talk (Rodriguez, 1964, 321–5), but neither the Liberal Vasconcelos of El Salvador nor the moderate Conservative Juan Lindo of Honduras would budge.[29] If anything, they became more committed to overthrow Chatfield's Guatemalan ally, Carrera. To that end, they supported the insurrection of José Dolores Nufio. In November 1850 Nufio invaded Guatemala to topple Carrera, but he was quickly defeated. Nufio then fled back to El Salvador and there gathered troops around him, including troops from Honduras, for a renewed attempt against Carrera (Bustamante Maceo, 1951, 44; Rodriguez, 1964, 322–3). By late 1850, Vasconcelos of El Salvador recognized that war with Guatemala was inevitable (Bustamante Maceo, 1951, 44).

---

[29] It deserves note that El Salvador had not recognized Guatemala's independence (Bancroft, 1887, 295).

On December 4, 1850, Vasconcelos therefore "announced to his people that the forces of Guatemala were about to invade the department of Sonsonate, with the view of inciting the inhabitants to rebel against their government" (Bancroft, 1887, 279, fn. 74). (Recall that Guatemala had invaded El Salvador twice in pursuit of fleeing rebels.) At the head of an allied force of Salvadorans, Hondurans, led by Trinidad Cabañas, and Nicaraguans, Vasconcelos invaded Guatemala on January 29, 1851.[30] Bustamante Maceo (1951, 44) explicitly notes that the Salvadoran forces aimed to "prevent the departure of a party of factional [e.g. exiled] Salvadorans . . . for an invasion of the Department of Sonsonate [in El Salvador] to launch a revolution against the Government of El Salvador." Although the invaders outnumbered his forces, on February 2 Carrera nevertheless managed to inflict a decisive defeat on the invaders at La Arada (ibid., 44–5).[31] Carrera's impressive victory gained him absolute power in 1851 and the title of president-for-life in 1854 (Rodriguez, 1965, 89–90). As a result of his defeat, the Salvadoran Congress replaced the Liberal Vasconcelos with the recently converted Conservative, Francisco Dueñas (Bancroft, 1887, 299).[32] With a Conservative in charge of El Salvador, Carrera's southwestern flank appeared secure. In Nicaragua, too, a Conservative, José Laureano Pineda, replaced a Liberal in May 1851. His Conservative government came under attack from Liberals and barely survived a Liberal revolt of August 4, 1851. For a short time, Guatemala, El Salvador, Honduras, and Nicaragua were all led by Conservatives, and a period of peace seemed at hand.

5.4.2 Cabañas comes to power

However, in Honduras Juan Lindo declared himself tired of his efforts, and stepped down. The man elected to take over the presidency

---

[30] On 9 January a new union had been born, a pact which combined El Salvador, Honduras, and Nicaragua into a *Representación Nacional.*

[31] While Bancroft (1887, 279, fn. 74) includes Nicaraguans among the invading forces, Bustamante Maceo (1951, 44) mentions only Salvadoran and Honduran forces. Hall and Brignoli (2003, 183), however, also include the Nicaraguans among the invading forces. The war dragged on at a low level and was settled officially in August 1853.

[32] Dueñas may have originally been a Liberal unionist, but soon saw where his advantage laid, and in substance and spirit adopted the Conservative cause (Bancroft, 1887, 299; Rodriguez, 1965, 89).

of Honduras in March 1852 was that by now familiar Liberal and *morazanista*, Trinidad Cabañas (Bancroft, 1887, 321). Cabañas' rise to power constituted an exogenous shock in favor of the Liberals in the other states. This quickly led to war.

Cabañas wasted little time to support the Guatemalan rebels of the montaña who had fought off Carrera for a number of years (ibid., 280). As one would expect, Carrera supported the Conservative opposition to Cabañas, led by Santos Guardiola (Scheina, 2003, 253–4). "Recriminations and border raids ensued, which culminated in a three years' war between the two countries, Guatemala aiding Guardiola and other enemies of Cabañas…" (Bancroft, 1887, 280). Bancroft (ibid., 322, fn. 51) notes that the contemporary "Astaburuaga attributes this war to Cabañas' attempt to promote an insurrection in Guat[emala] against his old enemy Carrera." According to Scheina (2003, 253), Guatemala initiated the hostilities, noting that "a Guatemalan army led by Gen. Joaquin Solares invaded the Honduran department of Copán" on October 31, 1852 (Bancroft, 1887, 322, Valenzuela, 1984, 165).[33] In July of 1853, Cabañas invaded Guatemala, but suffered a defeat at the hands of Vicente Cerna. Carrera attacked Honduras the next month, but Cabañas would not be fully defeated until 1855 (Hall and Brignoli, 2003, 183–4).

For our purposes, somewhat surprisingly perhaps, it does not really matter in this case who initiated the conflict, since it is clear both sides acted to preserve their position. Both Carrera and Cabañas were threatened by internal revolts and exiles organizing abroad. It seems reasonable, however, to argue that Carrera faced the additional threat of unionists and a multiple-front war and therefore had the greater incentive to initiate. The war ended only when Cabañas was driven from power and into exile in El Salvador.[34] He was replaced by the Conservative Guardiola, "a satellite of Carrera" according to Bancroft (1887, 322), who concluded a final peace treaty on February 13, 1856 (Scheina, 2003, 254).

---

[33] Bancroft (1887, 280) notes that Guatemalan sources date the start of the conflict to 1853 and claim that Honduras invaded first.

[34] Some sources date his fall from power to July 6, 1855 (Bancroft, 1887, 322), but we code his final defeat on 6 October as the date of his fall (see www.honduraseducacional.com/Presidentes/Jose%20Santiago%20Bueso.htm and Ramiro (1989, 221).)

All of the previous conflicts described above fit the pattern of exiles who obtain support from the leader's ideological opponents abroad, and one side initiates to either pre-empt an invasion by the exiles or follow the defeated exiles across the border to defeat them once and for all. Two minor conflicts initiated by Cabañas of Honduras in 1853 and 1854 are less easily traced to this dynamic, mainly because the available historical sources record few, if any, details. While Cabañas was engaged in a fully-fledged war with Guatemala, in 1853 a new dispute with El Salvador drew Honduras into another conflict on a second front (Bancroft, 1887, 299; Scheina, 2003, 253). Somewhat surprisingly, this conflict is not mentioned in Bustamante Maceo (1951) and details in the literature are very sparse indeed. In particular, we have been unable to find any explanation for Cabañas' behavior. While we know that Dueñas had joined the Conservative camp to obtain Carrera's blessings as leader of El Salvador, there is no record of Honduran exiles agitating in El Salvador or of any El Salvadoran support for Guardiola. Although the absence of evidence does not constitute evidence of absence, this crisis looks very much like a case in which Cabañas tried to dissuade Dueñas from opening up a second front against him.

As if he had not enough trouble on his hands already, Cabañas next decided to challenge Nicaragua as well. He threw in his lot with the Liberal opposition to Nicaragua's Conservative President, Fruto Chamorro. The only explanation in the literature for this conflict is that Honduras and Nicaragua had concluded a mutual assistance pact and Cabañas was thus outraged when Nicaragua refused to contribute troops for the war against Guatemala (Bancroft, 1887, 259, fn. 81). Cabañas supported the planned invasion by the Nicaraguan Liberal exiles and apparently even contributed a small number of Honduran troops (ibid., 260; Gámez, 1889, 593).[35] From the perspective of our theory, Cabañas' behavior is odd indeed, since by maximizing the number of his enemies, taking on Guatemala *and* El Salvador *and* Nicaragua, he also surely maximized the probability of his forcible removal from office. Other than a misplaced faith in his own military

---

[35] This episode is important to note mostly because it marked the beginning of the bloody and drawn-out civil war in Nicaragua, which drew in all the other states of Central America in what became known as the *Guerra Nacional* 1854–57 (Bancroft, 1887, 258).

abilities, the only explanation we tentatively proffer *ad hoc* though it may be, is that by trying to overthrow the Conservative leaders in El Salvador and Nicaragua, he hoped to obtain Liberal allies for his fight against Carrera. We find support for this explanation in Valenzuela (1984, 168, see also 185) who argues that Cabañas' objective was "the union of the three states [in order to] wage war against Guatemala, given that Honduras can not do it by itself." Another smidgen of evidence provides some additional support for this thesis. Gámez (1889, 587) notes an international conflict broke out between Nicaragua and Costa Rica in late February 1854, when negotiations of their common border broke down. It was this conflict, Gámez suggests, which convinced Cabañas that a good opportunity presented itself to replace the Conservative Chamorro with a friendly Liberal regime in Nicaragua. The conflict between Nicaragua and Costa Rica over their border at this time did not lead to a fully-fledged war. An explanation for this conflict probably must be found in a theory that specifically seeks to explain conflict over boundaries (Goemans, 2006).

5.4.3 *The* National War

The long struggle in Nicaragua, between Conservative and Liberal, the cities and elites of Granada and León, took a dramatic turn now that Carrera and the Conservatives controlled the other Central American states. With nowhere else left to turn, the Leónese Liberals turned to American filibusters to champion their cause.[36] The arrival of the American filibusters, with their relatively sophisticated weapons and superior training constituted yet another exogenous shock to the regional system. Conservative leaders everywhere had reason to fear not just an increase in power of their Liberal opposition, but also the potential for regional subjugation.

The American William Walker led these filibusters and proved himself a remarkably tenacious, skillful, and above all ambitious leader.

---

[36] The Liberal rebel, Castellón, negotiated a contract in December 1854 "with Byron Cole for North American filibusters to assist the Democrático [Liberal] cause in exchange for large land grants in Nicaragua. Among the adventurers enlisted by Cole was William Walker, who had already led an unsuccessful filibuster expedition to Baja California" (Hall and Brignoli, 2003, 184).

While nominally fighting on behalf of the Liberals and President Patricio Rivas, Walker had grand ambitions of his own. Walker

hoped to usurp power for himself in Nicaragua and ultimately throughout the isthmus, with a view to controlling the inter-oceanic routes being used for transportation to and from California and establishing an English-speaking slave state similar to those in the south of the United States.

(Hall and Brignoli, 2003, 184)

At the head of a small, but relatively well-armed group of Yankees and a smattering of Liberal troops, Walker successfully took on the Conservative Nicaraguan forces. As his successes mounted, his army quickly grew, as Liberal Nicaraguans flocked to his colors and as filibusters (totalling about 2,500 men) continued to stream in. By October 1855 Walker had accomplished the first of his ambitions when he became the head of the Nicaraguan armed forces. From there it was but a small step to have himself inaugurated as president on July 12, 1856. Walker then proceeded to make English the official language of the state and re-establish slavery. As Bustamante Maceo (1951, 46) notes, the governments of Costa Rica, El Salvador, Honduras, and Guatemala now were under a terrible and immediate threat. Once the Yankees controlled Nicaragua, what would prevent them from taking over the remaining Central American states?

In a truly remarkable display of common cause, or perhaps balancing, the Central American states quickly aligned against Walker. On March 19, 1856, Costa Rica declared war on Nicaragua, Walker and his filibusters, to be followed on 18 July by the governments of El Salvador, Guatemala, and Honduras (ibid., 45–6). It took the combined might of Guatemala, El Salvador, Honduras, and Costa Rica, as well as the efforts of the American tycoon, Cornelius Vanderbilt, to thwart Walker's plans. Walker was finally defeated in May 1857 and, taking sanctuary aboard the USS *Saint Mary*, returned to the United States.[37] The war had caused thousands of casualties on the battlefield and tens of thousands more deaths among civilians as a result of the spread of cholera by returning soldiers. As Hall and Brignoli (2003, 185) note,

[37] Walker attempted several times to return to Central America, only to be thwarted by US or British ships. The third and final time he attempted to return he was captured by the British, handed over to Honduran officials, and executed.

it is this war, rather than the struggle against imperial Spain or the struggle for independence, that is considered the great epic of Central American history. "Central Americans still celebrate the defeat of an enemy who threatened not only to destroy their sovereignty, but also to transform their culture and society beyond all recognition."

The historical record suggests several, not mutually exclusive, explanations for the *National War*. A primary cause surely was the exogenous shock in power in the Liberals' favor when Nicaragua and its Liberals obtained experienced fighters and advanced weaponry. Liberal insurgencies already threatened the Conservative leaders and with the increased strength of Nicaragua would surely become an even more dangerous concern. Along these lines Woodward (1993, 286) concludes that "[s]ome liberals joined the National Campaign against the filibusters, to be sure, but in the main it was a conservative effort aimed as much at liberal ideology and control as against the Walker invasion solely." A simpler commitment problem also played a role. Basically, Walker could not credibly commit not to overthrow the other Central American leaders. With a filibuster victory in Nicaragua, surely even more Yankees would join Walker in his attempt to control all of Central America. Finally, the leaders may also have fought for noble motives, against the re-imposition of slavery, and against the threat of future filibustering invasions.

After the Central American states had combined to defeat the filibusters, the war had a somewhat sordid aftermath when the leader of Costa Rica, Juan Rafael Mora, concluded this would be an opportune time to settle the boundary conflict with Nicaragua. Mora apparently estimated that Nicaragua would return to its vicious civil war among Liberals and Conservatives (Bancroft, 1887, 362–5). Costa Rica therefore declared war on Nicaragua on October 15, 1857. Mora, however, had miscalculated. Tomás Martínez and Máximo Jerez, the leaders of the two competing factions in Nicaragua, decided that enough blood had been spilled and that they would rule together. The war would continue until Walker attempted another invasion, and peace was restored on January 16, 1858. This war clearly came about because Mora saw what he perceived as a golden opportunity to take advantage of Nicaragua's weakened position. At the time Mora faced no particularly pressing threat of a forcible overthrow, and this case simply does not fit our theory.

5.4.4 Gerardo Barrios

For a short while, until June 1858, all countries in Central America were led by Conservatives. Under such conditions we would expect peace, and peace did indeed obtain. But a Liberal resurgence was almost inevitable. The change from the moderately Conservative Mora in Costa Rica to the more Liberal José María Montealegre might be condemned as "an illegal and inexcusable act" (quoted in Woodward (1993, 315)) by Carrera, but did not really constitute any significant threat to his rule. A strong Liberal leader in El Salvador, however, might be an entirely different matter. Such a leader emerged in El Salvador when Gerardo Barrios overthrew Miguel Santín de Castillo in June 1858. Initially, Gerardo Barrios played his hand very carefully and remained allied to Carrera, even receiving Guatemala's "Cross of Honor" in July 1858 (Woodward, 1993, 316). So securely into Carrera's good graces was Barrios in 1859, that "Carrera actually aided him by persuading [Conservative] Honduran President Santos Guardiola not to encourage Salvadoran exiles to use Honduran territory in efforts to oust Barrios" (ibid.; see also Bustamante Maceo, 1951, 51). Stronger yet, Carrera took active counter-measures against Salvadoran exiles in Guatemala who conspired against Barrios. Carrera ordered the army commander of Chiquimula to disarm the Salvadoran rebels who planned to invade El Salvador to overthrow Barrios (Vallecillos, 1967, 13). Barrios reciprocated Carrera's attitude when he promised at his official inauguration to pursue Conservative policies and good relations with El Salvador's neighbors (Woodward, 1993, 316).

According to our theory, the rise to power of the Liberal Gerardo Barrios should have led in fairly short order to an international conflict between El Salvador and Guatemala or Honduras. But no such conflict materialized in the first four years after Barrios' ascent. Several factors may have contributed to this anomaly. First, as a result of his victory at La Arada, Carrera had established himself as indisputably Central America's strongest and most capable military leader. Moreover, by the mid-1850s Carrera so dominated Guatemalan politics in his own right that rebellions and revolts were becoming more sporadic and very unlikely to succeed. Finally, Barrios "had been a confidant of ... Carrera throughout the 1850s" (Scheina, 2003, 254) and he took great pains to avoid giving offense and pursued accommodationist policies (Woodward, 1993, 320–1). In other words, as a result of his strong domestic and international position, Carrera faced a low probability of a forcible removal from office and therefore had little incentive to fight Barrios. While Barrios was under threat from Conservative Salvadoran exiles in Guatemala and Honduras, as we saw above, Carrera and Guardiola took efforts to lessen this threat by taking efforts to control these exiles.

It would take a second exogenous shock and the rise of a second Liberal leader in Central America to re-establish the old pattern leading to international conflict. The shock came when the Honduran Conservative leader, Santos Guardiola, was assassinated in early January 1862. Although there was no direct evidence, some curious coincidences led to rumors that Barrios was behind the assassination. Specifically, "Guardiola's vice-president, Victoriano Castellanos, was in El Salvador at the time of the assassination, and he promptly concluded a military alliance [both offensive and defensive] with El Salvador shortly after taking office as the new president of Honduras" (Woodward, 1993, 317).[38] Bancroft (1887, 324) notes that Barrios pressured Castellanos to take over the presidency, against the candidacy of the Conservatives, Senator José María Medina. With an ally now in Honduras, Barrios instigated an aggressive campaign in the Salvadoran and Honduran press against the governments of Guatemala and Nicaragua (ibid., 324–5). With a Liberal ally in power in Honduras, Barrios apparently felt strong enough to tack his sails more to his original Liberal convictions and initiated anti-clerical policies. This classic Liberal stance pitted Barrios directly against Carrera's preferences and policies. To add insult to injury, Trinidad Cabañas, who had been living in exile in El Salvador, now returned to Honduras to become a minister in Castellanos' government (Woodward, 1993, 318). When Castellanos fell ill in late 1862 and handed over power to José Francisco Montes, the latter continued the former's policies, both his alliance with Barrios and his hostility toward Guatemala and Nicaragua.[39] When Salvadoran exiles attempted to assassinate Barrios, regional tensions increased markedly, especially because the Salvadoran government blamed Guatemalan complicity. The evidence

---

[38] Woodward (1993, 318) notes: "Whether or not Barrios had any complicity in Guardiola's murder, the event tipped the scales in favor of the liberals."

[39] Castellanos died a natural death a week after he handed over power to Montes on December 4, 1862.

suggests this claim had merit, as Guatemala sheltered the leaders of the plot when they fled to Guatemala and refused to honor the treaty of extradition of 1853. Both sides were by now up to their familiar tricks: each side supported exiles attempting to overthrow the other.

As long as Carrera faced a threat from Mexico, it was necessary to prevent a two-front war and Carrera therefore bided his time. But when a French invasion eliminated the threat from Mexico, Carrera started to prepare for war in earnest. First, he cut off diplomatic relations on December 4, 1862. Barrios replied, condemning Carrera's tradition of intervening in the other Central American states. General Juan Ignacio Irigoyen now "warned Carrera of the Salvadoran danger on Christmas Day [1862] and counseled the Guatemalan caudillo that if he didn't oust Barrios during the first six months of 1863, Barrios would attempt to do just that to Carrera" (Woodward, 1993, 323). Taking care to blame the conflict on Barrios, "the man who has done so much evil to your country and yourselves" (quoted in ibid., 322), Carrera gathered his army and personally led the invasion in early February 1863. Uncharacteristically, Carrera was defeated at Coatepeque and forced to retreat into Guatemala (Bustamante Maceo, 1951, 52–3; Scheina, 2003, 254).[40] This defeat had two main consequences. First, Honduras now joined El Salvador in the war against Guatemala. Second, hoping to break Nicaragua's alliance with Guatemala, El Salvador and Honduras declared war on Nicaragua. Relatively quickly, however, the tide turned against El Salvador and Honduras. By the summer of 1863 Carrera had replaced the Liberal Montes with the Conservative Medina in Honduras.[41] Barrios held out until October, then, fearing for his life (Bancroft, 1887, 306), he fled the country first for Panama, then for New York City.[42] In Barrios' place, Carrera installed the

---

[40] Although this war is not listed in the Correlates of War project, Scheina (2003, 254) notes that in the initial battle at Coatepeque alone: "Some 6,500 Guatemalans attacked 5,000 Salvadorians [sic]....The battle lasted two days (February 22–23).... The Guatemalans lost 900 dead and 1,500 wounded as well as 9 cannon and 2,000 rifles. The Salvadorian losses were much smaller." Since this war saw several more battles, it is fairly certain that battle-deaths amounted to well over 1,000.

[41] Montes was declared an outlaw by Medina and surrendered unconditionally to Medina on 7 September. See www.honduraseducacional.com/Presidentes/Francisco%20Montes.htm.

[42] For extended details on the battles of this war, see Bustamante Maceo (1951, 52–67). Barrios' fear for his life is justified by subsequent events. As Woodward (1993, 327) notes, "Officials of the Barrios regime who failed to

Conservative Francisco Dueñas, who wasted no time to promulgate a decree with fulsome praise for the Guatemalan conqueror (Woodward, 1993, 327).

To sum up, the entry into power of the Liberal Gerardo Barrios was not sufficient to change the Central American landscape, it would take the assassination of Guardiola to tip the balance in favor of the Liberals (ibid., 318). It was thus this assassination which constituted an exogenous shock sufficiently powerful to lead to war. A Liberal regime in Honduras opened up another safe haven for the eastern Guatemalan opposition to Carrera, who had always found the *montaña* difficult to control and a source of seemingly endless rebellions. To deal with this threat, Carrera initiated a conflict against El Salvador and Honduras, which solved his two-front problem.

Carrera had once again bested the Liberals. He would not have to fight them again. Carrera died, probably from vascular dysentery, two years later, at 9:30 a.m. on Good Friday, April 15, 1865. With him passed a remarkable figure, an Indian who against enormous odds had risen to the highest position in Central America and held it through sheer force of will and, above all, competence. Whatever a reader might think of his policies, Rafael Carrera was a most unusual man (Woodward, 1993). On his deathbed, Carrera appointed a competent and loyal Conservative, Vicente Cerna, his successor. Cerna benefited from the unchallenged dominance of Conservatives in Central America bequeathed to him by Carrera. The only country ruled by a Liberal was Costa Rica, the smallest and least powerful of the Central American states, and Costa Rica had learned its lesson when Barrios' attempted return failed miserably.[43] Under these circumstances, our theory would

escape, including the Foreign Minister Manuel Irungaray and several generals, were shot. Many more were marched back to Guatemala and imprisoned in the San José fortress in the capital...." Bancroft (1887, 306) notes that like other deposed leaders, Barrios, too, tried to return to power. He returned to Central America, precisely to Costa Rica, in 1864. Barrios' return to Central America provoked an international crisis, as the other Central American states broke off diplomatic relations with Costa Rica, El Salvador being the first to do so on January 3, 1865 (Bustamante Maceo, 1951, 67). When Barrios sailed forth to launch his invasion, Barrios was captured by the Nicaraguans, who handed him over to El Salvador, under the explicit condition that he should not be put to death. The government of El Salvador, or rather its leader, Francisco Dueñas, proceeded to break this promise and court-martialed and then executed Barrios on August 29, 1865.

[43] See fn. 42.

predict an absence of international conflict. For five long years, peace did indeed obtain on the isthmus.

5.5 The return of Liberalism 1872–1918

While prospects looked bleak for Liberals in Central America when Conservatives ruled all states except Costa Rica, a ray of light broke through when the Liberal Benito Juárez rose to power in Mexico in 1867. However, even before the return of a Liberal leader to Central America, conflict erupted.

5.5.1 The rise and demise of Justo Rufino Barrios

Beginning in 1870, the Conservative leader of Honduras, José Medina, started to accuse his fellow Conservative leader of El Salvador, Francisco Dueñas, of aiding and abetting plots to overthrow him and thereby violating article 8 of the Treaty of Santa Rosa of March 1862 (Bancroft, 1887, 393). In return, El Salvador claimed that Honduras had violated article 9 of that treaty by allowing the executive – e.g. President Medina – to declare war against El Salvador without first complying with that clause. Moreover, as Honduras accused El Salvador of harboring hostile exiles, so did El Salvador accuse Honduras of giving "asylum to Salvadoran refugees, giving them employment on the frontier of Salv[ador], where they had been constantly plotting and uttering menaces against their gov[ernmen]t, using arms obtained from gov[erment]t warehouses" (quoted in ibid., 394, fn. 4). Why Conservative Dueñas would support the opposition to his fellow Conservative Medina, or vice versa, remains unfortunately unclear, but from here on things followed a familiar pattern. As Scheina (2003, 255) summarizes it nicely: "The immediate cause [of the war] was the sanctuary that El Salvador and Honduras were giving to each other's dissidents."

President Medina of Honduras first abrogated all treaty obligations between Honduras and El Salvador on February 7, 1871. We would argue that this does not quite reach the level of conflict initiation – although whether it was Medina or Dueñas who initiated the conflict, both had incentives to do so to avoid a forcible overthrow. An international war broke out when later that same month Dueñas of El Salvador dispatched troops to invade Honduras (Bancroft, 1887,

395).[44] Recognizing an opportunity, the Liberal opposition in El Salvador, led by General Santiago González, organized to overthrow Dueñas and appealed to Medina for help. Medina, about to fight Dueñas, saw the value of a fifth column and supported González "with the forces he had organized to invade Salvador through Sensuntepeque" (ibid.).[45] After less than a week of fighting, Dueñas' forces, though superior in numbers, were decisively defeated and he and Tomás Martinez (ex-president of Nicaragua) were temporarily imprisoned and then allowed to leave the country.[46] González took power, El Salvador was once again ruled by a Liberal, and Medina would rue the day he brought a Liberal back into power.

On the one hand, we found no *ex ante* indicator of a shock that set the familiar pattern of exiles and conflict into motion. On the other hand, the war was clearly caused by the threat posed by Salvadoran exiles in Honduras to Dueñas' rule. Like many of the other wars we discussed, this war thus also clearly qualifies as a pre-emptive internationalized civil war. While our theory therefore fares poorly in explaining the exact timing of the conflict, it does well in predicting that there would be war once each side perceived a threat from its exiles across the border.

The success of the Liberal revolution in El Salvador bode ill for Cerna's rule in Guatemala, because it allowed the Liberal opposition there to open up a second front in the east (Woodward, 1993, 347). González' victory thus constituted a shock which we would expect to

---

[44] Scheina (2003, 255) records that "[o]n March 5, 1871, Honduras declared war on El Salvador," but it seems unreasonable to trace the initiation to this declaration of war when Salvadoran troops had already invaded Honduras a month earlier.

[45] According to our analysis, it is odd indeed for a Conservative to support Liberal rebels. We would expect something like that to happen only in times of dire need. Bancroft (1887, 395, fn. 7) notes: "It was said that Medina was enticed into assisting the liberals, under the delusion that they would call him to rule over the united states of Guat[emala], Salv[ador] and Hond[uras]." Such innocence on Medina's part, however, we find hard to believe.

[46] Notably, Bancroft (1887, 396) records that González' "first step was to protect the person of Dueñas against possible violence from his exasperated enemies." Dueñas had to post a $100,000 bond promising he would not return to any port in Central America before he was allowed to leave first for Europe, then New York, subsequently residing in San Francisco. In later years he was allowed back into El Salvador and was treated with the utmost respect.

lead to war. Liberals, led by "the elderly general Miguel Garcia Granados" (Rodriguez, 1965, 94), had continued an unsuccessful opposition to the Conservative regime since 1867. (Two other generals played important roles in the revolution, Serapio Cruz and Justo Rufino Barrios. One of these would end up with his head fried in a bucket of oil, the other became master of Guatemala.) Cerna could never decisively defeat the rebels, but neither did the rebels make much headway. In 1871, however, the Mexican Liberal leader, Benito Juárez, provided crucial assistance to the Guatemalan Liberals. "With help from the Juárez government, they gained territory and confidence early [in 1871], forcing the government to put more and more resources into its defense" (Woodward, 1993, 346). Given that Mexican support proved so crucial to the Guatemalan Liberals, our theory would predict a high likelihood of an international conflict between Guatemala and Mexico. Two facts, however, explain why that did not happen. First, Mexico was incomparably stronger than Guatemala, and any invasion of Mexico would surely only have increased the probability of Cerna's forcible removal from office. Second, events moved too quickly; in particular, the successful Liberal revolution in El Salvador forced Cerna to divide his forces to deal with rebels in the east as well as rebels in the north. Two-and-a-half months after the Liberals re-took El Salvador, on June 29, 1871, the Liberal Justo Rufino Barrios defeated Cerna's army.[47] When he led the army into the capital without opposition the next day, the Liberals had finally won (ibid., 347). While Justo Rufino Barrios led the troops into Guatemala City, the new leader of Guatemala was Miguel Garcia Granados, who had been provisional president. Justo Rufino Barrios, still only in his mid-thirties by then, was assigned to the military district of Los Altos (Rodriguez, 1965, 94).

   We would have expected that Cerna react against González' entry into power and attempt to stop dissidents from entering Guatemala from El Salvador by launching a war against El Salvador. No such war occurred. Perhaps Cerna lacked the time to mobilize forces against González, perhaps he had to fight on too many fronts. But these *ad hoc* explanations are unconvincing, and this case thus should count as a failure for our theory.

---

[47] Cerna fled first to Honduras, subsequently taking up residence in Costa Rica.

The rising tide of Liberalism could not but engender a strong Conservative reaction. As had happened almost a decade earlier, it would be the rise of a second strong Liberal leader that shocked the system and led to war. The leader most threatened by the new Liberal regimes in Guatemala and El Salvador, ironically, was José Medina of Honduras, who had helped create the Liberal wave spreading across Central America when he helped to oust Dueñas in El Salvador. Now Medina himself faced a Liberal revolt at home (Woodward, 1993, 341). In an attempt to deal with his troubles, as Scheina (2003, 255) notes: "Honduran President Medina was becoming the champion of Conservative Salvadorian [*sic*] and Guatemalan dissidents." Medina not only permitted the Conservative Guatemalan exiles "to recoup their forces on [Honduran] territory" (Rodriguez, 1965, 97) but had the audacity at the same time to demand recompense for his efforts to depose Dueñas. War now seemed inevitable, and indeed on March 25, 1872, Honduras declared war on El Salvador. Both González and Garcia Granados in turn declared war on Honduras (Bancroft, 1887, 398, fn. 17). We present Garcia Granados' declaration of war (reproduced in Burgess (1926, 106–7)) at length:

In view of the fact that the President of Honduras, don José María Medina, has constituted himself chief of the reactionaries against the liberal principles and institutions, implanted in this republic and in Salvador, that he has received the shattered fragments of the revolutionary factions which have disturbed our peace, giving military positions to many of the revolutionary chiefs, that he has refused to return to this country the arms, property of the nation, which these revolutionaries took with them to Honduras, alleging frivolous excuses for not doing so, that in an effort to hide his aggressive intentions he has declared himself to be in a defensive war, seeking in this way to deceive the governments against which he is preparing his forces and to frustrate their union and common defense, that furthermore the government of the Republic of Salvador having declared war on the ruler of Honduras for such causes as have been expressed, has asked for the aid which this Government is obliged to give, according to Article 13 of the treaty of friendship and alliance made effective the 24th of January of this year, and that for all of these reasons war has become necessary, and furthermore in the view of the fact that I should myself direct the operations of the army if I am to exercise the authority with which I have been entrusted, I hereby decree, Article 1. The Republic of Guatemala is at war with the Government of Honduras. Article 2. As I must take over the command of the army, Lieutenant General don. J. Rufino Barrios shall have charge of the

Presidency in my absence, enjoying all the ample powers with which I have been invested. Article 3. The ministers of the government shall execute this decree, each in his own sphere. Given in Guatemala, May 8, 1872. [Signed] Miguel García Granados.

As so many times before, both sides were fighting to prevent a forcible overthrow. On the one hand, Medina faced an emboldened and strengthened Liberal opposition at home. On the other hand, García Granados and Justo Rufino Barrios sought to "starve the revolt of eastern Guatemala" (Rodriguez, 1965, 97) and protect their revolutions from a Conservative backlash. As a result of this familiar dynamic, in the words of Bustamante Maceo (1951, 70), "[t]o contain the conservative reaction, the governments of El Salvador and Guatemala decided to go to war with Honduras."[48] After three months of intermittent fighting, Medina was finally defeated on July 12 and 28, 1872 and taken prisoner a few days later (ibid.).[49] Guatemala and El Salvador installed the ardent Liberal Céleo Arias as President of Honduras, and the three countries concluded an alliance to maintain the Liberal regime (Burgess, 1926, 107).

In March 1873, García Granados called elections in Guatemala, which were won by Justo Rufino Barrios. In a rare peaceful transfer of power, García Granados accepted the results of the election and gracefully stepped down. Burgess (ibid., 120–1) speculates that three factors played a role in Granados' decision to call elections. First, Granados apparently was aware of "a certain friction with Barrios and wished it to be decided once and for all which was to be the master. [Second,] friends had given him to understand that he had better step aside. [And third, he] was tired of the responsibilities of his post." All three, arguably, played a part. In addition, it may have been important that "a really cordial feeling seemed to exist between the retiring and the incoming presidents" (ibid.). The aging García Granados, by then 64 years old, could moreover safely hand over power to a leader who had demonstrated a high degree of ability and

[48] As implicitly does Bustamante Maceo (1951), Rodriguez (1965, 97) also seems to consider the war to be initiated by Guatemala and El Salvador. "The pattern of intervention in Honduras – a defense measure with an ideological base – was repeated" in subsequent episodes.

[49] Scheina (2003, 255–6) notes that the Salvadorans had gotten 700 Remington repeating rifles from the Guatemalans. These rifles had also been decisive in the Liberal uprising in Guatemala.

competence. Garcia Granados returned to private life, with the title "*Benemérito de la Patria*" and lived peacefully in Guatemala City until his death in 1878.

One might expect that now that Liberals ruled all Central American states with the exception of Nicaragua, peace would prevail. However, while Tomás Guardia of Costa Rica had come to power as a Liberal in 1870, a marked shift in his policies became evident in subsequent years. This shift was probably best exemplified by his stance to the Conservative exiles from other countries, whom he welcomed into the country (Bancroft, 1887, 382). Residing in Costa Rica were now prominent Conservatives such as ex-President Cerna of Guatemala, a great many clergy expelled by the new Liberal regimes, and a number of discontented Nicaraguan army officers. As per usual, these "exiles busied themselves preparing for counter-revolutions in all the republics where the liberal regime was established" (Burgess, 1926, 122). In particular, the Conservatives gathered in Costa Rica raised a force, led by Enrique Palacios, which moved into Honduras in preparation for an invasion of Guatemala. Such an invasion obviously was of concern to Justo Rufino Barrios and Santiago González. They convinced President Quadra of Nicaragua of the dangers posed by Guardia's meddlesome policies and on August 26, 1873 the three countries concluded a defensive alliance against Costa Rica "to effectively isolate Costa Rica and assure the liberal regime throughout Central America" (ibid., 126; see also Bancroft, 1887, 479–80). In spite of all this sound and fury, no international conflict with Costa Rica occurred in 1873, most likely because Guatemala and El Salvador were otherwise engaged in a war with Honduras

Enrique Palacios, the leader of the Guatemalan Conservative invading forces mentioned above, was driven back across the border into Honduras in July 1873. There, he more or less successfully tried to reconstitute his forces (Bustamante Maceo, 1951, 70–1). President Justo Rufino Barrios of Guatemala and President González of El Salvador now concluded that "Arias proved incapable of suppressing Guatemalan and Salvadoran Conservatives who were operating from Honduras" (Scheina, 2003, 256; see also Bancroft, 1887, 460).[50]

---

[50] Burgess (1926, 126–7) claims that González tricked Barrios into replacing Arias with Leiva. "It was made to appear that the Honduras Government had favored the filibusters [e.g. Palacios]. González, President of Salavador, was

Barrios and González therefore asked Arias to step down. When he refused, El Salvador and Guatemala fought a second campaign against Honduras, and replaced Arias with the moderate Ponciano Leiva in mid-January 1874 (Bustamante Maceo, 1951, 71; Scheina, 2003, 256). Our theory fails to predict the timing of this conflict, because there is no clear *ex ante* exogenous shock. However, the motive for the war clearly follows the logic of our theory, the leaders invaded Honduras in another pre-emptive internationalized civil war. In other words, they invaded to prevent their own forcible overthrow at the hands of the domestic opposition in exile across the border.

In 1874 it looked as if the promise of an ideologically united Central America would finally yield its rewards and bring peace. Burgess (1926, 137) goes so far as to argue that:

1874 proved to be one of those rare lulls in the political life of Central America when there are neither revolutions nor wars nor rumors of the same. The efforts of the clericals to overthrow the liberal regime by revolution from within the republics themselves had signally failed. Their machinations with a view to bringing about the fall of the new governments from without had been equally fruitless.

In the background, however, tensions between Costa Rica and Nicaragua still simmered. When Fruto Chamorro took over in 1875 as (Conservative) President of Nicaragua, one of his first acts was to grant an unconditional pardon to individuals and groups associated with previous attempts to instigate a revolution. His gesture was fruitless, as a series of plots to overthrow him quickly sprouted around him. Chamorro, on November 17, 1875 therefore expelled the troublemakers, who were granted asylum in Costa Rica. Once there, these exiles sought to promote a war between Costa Rica and Nicaragua to regain power. As tensions rose to a boil, Costa Rica suspended diplomatic relations with Nicaragua. "No actual war existed, but it might break out at any moment, in view of Costa Rica's menacing attitude" (Bancroft, 1887, 481). The crisis between Nicaragua and Costa Rica slowly ebbed, but then a complicated tale of intrigue led to a war between Guatemala and El Salvador.[51]

anxious to see Arias removed from the presidency of Honduras and succeeded in making Barrios think that the latter had not been true to the liberal cause."
[51] Bancroft (1887, 256) records an international crisis between Germany and Nicaragua. "A squabble occurred in 1876 at Leon, in which the German

An unexpected and sudden change in attitude by González of El Salvador now led him to favor Conservatives. This change of heart is reminiscent of Malespín's earlier change of heart and it would have the same result: war. According to Bancroft (ibid., 401–3), Santiago González of El Salvador began to conspire with Guatemalan exiles in El Salvador and with the ideologically moderate leader of Honduras, Ponciano Leiva, to overthrow Barrios. Because of Leiva's alleged subservience to González, the latter promised that he would support Leiva with the Salvadoran army against the insurrection led by the former Conservative President, José Medina. Enrique Palacios, now living in exile in El Salvador, then wrote in mid-February 1876 to Medina, "urging him to desist from the campaign and arrange matters with Leiva, as both the latter and González were conservatives at heart and when once more Honduras was at peace, it could unite with El Salvador to overthrow the liberal regime in Guatemala" (Burgess, 1926, 154). Although it is unclear whether Barrios was aware of all the details of the game afoot, he clearly had become suspicious and "González was notified that if he persisted in that course, Guatemala would then interfere in favor of General Medina" (Bancroft, 1887, 402). Barrios' threat was all the more credible because he had detected a marked shift in Leiva's policies in favor of Conservatives as well, and accused him of no longer honoring his commitments with regard to the Guatemalan Conservatives in Honduras (Bustamante Maceo, 1951, 72). Chastized, González backed down for the moment, and in a conference at Chingo, the leaders of El Salvador and Guatemala agreed on a common policy to deal with the Honduran troubles. (On February 1, 1876 González' term ended. While he duly turned over the presidency to Andrés del Valle, an inexperienced and apparently untalented politician, Santiago González managed to hold onto the effective leadership as vice-president of El Salvador (Burgess, 1926, 152–3; Bancroft, 1887, 402).) At Chingo, the leaders from El Salvador and Guatemala agreed to send an army composed of 1,000 soldiers each from Guatemala and El Salvador to pacify Honduras. This army

consul and a Nicaraguan citizen were concerned, giving rise to a conflict between the German and Nicaraguan governments, the former making of it a casus belli, and demanded, backed by a naval force, a considerable sum of money." For another incident in 1875 between Nicaragua and Costa Rica, see Bancroft (ibid., 383).

would be led by the Guatemalan Minister of War, Marco Aurelio Soto, a Honduran by birth. This agreement, however, did not last long. Both sides seem to have thoroughly distrusted each other by now, and kept troops ready to battle the other, rather than fight as promised in Honduras (ibid.). In El Salvador, meanwhile, González allowed Palacios to form a provisional Guatemalan government, with a Conservative Cabinet (Burgess, 1926, 154). Barrios' patience had now run out, writing to Medina on 10 March 1876: "We are now at war with the Republic of Salvador, or rather with the traitor González" (ibid.). Barrios

came himself with a force to threaten Salvador on the west, and actually invaded the latter without a previous declaration of war. At last, on the 20th of March, José María Samayoa, minister of war in charge of the executive of Guatemala, formally declared all official relations with Salvador at an end, and then again on the 27th, alleging that Salvadoran troops had invaded Guatemala, decreed the existence of war.

(Bancroft, 1887, 402)

The Guatemalan decree of March 20, 1876 laid out Barrios' case against González:

Salvador was fostering a revolution against Guatemala under Enrique Palacios; . . . it had not kept its part of the agreement of Chingo; . . . it had changed the sense of the agreement of Chingo in sending a copy of the same to Honduras; . . . the Salvadoran Government was spreading the rumor that Barrios was trying to conquer and rule over Salvador; and . . . González and Valle were plotting for the aid of Honduras against Guatemala.

(Burgess, 1926, 155)

The war was mercifully short. By 25 April, El Salvador recognized the war was lost and accepted Barrios' terms (ibid., 157).[52] Del Valle was to give up the presidency and González would have to give up command of the Salvadoran forces. In return, both were guaranteed their "persons and property" (Bancroft, 1887, 405) and allowed to leave the country. To demonstrate to the Salvadoran people that the

---

[52] For details, see Burgess (1926, 156–60) and Bustamante Maceo (1951, 72–6). Notably, Barrios took pains to demonstrate that "he was not making war on the people of the country but on its Government. He required no indemnity at the hands of the conquered, though the war had cost Guatemala fully a million dollars. He did not even go on to the capital city, in spite of the fact that its gates were open to him" (Burgess, 1926, 158).

war was aimed only at the persons of del Valle and González, Barrios claimed no war indemnity – even though the war had cost over a million dollars – and did not even stage a triumphant entry into the capital (Burgess, 1926, 158). The new Salvadoran president, hand-picked by Barrios, of course, would be Rafael Zaldivar (Bustamante Maceo, 1951, 75).[53]

In the meantime, the civil struggle in Honduras had continued. Try-ing to prevent a two-front war and an alliance between Medina and Palacios, Barrios directed Soto to support Medina as the leader of Honduras on 28 March (Burgess, 1926, 156). The new government, however, proved unable to control the situation to Barrios' liking and he therefore backed Marco Aurelio Soto to become president. Medina threw in his lot with Soto and the latter became president at the end of August 1877 (ibid., 158). The new government managed to relatively quickly stabilize the situation.

Although these wars conform to our theory, they raise some puz-zling questions. Both González and Leiva seem to have fundamentally changed their attitude towards the Conservatives, which constitutes the shock which sets the events in motion. And as we have seen so often before, a crucial role is once again played by exiles who pose a threat to other leaders, in this case to the Guatemalan leader, Justo Rufino Barrios. However, we are left completely in the dark as to why González and Leiva turned to the Conservatives. The relevant sources leave no doubt that they both did, but any exploration of their motives is unfortunately absent. It is unlikely that Justo Rufino Barrios presented any kind of immediate threat to González.

The war of 1876 had shown that Barrios, and the Liberals, would brook no threat to their power. Justo Rufino Barrios had proved his mettle. The Liberals were in a stronger position than ever before. Our theory would predict that with such ideological homogeneity and in absence of exogenous shocks such as the rise of an ideologically hostile

---

[53] Burgess (1926, 158–9) calls this war the Central American war *par excellence.* "There is a real line of cleavage between Liberals and Conservatives and yet these two shibboleths often serve simply as a smoke screen to hide naked personal ambition. Politics in Central America is first, last, and all the time personal. Parties are born and die. The *jefecillos*, the different outstanding men who are able to secure a personal following, are always the real factor in the situation. Most of them [belong] to parties of many names, but the one party to which they are infallibly faithful is the party of self."

leader, natural disasters or interference from beyond the isthmus, peace should prevail. And peace did indeed prevail. For almost a decade, Central America experienced neither crisis nor war.[54] By the standards of nineteenth-century Central America, this constituted an unusually long era of peace.

Barrios apparently felt so secure that he could afford a trip to the United States of America and an extended voyage to Europe in 1884 (Burgess, 1926, 240). He returned to office in January 1885, filled with dreams of a Central American union to be led, obviously, by the "Great Reformer" Justo Rufino Barrios himself. Whether his vision was inspired by the recent German and Italian unifications, or by Soto's plan for a reconstituted union, Barrios now announced, on February 28, 1885, the re-establishment of a Central American union, under his leadership, of course. With alacrity, Soto's successor as the President of Honduras, Luis Bográn, fell in line with his Guatemalan protector (Rodriguez, 1965, 101–2). Others, however, were less than enthusiastic about their prospects in this new union.

Traditionally isolationist, Costa Rica marshalled her forces for the show-down. So did Nicaragua's conservative regime, alarmed at the possibility of having liberalism forced upon it by a strong central government. Porfirio Díaz of Mexico deployed troops along the Guatemalan border and encouraged defiance of Barrios' call; a powerful neighbor to the south was not to his liking. The opposition to union gained precious time because of the stalling tactics of Rafael Zaldivar, the Salvadorean [sic] president who owed his office to Barrios.

(ibid., 101; see also Cruz, 2002, 111–13)

Following in Barrios' footsteps, Zaldivar tried to buy time by taking a leave of absence to travel to Europe (Burgess, 1926, 241). However, the political landscape had not changed by the time he returned in August 1884. Barrios still pushed for union with Bográn's support and on February 28, 1885 unilaterally proclaimed the re-establishment of the union, with himself as the "General-in-Chief of the Central American forces" (Scheina, 2003, 257). Finally, Zaldivar had to decide: support or fight Barrios. Two factors probably were decisive: fierce domestic opposition to the plan, and Zaldivar's desire to remain in control. Both

---

[54] Justo Rufino Barrios apparently even felt strong enough domestically to settle a long-standing boundary issue with Mexico in 1881 (Burgess, 1926, 204–5).

factors were highlighted by the Spanish Minister to both Guatemala and El Salvador, who sent Justo Rufino Barrios a lengthy telegram. According to Burgess (1926, 251, emphasis added; see also 254):

the essence of the message was to the effect that he (the Spanish Minister), then on a visit to San Salvador, was a witness to the fact that the form in which it was proposed to carry out the Union of the separate Republics of Central America, had raised a storm of opposition in El Salvador, and that in consequence Zaldivar was utterly unable to dominate public opinion in favor of Barrios and Union. *To attempt to do so might cost Zaldivar his life and would most certainly cost him his position.*

Burgess (ibid., 252–3) himself, though, puts more weight on the second factor, that Zaldivar did not want to give up power. Whichever factor weighed more heavily, Zaldivar finally and decisively came out against the union. Furious, Barrios prepared to invade El Salvador and personally fired the first shot of the war, as a 14,500-man-strong Guatemalan army crossed the border into El Salvador on March 30, 1885 (ibid., 271; Scheina, 2003, 257). The war was over three days later, when a sniper's bullet felled J. R. Barrios as he was leading his troops in battle (ibid.).[55]

Our analysis has shown that Justo Rufino Barrios initiated a war against El Salvador because he intended to re-establish the union, and Salvador opposed him. Why Barrios thought the time for union had come remains somewhat of a mystery. To be sure, his announcement was welcomed with great enthusiasm in Guatemala (Burgess, 1926, 244–5). However, it is extremely unlikely that Barrios declared the union re-established or went to war to bolster his popularity at home. At the time Barrios faced a low threat of a forcible removal from office and a (very) low threat of a regular removal from office. If anyone had reason to fear a forcible removal from office it would have been Rafael Zaldivar of El Salvador, but he did not initiate the conflict. That

---

[55] For details on the battles and subsequent developments, see Bustamante Maceo (1951, 76–81). Ironically, perhaps, Zaldivar did not benefit from Barrios' death. Helped by the new Guatemalan President, Manuel Lisandro Barillas, General Francisco Menéndez launched a revolt against Zaldivar in early May 1885. When Zaldivar learned of the fall of Santa Ana to the revolutionary forces (13–15 May), he handed over power to Fernando Figueroa and went into exile. Nicaraguan forces then invaded El Salvador in support of Zaldivar and Figueroa, but were defeated. Menéndez finally triumphantly entered San Salvador on June 22, 1885.

distinction clearly befalls Barrios. On the one hand, Barrios' low risk of a regular removal may have given him the opportunity to initiate the conflict; on the other hand, the low risk of a forcible removal from office gave him little incentive. In sum, this war is not convincingly explained by our theory.

5.5.2 The era of Zelaya and Estrada Cabrera

After Barrios' death, Central America remained by and large ruled by Liberal leaders. The exception was Nicaragua, with its line of moderate Conservative leaders since 1857. Nicaragua, however, joined the camp of the Liberals when José Santiago Zelaya took over the presidency in 1893. On the other hand, a Conservative leader took over from a Liberal leader four times between 1885 and 1919 (see Tables 5.10–5.11). First, a Conservative leader rose to power in Costa Rica in 1890. Second, in Honduras Domingo Vásquez took over power from the moderate Leiva in 1893, only to quickly be replaced by another Liberal; a decade later, in 1904, another Conservative, Manuel Bonilla, took power in Honduras. Finally, in 1911, Conservatives once again took control of Nicaragua. The latter case, however, occurs after the regional dynamics were fundamentally altered because of increasing US pressure, and the Corinto Pact and the 1907 Washington Treaty.

Our theory would predict sustained periods of peace when the ideological stars were aligned, in other words, when the Central American countries were led by uniformly Liberal leaders.[56] We would predict an increased probability of war, however, during those periods when a Conservative replaced a Liberal leader. Tables 5.10–5.11 show the theory fares very well. In the twenty-four years between 1885 and 1919 Central America experienced only four wars, far less than in earlier, ideologically more diverse times. Moreover, the introduction of a new Conservative leader explains at least two out of the four wars, those of 1893 and 1907. We now turn to a deeper examination of the forces at work in Central America during this period.

---

[56] There is good evidence of a substantial amount of cross-national cooperation among the Liberal leaders. For example, in 1889 Conservative Salvadoran exiles were preparing to invade El Salvador but were attacked and defeated by Honduran troops (Bustamante Maceo, 1951, 83).

June 22, 1890 was supposed to be a day of celebration for Francisco Menéndez. It was, after all, the anniversary of his official ascent to power as President of El Salvador. A ball in his honor was organized, with dignitaries from the neighboring republics in attendance. One of those, a general by the name of Melecio Marcial, accompanied by other officers, walked up to Menéndez to demand his immediate resignation, followed by a request that the ladies leave the building. In response, Menéndez had a heart attack and died on the spot (Bustamante Maceo, 1951, 83–4). The mastermind behind this coup, Carlos Ezeta, now quickly took over power in El Salvador.

Ezeta's coup did not go over well with the other leaders in the region. Both Manuel Lisandro Barillas of Guatemala and Luis Bográn of Honduras refused to recognize the new regime in El Salvador. On June 28, 1890 Guatemala declared war and on 16 July Guatemalan forces invaded El Salvador. This war ended in more or less of a draw, with a peace treaty in August, where all leaders involved managed to hold on to power (ibid., 84–6). While the war was clearly associated with a turnover of the leadership in El Salvador, Ezeta had been solidly in the Liberal camp, and the underlying motives for this war remain opaque. Specifically, we have found no traces in the historical record to explain why Manuel Lisandro Barillas and Luis Bográn refused to accept the new government of Carlos and Antonio Ezeta. Thus, this case presents a puzzle for our theory. Nonetheless, we feel confident that this war was not caused by some well-established state- or system-level factors.

As the result of an unusual set of coincidences and exogenous shocks, the year 1893 brought a fundamental ideological shift in two Central American countries. According to our theory, this should produce an unusually high probability of war. After a complicated series of events, featuring both old rivalries among cities (pitting the old rivals León, Granada, and more recently Managua against each other), and cross-cutting cleavages, the Liberal José Santos Zelaya had skillfully outmaneuvered all other contenders and gained the presidency of Nicaragua, which he would control with an iron, and greedy, grasp until 1909.[57]

---

[57] For background on the twists and turns of Zelaya's rise to power, see Cruz (2002, 127–38). Zelaya was notoriously greedy and ruthless. Estrada Cabrera accused him of giving his enemies enemas of alcohol and chili peppers (Palmer, 1910, 229). Palmer (ibid., 177) notes he also had a sense of humor: "He

At the same time a Conservative leader, Domingo Vásquez, replaced the moderate Leiva in Honduras.[58] It should not come as a surprise that accusations and dissidents streamed across the border. Each side accused the other of conniving with his domestic enemies and preparing for revolution (Cruz, 2002, 136–7). Zelaya declared war first and Vice-President General Ortiz personally led the Nicaraguan troops into Honduras (ibid.).[59]

Scheina (2003, 258–9, emphasis added) aptly summarizes the developments of 1893:

> In late 1893 recently elected Conservative Honduran President Domingo Vásquez threatened Zelaya that if he did not expel dissident Liberal Hondurans from Nicaragua, Vásquez would declare war on Nicaragua. Zelaya formed an alliance with Honduran Liberal Policarpo Bonilla. On December 23 Bonilla invaded Honduras at the head of Honduran Liberals and *Nicaraguan troops.*... Vásquez fled into El Salvador and ardent Liberal Policarpo Bonilla became president.[60]

The events in 1893 made war particularly likely, because both sides had reason to fear hostile action by exiles supported by the other government. In other words, in terms of our theory, therefore, both sides had strong incentives to initiate conflict. Zelaya emerged victorious from the conflict, in a better position to deal with the Conservative opposition and with increased legitimacy. His legitimacy was further increased when he emerged victorious from a crisis with the United Kingdom over the Mosquito Coast.[61]

---

enjoyed the farces of re-elections, and on one occasion put three candidates in the field, Señores José, Santos and Zelaya, and he solemnly announced José Santos Zelaya as having been elected."

[58] Honduras had been experiencing civil conflict since at least 1891, see Scheina (2003, 258).

[59] Even though generally sympathetic to Nicaraguan leaders, Aquino (1944, 56–7) explicitly agrees that Zelaya declared war first, albeit in anticipation of a Honduran onslaught. Ortiz decisively defeated the Hondurans on January 4, 1894 at Choluteca where, in Ortiz's words, "I believe that General Vázquez has lost the flower of his army. The campaign will be short, and victory complete" (quoted in Cruz (2002, 136)).

[60] The next year, in 1894, Policarpo Bonilla promulgated a new Liberal constitution which forbade presidential re-election (Parker, 1964, 187).

[61] Cruz (2002, 140) claims Zelaya's victory was the result of American support and British indifference. See also Hall and Brignoli (2003, 224–5) and Rodriguez (1965, 107). The latter claims that, "Hailed as a national hero,

In 1898, another change in leadership, this time in El Salvador, where Tomás Regalado replaced R.A. Gutiérrez, produced a minor crisis between El Salvador and Nicaragua and Honduras. Regalado was uncertain about the reaction of both Nicaragua and Honduras to his revolution, and as a result sent off two armies to confront potential invaders.[62] However, Zelaya, and subsequently Policarpo Bonilla as well, accepted the change in leadership in El Salvador and the crisis was resolved (Bustamante Maceo, 1951, 95–8). Although this case does not fit the pattern whereby wars and crises occur when the leadership of a country changes its ideological orientation and as a result changes its attitudes to exiles on its soil, it does conform with our more general pattern where a leader initiated a crisis to protect himself against a forcible removal from office.

In 1904, the Conservative Manuel Bonilla gained the presidency in Honduras, replacing the Liberal Terencio Sierra. As we have proposed and shown, the replacement of a Conservative leader by a Liberal leader proved a harbinger of war in the era of Carrera (roughly 1840–71). Subsequently (1885–1919), the obverse held: the replacement of a Liberal leader by a Conservative leader was almost sure to create international conflict. It took about two years, but war did indeed follow, although not until El Salvador and Guatemala fought a rather peculiar war first.

By the turn of the century a new dynamic had established itself. Now that Liberalism ruled secure, regional tensions focused on the two dominating characters on the isthmus, Manuel Estrada Cabrera of Guatemala and José Santos Zelaya of Nicaragua. Zelaya and Regalado of El Salvador both supported insurrectionary forces invading Guatemala from both Mexico and El Salvador (Bustamante Maceo, 1951, 99; Hall and Brignoli, 2003, 225). (Officially Pedro José Escalon was president of El Salvador since 1903. In reality, Regalado remained Salvador's effective leader (ibid.; Rendón, 1988, 186).) Three times in May 1906 the exiles invaded from El Salvador, each time they were

---

Zelaya had no trouble asserting his will over the politicians of León who had hoped to dominate the young Managuan in the elections of 1896. He was now undisputed ruler of Nicaragua."

[62] Regalado was uncertain because El Salvador had earlier in the decade signed on to a new project to establish union. His ascent to power would, and indeed did, spell an end to yet another attempt at re-establishment of union.

beaten back. No national forces were involved, in other words, no Salvadoran, Nicaraguan or Mexican troops were involved and this would have remained one of the countless petty insurgencies, until, well, to put it bluntly, Regalado had one too many. As Scheina (2003, 259) puts it:

On May 27 exiled Guatemalan Gen. Manuel [Lisandro] Barillas invaded Guatemala from El Salvador with the objective of overthrowing President Manuel Estrada Cabrera but was defeated at Ayutla... on June 11. *On July 9 Gen. Tomás Regalado, the Salvadorian Minister of War who was frequently inebriated, spontaneously led a second invasion*; he was killed in the first engagement four days later. Guatemala then invaded El Salvador. Some 7,000 Guatemalans attacked 2,000 Salvadorians in bloody, indecisive fighting... between July 12 and 17. Mexico and the United States intervened and restored peace.[63]

Frederick Palmer tells a very similar tale in the *Chicago Daily Tribune* (February 27, 1909, p. 1 "Pocket Republic Minus A Dictator"):

Ex-President Regallado, for example, had no more official position than Miles or Corbin or any other retired general. Whenever he went on one of his long sprees his cry was for something to break the monotony of orderly government. While he lived the old customs should not die out, and the army thought him a devil of a fellow and unconquerable – especially when drunk. Early one morning in the spring of 1906 he planted the artillery in the plaza and blew off the front of the Salvadorean White house. His action was due to his personal dislike of Escalon, who was president at the time. Having paid this grudge he set out to pay another. That Cabrera of Guatemala was a mean, half caste Indian, who deserved to have his face slapped. So Regallado led the troops across the Guatemalan frontier without any declaration of war. He had not yet sobered up when he was killed in battle, while the issue of the war was still undecided at the time that Secretary Root offered his "good offices," which is diplomacy's name for the big stick.

Rendón (1988, 192–3) provides some intriguing detail that makes the story of of a drunk Regalado invading Guatemala rather plausible:

---

[63] It perhaps deserves mention that on his way to the front, Regalado cannonaded the presidential palace (Bustamante Maceo, 1951, 99) out of anger with President Escalon.

Many accounts say that Regalado had been drunk for several days before he attacked. . . . two [Guatemalan] regiments [who had moved near the border] wore blue-coloured uniforms which made them almost indistinguishable from the Salvadorean army. The drunk General Regalado may therefore have inadvertently entered Guatemalan-held territory thinking that his troops had preceded him.

With Regalado's death, the driving force behind this war was gone. Mexico and the United States led a peace conference on the USS *Marblehead* and peace was re-established in mid-July 1906 (for the conference on the USS *Marblehead*, see Hall and Brignoli (2003, 225) and Rendón (1988, 197–9)).

This war, known as the *War of Totoposte*, is unusual in several aspects. While it seems clear that Regalado was the first to cross the border, it is significantly less clear who initiated the crisis that preceded it. Bustamante Maceo (1951, 99) claims that a state of war was declared between El Salvador and Guatemala because of the invasion of the Guatemalan exiles into Guatemala, but does not record the date, nor who declared war first. Rendón (1988, 187–96) describes some striking details of events leading up to the war, including the wretched condition of the Guatemalan army stationed along the border, but does not mention any declaration of war and leaves it unclear who moved troops to the border first.[64] We have found only one source to indicate the initiator; that source puts the burden on Estrada Cabrera and Guatemala. Karnes (1961, 185–6) writes: "Guatemalan troops were successful in repulsing [the invading exiles], and, blaming Honduras and El Salvador in particular for permitting the attacks, Estrada Cabrera mounted an offense against them."

---

[64] Rendón does make several other noteworthy points. First, she points out that by 1905 the economy was in bad shape as coffee prices had dramatically fallen, and the pesos had undergone a serious devaluation. Such an exogenous shock, of course, worked to Cabrera's disadvantage. Second, wary of an army coup against him, Cabrera "used this war as a further opportunity for waging his own war on the national army" (Rendón, 1988, 188). Third, and in seeming contradiction to this second point, she notes that "Cabrera recognized that if he lost the war, his arbitrary reprisals against so many citizens, innocent or otherwise, would lead to his own imprisonment or death. He therefore made preparations in case of possible defeat, arranging funds and transport for a safe passage from Guatemala. These plans were so secret that when the war was won, Cabrera chose to shoot those men who had been involved with arranging his finances" (ibid., 191–2).

The question who initiated is, of course, important for our theory. If Guatemala initiated the war, our theory would provide a very convincing explanation. Guatemala's economy had turned sour, and exiles invaded from El Salvador and Mexico to overthrow Estrada Cabrera. As a result, Cabrera had strong incentives to initiate a war against El Salvador to deal the rebels a decisive defeat. If El Salvador initiated the war, our theory would not offer a convincing explanation. It also deserves consideration that this war is the result of truly unique circumstances – Regalado's inebriety and the color of some soldiers' uniforms – and therefore escapes systematic explanation.

Two more crises occurred in 1906. First, Nicaraguan leader Zelaya supported an attempt by General Manuel Rivas and Dr. Prudencio Alfaro to overthrow the Salvadoran leader, Pedro José Escalon (Bustamante Maceo, 1951, 101). Second, Estrada Cabrera moved troops to the Mexican border and initiated an international crisis with Mexico, to prevent another incursion by Guatemalan exiles (Rendón, 1988, 198–9). The first of these seems to derive from Zelaya's ambition to control the isthmus, an ambition perhaps given free rein because of his very low risk of a regular, and only medium risk of an irregular removal from office. The second crisis, recorded only in Rendón (ibid.), follows the established pattern whereby leaders try to block, thwart or pre-empt exiles from invading their country and thus initiate a crisis or war in order to forestall a forcible overthrow.

The rise of the Conservative Manuel Bonilla in Honduras would, as anticipated, cause a major war. As Rodriguez (1965, 111–13) notes:

A...powder keg was lit in Honduras in 1903 when Manuel Bonilla took over the government by force, ending the rule of liberals like Policarpo Bonilla (1893–99) and his hand-picked successor Terencio Sierra (1899–1903), whom Zelaya had aided to power. A conservative, this new Bonilla (who was not related to the former President) constituted another threat to Zelaya's position in Nicaragua and his hopes of uniting the five states of Central America.

Unhappy with a Conservative leader as his neighbor and its effect on his own Conservative opposition, the ambitious Zelaya sought to eliminate this threat from the north. To that end, Zelaya supported Dionisio Gutierrez with about 3,000 Nicaraguan troops in an invasion of Honduras (Bustamante Maceo, 1951, 102; Scheina, 2003, 259). The invasion, on December 23, 1906, was beaten back and pursued back into Nicaragua. In hot pursuit, Bonilla's army killed not only invaders, but also some Nicaraguan citizens (Karnes, 1961, 188).[65] In response, Zelaya demanded compensation and reparation (Scheina, 2003, 259–60).[66] When Bonilla refused, Zelaya organized an army composed of Honduran Liberals and the Nicaraguan army to invade Honduras in February 1907 (ibid., 259). After some bloody battles in which the Honduran army and its Salvadoran allies faced a Nicaraguan army equipped with Maxim machine guns, Bonilla was decisively defeated on March 23, 1907. He fled aboard the US cruiser, the *Chicago*, and went into exile in Guatemala.[67] After some skirmishes between Terencio Sierra and Miguel Rafael Dávila, the latter emerged victorious as the new Liberal President of Honduras.

In contrast to the 1906 *War of Totoposte*, the exact identity of the initiator is not crucial for our theory in this war. Manuel Bonilla's ascent to the presidency in Honduras constituted an exogenous shock with dangerous consequences for Zelaya's domestic balance of power with the Conservative Nicaraguan opposition. Our theory would thus predict that Zelaya would initiate a conflict to remove this threat. At the same time, it could be argued that Zelaya's support of the Liberal Honduran exiles provided Bonilla strong incentives to remove this threat. We conclude that Zelaya's decision to contribute 3,000 Nicaraguan troops to Gutierrez' army of exiles makes him the initiator in this conflict. This war thus also conforms nicely to our theory.

5.6 A problem (largely) solved: the Washington Treaty

In our analysis, we pointed out how the support of exiles time and again led to war. When, for example, Honduras and Nicaragua were ruled by a Conservative and a Liberal respectively, the Conservative leader of Honduras would support the Conservative exiles from Nicaragua,

---

[65] For details of the battles in this war, see Bustamante Maceo (1951, 101–4).

[66] Aquino (1944, 102) places the blame for this war squarely on the shoulders of "western Liberal exiles" and "Conservative conspirators" who conspired with General Manuel Bonilla.

[67] Palmer gave a scathing assessment of the role of exiles in Central America when he wrote: "Manuel Bonilla is now in the cattle and revolutionary business in Honduras and waiting for his chance, while poor Dávila sits up nights scanning the first signs of an outbreak." Frederick Palmer, *The New York Times*, March 1, 1909, p. 8, "Honduras Wants Intervention."

while the Liberal leader of Nicaragua would support the Liberal exiles from Honduras. This pattern poses a puzzle: why would leaders make what might appear as the same mistake over and over again, especially when it often led to war and their forcible removal from office?[68] The answer is simple. To maintain support among home Liberals (or Conservatives), the Liberal leader had to support Liberal exiles. In a nutshell, the strategy of supporting exiles with a similar ideology strictly dominated the strategy of not supporting such exiles. As a result, leaders found themselves in a classic Prisoner's Dilemma. While both sides would have been better off if neither supported exiles, the logic of their strategic interaction ensured they ended up in a situation where both sides supported the exiles, with an increased probability of war. What was necessary to escape this dilemma was a credible enforcer, a party who would hold accountable a leader who against his promises supported exiles.[69] The Washington Treaty of December 1907 would finally provide such an enforcer.

The 1907 war marked a turning point in Central American relations, because by now the United States of America had taken an active interest in the region. Secretary Root now determined that wars in Central America were against the interests of the United States. He therefore organized a conference of all five states in December 1907 in Washington, under the auspices of Mexico and the United States (Palmer, 1910, 292–4). In the Washington Treaty of December 20, 1907, the parties attempted to deal with the fundamental causes of the recurrent warfare on the isthmus. Articles XVI and XVII declared:

Article XVI Desiring to prevent one of the most frequent causes of disturbances in the Republics, the contracting Governments shall not permit the leaders or principal chiefs of political refugees, nor their agents, to reside in the departments bordering on the countries whose peace they might disturb.

---

[68] Palmer (1910, 293) provides an interesting explanation for why exiles always constituted a greater threat than purely domestic rebellion. "[B]ecause of recent years, with the line of telegraph instantly apprising a dictator of any movement against him, the only hope of turning him out was by a force organized across the frontier, or by assassination or a palace plot."

[69] The Central American states had many times signed treaties in which both sides promised not to support exiles. In 1902, for example, the Central American states minus Guatemala agreed to a pact at Corinto whereby they agreed to the principle of arbitration of their difficulties and differences (Rodriguez, 1965, 108–9). Not surprisingly, without an enforcer none of these agreements stuck.

Those who may have established their permanent residence in a frontier department may remain in the place of their residence under the immediate surveillance of the Government affording them an asylum, but from the moment when they become a menace to public order they shall be included in the rule of the preceding paragraph.

Article XVII Every person, no matter what nationality, who, within the territory of one of the contracting Parties, shall initiate or foster revolutionary movements against any of the others, shall be immediately brought to the capital of the Republic, where he shall be submitted to trial according to law.

> (Reproduced in Palmer (ibid., 307–17, Appendix A))

An Additional Convention to the General Treaty contained three further clauses aimed to remove the threat of a forcible removal from office, which we have identified as a fundamental cause of international conflict. It stated:

Article I – The Governments of the High Contracting Parties shall not recognize any other Government which may come into power in any of the five Republics as a consequence of a *coup d'état*, or of a revolution against the recognized Government, so long as the freely elected representatives of the people thereof, have not constitutionally reorganized the country.

Article II – No Government of Central America shall in case of civil war intervene in favor of or against the Government of the country where the struggle take place.

Article III – The Governments of Central America, in the first place, are recommended to endeavor to bring about, by the means at their command, a constitutional reform in the sense of prohibiting the re-election of the President of a Republic, where such prohibition does not exist, secondly to adopt all measures necessary to effect a complete guarantee of the principle of alternation in power.

> (Reproduced in Palmer (ibid., 316–17))

To enforce these terms, the treaty established a Central American Court of Justice residing in Cartago.

Notwithstanding the new treaty, tensions in the region remained high. A new crisis in 1908 between Nicaragua and Honduras on the one hand and Guatemala and El Salvador on the other, seemed about to explode into fully-fledged war (ibid., 103).[70] As so often before, the core issue was the support of rebels-in-exile (Rodriguez, 1965, 112–13). What was different this time was that in this case, invoking the Washington Treaty, "[t]he United States and Mexico forced the...issue to come before the Central American Court of Justice" (Scheina, 2003, 261). The Court took up the case with alacrity and dispatch. As Karnes (1961, 194) summarizes the developments:

Three days after the complaint was filed, interlocutory decrees were issued against Honduras, Guatemala, and El Salvador, requesting that they withdraw their forces from the frontiers, restrict the activities of their exiles, and remove from command certain Salvadorean officers....Within five days the decrees had been carried out, and the revolution had subsided. While the court debated, other factors helped to bring about a peaceful solution. In Washington, Secretary of State Robert Bacon told the Central American ministers that if the states failed to permit the operation of the peace machinery, the United States might be forced to intervene.

The actions of the Court managed to avoid war. Moreover, when Federico Tinoco rose to power in Costa Rica as a result of a coup in 1917, US President Woodraw Wilson abided by the non-recognition policy prescribed by the Washington Treaty until Tinoco was finally forced to step down (Rodriguez, 1965, 120). To be sure, when a leader was removed under threat of force, as was Zelaya in 1909, if this occurred at the instigation, or at least passive concurrence of the United States,

[70] In his article on this situation, Frederick Palmer (*The New York Times*, March 1, 1909, p. 8, "Honduras Wants Intervention," emphasis added) describes Dávila's concerns:

Of course I heard of revolutionary possibilities on the way. They are always in the air, and they were in the mind of President Davilla when I talked with him. He is said to be the one clean-handed President in money matters in Central America.... "*All I ask is to get out alive*," pleaded the old President. "I go to bed every night without knowing what may happen in the morning. I have no one whom I can trust. I have to do all for myself. What hope of peace or development has Honduras, lying between Guatemala and Nicaragua? None, except by interference by the United States. It is for you to see that the Central American court is not the plaything of Nicaraguan and Guatemalan politicians. Will you not drive out their spies? Will you not use your strong arm to give us peace–peace long enough to learn that continual revolution is not the natural order of a nation's existence?"
    We are confident that many previous Central American leaders shared such sentiments.

the new leader had little trouble obtaining recognition (Schoonover, 1991, 132–45). But while these cases show that the United States did not uphold the letter of the law, they do show that the United States now had become the arbitrator of Central American affairs. The United States had shown it intended to hold the Central American states to their promises. Henceforth, "The United States become the enforcer of the 1907 treaty" (Scheina, 2003, 261).[71] Now that the United States proved willing to accept a pre-eminent role in Central America, the old pattern was broken. Even though a Conservative leader replaced a Liberal leader in Nicaragua in 1911, and the Conservative Manuel Bonilla regained power in Honduras in 1913, these exogenous shocks did not trigger international crises or wars as they had so many times before. In a way we did not anticipate, the 1907 Washington Treaty solved the commitment problem by cushioning the effects of any temporary shock in the leader's capabilities and legitimacy. With the credible threat not to recognize any leader who came to power through a coup, the Washington Treaty fundamentally altered the fundamental costs and benefits of any coup or revolt.

5.7 Conclusions

Our analysis of almost eighty years of Central American history has discovered some surprising and hithertofore largely unknown patterns. We should note that, unbeknownst to us when we began our research, our empirical focus on Central America fits well with our theoretical focus on leaders. There is no doubt who made decisions about peace or war in Central America between 1840 and 1919: it was the individual leader, the *caudillo*. Bureaucratic politics played little or no role, not least because these countries' bureaucracies were woefully underdeveloped and staffed. Nor did public opinion in the form of elections hold much sway, as elections almost always were rigged and the outcome known well before any voter went to the polls.

A striking pattern emerges from our historical analysis. Our theory enabled us to identify the crucial sources of variation that induced leaders to initiate war. In other words, we were able to predict not

---

[71] Scheina (2003, 261) adds the unnecessary qualifier, "when it chose to do so."

just whether, but also *when* leaders would choose to initiate conflict. Leaders in Central America became increasingly likely to lose office through the use of force when the replacement of a leader in a neighboring country changed the ideological balance of power in the region, or when a neighboring leader changed his allegiance and thereby changed the ideological balance of power in the region. When the ideological balance of power in the region changed, exiles would become more likely to obtain foreign support and the domestic balance of power between Conservatives and Liberals would shift against the leader. But the leader could not make a deal to share power, because it was not credible that this deal would stick if circumstances changed in his favor. As a result, violent conflict between the leader and the opposition became more likely. The opposition would gather abroad, where the leader's ideological opponent would give them shelter, arms, and a safe place to organize and prepare an invasion.

Exiles across the border, organizing to invade and overthrow the leader, often were the cause of interstate war. As Palmer (1910, 293) put it: "A favorite means of warfare of one President on another was to support the organization of a revolutionary army within his borders to invade his neighbor's territory when it was ready."[72] Small wonder, then, that leaders would try to pick the time and place to pre-empt such invasions by invading their hostile neighbor first. When leaders – often at the head of their army – invaded their neighbors to deal with a dangerous domestic threat, international war ensued. These wars clearly fit the general causal mechanism we developed in Chapter 2, although the relationship between an exogenous shock, the increase in the risk of a forcible removal from office and conflict initiation manifests itself in way we did not (could not?) anticipate. With the benefit of hindsight, we are, however, confident that this specific pattern occurred at other places and times in recent history.

---

[72] Note how this pattern gives successful coup plotters and revolutionists an incentive to kill the former leader and his supporters. Elsewhere Palmer (1910, 230–1) highlights how common the threat from exiles truly was. "It seemed to me – and, generally speaking, this is correct, – that every man in Central America, outside of Costa Rica, who had a smattering of education was, in one form or another, potentially a revolutionist. The 'out' often goes to the rival dictator's country and seeks a little allowance as an ally in planning trouble for his own country."

We have not held back our doubts about cases which appear poor, marginal, or at least somewhat doubtful fits with our theory. Our theory fared particularly poorly in explaining conflicts with European (Great) Powers, but we would not have expected it to offer success-ful explanations of those conflicts. Nevertheless, overall our theory did fairly well. Counting only *ex ante* identifiable exogenous shocks and dismissing relatively ambiguous cases, our theory correctly pre-dicted about two-thirds of the Central American wars between 1840 and 1919 (11 out of 17 wars). (We note in passing that we did not expect to find so many wars in Central America in this period, and this many wars will surely come as a surprise to most readers as well.) As cases that fit the pattern postulated by our theory, we count the war between Guatemala and El Salvador of 1844, the war between Hon-duras and El Salvador of 1844, the war of 1851 between El Salvador and Honduras against Guatemala, the 1851 war between Guatemala and Honduras, the *National War* of 1856 between Costa Rica, El Sal-vador, Guatemala, and Honduras on one side against Nicaragua and William Walker on the other, the war of 1863 between Guatemala and Nicaragua against El Salvador and Honduras, the 1872 war of Hon-duras against El Salvador and Guatemala, the 1876 wars of Guatemala against Honduras and Guatemala against El Salvador, the 1893 war between Nicaragua and Honduras, and finally, the 1907 war between Nicaragua on one side against El Salvador and Honduras on the other. Some of the other wars seem to have been driven by decidedly idiosyn-cratic motives, such as Justo Rufino Barrios' dreams to replicate Bis-marck's unification of Germany and Regalado's keen eye for the bottle and his soldiers' uniforms. It is safe to say that no theories of democra-tization, of democratic dyads, of selectorates or of multipolarity have much, if anything, to contribute to explain the wars of Central America in this period.

Admittedly, however, our theory fares less well in explaining intra-regional crises, explaining only somewhat less than half (6 out of 13) of the international intra-regional crises between 1840 and 1918. The following cases conform to our theoretical explanations, beginning most prominently with the crisis engendered by Morazán's return to power in Costa Rica, the crisis of 1842 that pitted Guatemala, El Salvador, Honduras, and Nicaragua against Costa Rica, the crisis of 1843 between Guatemala and El Salvador, as well as the 1848 crisis between the same protagonists, the crisis of 1866 that figured the same configuration of belligerents, the crisis between Guatemala and Mexico of 1906, and the crisis between Nicaragua and El Salvador of 1907. On the one hand, this finding might appear to undercut our theory. On the other hand, it deserves emphasis that we seek to explain not only the presence, but also the *timing* of international crises and wars. On that front, our theory easily beats all competitors.

We know of few theories, indeed, that successfully predict the timing of peace and war. As our historical analysis of Central America between 1840 and 1918 has shown, our theory is able to do just that. The probability of international conflict was high when the ideological balance of power shifted in the region. The probability of international conflict was low when one ideology ruled hegemonic on the isthmus. These are new findings which overall lend strong support to our theory.

6 | Conclusions

6.1 Summary

What did the late King Prajadhipok, the last absolute ruler of Siam (now Thailand), do to prepare himself financially for life after his anticipated overthrow in the early 1930s? He took out unemployment insurance with French and British insurance companies. Then, having failed to suppress the newly formed constitutional government, he accepted his ouster, collected on the policies and lived comfortably in England for the remaining six years of his life.[1]

This book makes a simple point: leaders decide to initiate conflict at least partly on how conflict in turn affects not just the probability, but especially the manner of losing office. In particular, we argue that as the risk of a forcible removal increases, leaders become more likely to initiate international conflict. To establish this point, in Chapter 2 we developed a theoretical framework to explain which, when, and why leaders can obtain private benefits from international conflict. The answer, we argue, turns on leaders' expectations about their personal fate out of office. In countries that have established norms, procedures, and institutions *to protect leaders after they lose office*, leaders can afford to lose office gracefully and participate in an institutionalized process of regular transfers of power. In countries that lack the institutions to protect leaders, they will be loath to turn over the reins of power, because that exposes them to significant personal punishments such as exile, imprisonment or death. The removal of such leaders then typically requires the threat or use of force.

The lack of domestic institutions enforcing a credible commitment not to punish leaders can induce a second commitment problem when

---

[1] From http://anecdotage.com/index.php?aid=8306.

a temporary shock weakens the leader *vis-à-vis* his domestic opposition. Because the leader cannot credibly promise not to renege on any deal when his circumstances improve, costly domestic conflict can rationally emerge. In other words, if no peaceful bargain that avoids the costs of domestic conflict can be struck between leader and the opposition, the two sides can rationally fight in an attempt to redistribute or maintain power and control over domestic resources. This conflict can take several forms, such as coups, rebellions, revolution as well as insurgencies, but they revolve around the same central commitment problem (Fearon, 2004). Leaders can then choose to initiate international conflict if that offers an increased chance to eliminate their domestic opponents, for example by defeating rebels and exiles who have found a safe haven abroad.

We offered two mechanisms whereby conflict could pay for leaders who anticipate a forcible removal from office. In the first, *fighting for survival*, leaders can decrease the hazard of a forcible removal from office more or less independent of the outcome of the international conflict. For example, leaders could fight for survival if they can send coup plotters to the front to fight and die, or if they can disrupt a planned invasion by rebels. In our second mechanism, *gambling for survival*, it is the outcome against the international opponent that is fundamental to the leader's survival. Victory against the international opponent gives increased legitimacy or resources that enable the leader to also defeat his domestic enemies.

Because defeat increases the probability of a forcible removal from office with its associated unpleasant consequences, we proposed a third mechanism, *peace through insecurity*, whereby an increase only in the risk of a *regular* removal from office makes leaders less likely to initiate conflict. For such leaders, not much is to be gained, but much – indeed, their very lives – can be lost in case of defeat. Taken together, these arguments amount to a fundamental reformulation of theories of diversionary war.

The rest of this book was devoted to testing our claims. The statistical analysis in Chapter 3 showed that between 1919 and 2003 conflict initiation – the Challengers in international conflict – decreased the risk of a forcible removal from office, as posited by our *fighting for survival* mechanism. To offer a finer-grained examination of our arguments, one that would articulate the conditions under which our proposed mechanisms are more likely to be at work, we split our sample into various sub-samples. Thus, to differentiate countries that can credibly commit to safeguard their leaders after they lose office from countries that lack the institutions, norms, and procedures to make such a commitment credible, we split the sample into four sub-samples, one each for leaders of autocracies, mixed regimes, presidential, and parliamentary democracies. Following Riker (1982), we postulate that democracies do have the institutions, norms, and procedures to guarantee leaders their safety, whereas autocracies and mixed regimes lack such institutional protections for their leaders. Leaders of autocracies and mixed regimes, therefore, are more likely to face a forcible removal from office and as a result have more to gain from conflict initiation.

Our competing risks model showed that leaders of autocracies who initiated an international conflict did indeed gain a significantly decreased hazard of a forcible removal from office. While the effect for mixed regime was similarly negative, it just barely missed significance at the 5% level. Autocratic leaders, moreover, also gained a significantly decreased hazard of a forcible removal if they managed to gain a victory in a crisis. These results show, in other words, that leaders of autocracies do have the incentives to both *fight* and *gamble for survival*. Leaders of presidential and parliamentary democracies need fear only a regular removal from office, and enjoy a low hazard of a forcible removal from office. They are therefore not expected to gain any benefits from conflict initiation. As expected, for those leaders conflict initiation did not significantly affect the hazard of a forcible nor of a regular removal from office.

In the broadest terms, we argue that an increase in the risk of a forcible removal in turn increases the probability of conflict initiation because international conflict can, in turn, decrease the probability of a forcible removal. To examine this empirically, we split the sample into one sub-sample of leaders engaged in a civil war and thus at an increased risk of a forcible removal, and a sub-sample of leaders at civil peace. As expected, leaders involved in civil war obtained a decreased hazard of a forcible removal from office when they initiated an international conflict.

Finally, to approximate leaders experiencing a temporary shock in their capabilities, we split the sample into a sub-sample with negative economic growth and another with positive economic growth. As expected, leaders experiencing negative economic growth gain a decreased hazard of a forcible removal when they initiate an international conflict. They also gain a lower hazard of a regular removal from office. According to our theory, leaders enjoying positive economic growth have little to gain from international conflict. Thus, it came as no surprise to find that conflict initiation did not significantly affect either hazard of removal from office. Taken together, the results in Chapter 3 provide strong support for the *fighting for survival* and weaker support for the *gambling for survival* mechanism.

In Chapter 4, we presented a statistical test of the two central claims of our theory – (*a*) leaders are more likely to initiate an international conflict when they face higher risk of forcible removal from office; (*b*) leaders are less likely to initiate an international conflict when they face higher risk of regular removal from office. To this end, we developed one instrument to measure the risk of a regular removal and a second instrument to measure the risk of a forcible removal from office. When we included these two endogenous regressors with the standard variables used to predict conflict, we found that as proposed by our *peace through insecurity* mechanism, as a leader's risk of a regular removal from office increases, the probability he will initiate an international conflict decreases. In addition, as proposed by our *fighting* and *gambling for survival* mechanisms, as the leader's risk of a forcible removal from office increases, he becomes more likely to initiate international conflict. While these results increase our confidence in the theoretical framework we developed, we recognized in Chapter 2 that international conflict can affect the probability of a forcible removal from office in several different ways. To put it bluntly, several stories fit the general mechanisms, and the statistical tests offer no way to differentiate among the alternatives.

To trace the causal mechanism that connects the fate of leaders to the initiation of international conflict, in Chapter 5 we examined the history of Central America, a region where the threat of a forcible removal from office loomed large in the nineteenth century. We focused on a period which deliberately falls outside of the sample used for our statistical analysis – the period between 1840 and 1918. During that time – and even well before – Guatemala, El Salvador, Nicaragua, Honduras, and Costa Rica finally broke free from the Federal Republic of Central America in 1840, rival *caudillos* were locked in an ideological battle between "Liberals" and "Conservatives." If a Liberal leader in one country lost power to a Conservative, this would constitute a (temporary?) shock to the relative power of neighboring Liberal leaders, since their Conservative opponents would typically be offered a safe haven and even arms to organize for revolt. In response, those leaders, now at an increased risk of a forcible removal form office, would both *fight* and *gamble for survival*. They would fight for survival when they invaded their neighbor in pursuit of fleeing rebel forces or to deal a quick devastating blow to the organizing invasion force. They would gamble for survival if they decided to tackle the root of the problem and fight and remove the offending leader and replace him with someone of their own ideological stripe. Our theory successfully predicted not only 11 out of 17 wars, it also successfully predicted long periods of peace, in particular the peace that followed the 1907 Washington Treaty.

Our empirical analysis leaves us confident of our core claim: leaders initiate conflict when they anticipate a forcible removal from office. We are also confident that leaders at risk of a regular removal from office have *dis*-incentives to initiate conflict. These are new theoretical claims and new empirical results. We make no grand claims that every other theory out there is wrong. Indeed, we strongly believe that international conflict can occur for a variety of reasons, through a variety of mechanisms. We do urge, however, more attention to explanations for war based on the incentives of political leaders.

6.2 Implications

The material developed in and for this book, we believe, has important implications for both scholars and policy-makers. To address academics first, there is remarkably little research on leaders and international conflict, barring research on traditional versions of diversionary war and the path-breaking work of Bueno de Mesquita and his co-authors (Bueno de Mesquita, Siverson and Woller, 1992; Bueno de Mesquita and Siverson, 1995; Bueno de Mesquita and Siverson, 1997; Bueno de Mesquita et al., 1999; McGillivray and Smith, 2000; Bueno de Mesquita et al., 2003). Much, we believe, is to be gained by renewed attention to the role and incentives of leaders in the study of international conflict.

While our focus on leaders allowed us to develop new theoretical explanations for war and peace, it would be easy to dismiss our approach by arguing that a focus on leaders explains only a few marginal cases of international conflict. Not much, in such a critique, would be gained by switching our focus away from systems and states to leaders. In response, it is not difficult to make a compelling case for a focus on leaders: there is more variation at the leader level, since leaders vary in their characteristics and enjoy a median tenure of about two years. Systems, in contrast, change their polarity only at a glacial pace, while states typically also remain democratic or non-democratic for long periods of time. If system- and state-level attributes change slowly, they are unlikely to be able to predict sudden shifts from peace to war.[2]

The ultimate answer must come from the empirical record, to which we now briefly return. For our data, we again rely on the *Archigos* data. The *Archigos* data allows us to explore the explanatory power of a focus on leaders from a straightforward empirical angle. We assess the extent to which each of the three traditional levels of analysis – system, state, and leader – captures the variation in 85 years of conflict in the international arena. To do so, we estimate a hierarchical model where we partition the total variability in international conflict among systems, countries, and leaders. A fourth category – the residual category – represents the variation that occurs over time for each given leader. In our data, we have 2,134 leaders, 163 countries, and four different configurations of the international system, in the period from 1919 to 1938; World War II; the Cold War from 1946 to 1990; and the post-Cold War period from 1991 to 2003. The model estimates the relative contribution that each level offers to the overall variability in the patterns of conflict involvement.[3]

We report the findings from the hierarchical model in the simplest form in Figure 6.1, where we use a box-plot to report the four parameters that measure variability in conflict. In sum, we find that about 27% of the variation in patterns of conflict occurs at the level of leaders; about 24% occurs at the state level; about 14% occurs at the system level. The lion's share of the variation, about 35%, occurs during the leaders' individual spells in office. Of the three systematic components

---

[2] With little variation on the right-hand side, we can expect little power to explain variation on the left-hand side.
[3] We present the model in the Appendix. Here suffice it to say that we estimated a Bayesian hierarchical model with random intercepts, a binary dependent variable, and a probit link. We also report the results of the tests for the convergence of the estimation in the Appendix.

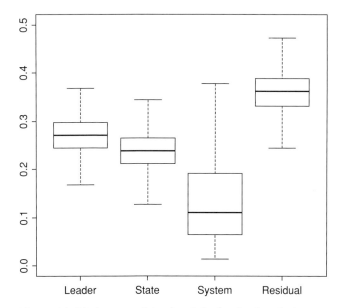

Figure 6.1: Variance explained and the levels of analysis

Note: Box-plots of the ratios of the variances at each of the four data clusters over total variance. Estimates obtained from a Bayesian hierarchical model of conflict involvement with random intercepts and a probit link.

associated with the levels of analysis, leaders capture the largest portion of the variation. State-level variability comes second. The system-level variability is both the smallest and the most uncertain, as the larger confidence bounds in the box-plot indicate.

From this illustration, we can conclude that all levels of analysis can claim some support. Given the rich intellectual history each level of analysis can invoke, this finding should not come as a surprise. But if no level of analysis can be entirely dismissed, the results we report in Figure 6.1 raise two important points about leaders and conflict. First, about one-third of the variation in international conflict derives from the personal characteristics and attributes of leaders. This straightforward analysis, therefore, validates the importance of leaders in the study of international conflict.

The results of the hierarchical model raise a second important point. About 35 percent of the variation is allocated to the residual category, the variation that occurs over time for each leader. In our attempt to explain conflict, therefore, we should not just assess the *types* of systems, countries, and leaders who are most likely to be embroiled in conflict. It is perhaps even more important to explain when leaders would make the decision to go from peace to conflict and from conflict to peace. Our theory attempts to do just that. We developed arguments to explain why leaders who need fear only a regular removal from office will go to war only when they are secure in office, while leaders exposed to the threat or use of force will initiate conflict when they anticipate a forcible removal from office.

Second, and perhaps more fundamental, we believe, there is much promise in research which explores the relationship between domestic and international conflict (Wagner, 2007). As our theory highlights, many international wars are fought to gain the upper hand against a domestic enemy (see also Gleditsch, Salehyan and Schultz (2008)). More striking yet, in many "international" conflicts, the goal may not by any means be the defeat of the international opponent. These "wars", commonly called internationalized civil wars, asymmetric wars, or insurgent wars, are becoming a feature of the current international system (Kaldor, 1999; Gleditsch *et al.*, 2002; Jervis, 2002; Record, 2002; Mueller, 2004). Should these cases even count as international wars? We believe the field is long overdue a discussion about war in its most basic form: which events constitute a war, and why? Is war by definition mutual? Can it be unilateral? What to do with cases like Denmark in 1940? After all, Denmark surrendered after the death of less than a dozen of its soldiers, but did so in full recognition of its military capabilities and prospects relative to Germany. Notably, there is no Germany–Denmark war in the Correlates of War project.

Finally, and perhaps more fundamentally still, a focus on leaders makes it possible to explore avenues how war can *pay*. It is particularly unclear how war can pay from a systemic perspective. Supposedly, states can rationally launch pre-emptive war, in an attempt to prevent their enemy from growing stronger. Supposedly, again, once the enemy grows stronger he would or might attack, but by systemic theory it is unclear why he would. In essence, the only reason to go to war would be to prevent any future attempts at prevention which aimed to prevent . . . ad infinitum, which of course leaves us with no reason for war at all. In the formal literature states often bargain over a pie, but it is unclear why states get more utility from more pie. States are better off by more of what, exactly?[4] From a second image perspective, it is also unclear how war could pay for states, with the potential exception that wars "to make the world safe for democracies" might pay because of the so-called "democratic peace." Leader-level theories, in contrast, make much more concrete what leaders can gain from war: loot to be redistributed, opportunities to outflank, de-legitimate or outright defeat domestic opponents. The increased clarity of what leaders, as opposed to states or regime types, could gain from international conflict greatly enhances the prospects for empirical research. It may even help to move from explanations of war in the abstract, to a rigorous theory that can explain when, why, and which wars occurred ... or are likely to occur.

Policy-makers, we propose, should keep a sharp eye out for domestic unrest and threats to leaders that could result in their forcible removal from office and subsequent punishment. During the writing of this book, in the late summer of 2008, we agreed that the military leaders who had replaced Prime Minister Thaksin in Thailand feared a coup or a revolt against them. As a result, we concluded, Thailand would be likely to initiate an international conflict. And it did, against Cambodia – apparently over the issue of a sacred temple. Analysts and policy-makers, we urge, should trace and take into account the post-tenure prospects of leaders. In some cases, this may require a careful weighing of the short-term costs of international prosecutions of leaders against its long-term hoped-for deterrent benefits. Leaders accused of war crimes or crimes against humanity, we would argue, have little incentive to hand over the reins of power. Shoving a leader to the precipice may leave him with no way out, except through international conflict. The trade-off here for policy-makers is stark. Seek justice and deter future criminals? A worthy goal. But at the cost of an international conflict with potentially many additional victims? "Do not prosecute, do not punish, do not forgive, and, above all, do not forget." This was the impassionate guideline for democratizers that Samuel Huntington (1991, 231) offered in his celebrated treatise on the third wave of democratization in the late twentieth century. Our

---

[4] If more territory would always be better, we are left with many puzzles, including the existence of San Marino, Monaco, Liechtenstein, and many other small states. More territory is not always necessarily better, since more territory can bring strategic, demographic, and perhaps electoral problems.

book shows that not just democracy – as Huntington argued – but also international peace is caught in this moral dilemma.

6.3 Conclusions

Leaders sometimes seek international conflict to protect themselves from severe punishments. Few kings are as wise and rational as was King Prajadhipok, Rama VII of Thailand, whose far-sightedness we illustrated in the epigraph of this chapter. As we illustrated in Chapter 1, the Mo Ibrahim Foundation, however, is trying to create incentives to induce a similar far-sightedness among African leaders. His noble goal and his solution, for once, seems to go to the heart of the problem. The promise of a retirement free from want and full of possibilities may well change the behavior of African leaders. African leaders may well not just strive to become better leaders of their own people, they may also have fewer incentives to initiate international conflict. This book suggests that Dr. Ibrahim is onto something, perhaps even bigger than he had initially intended. The flower of peace may grow out of the solution to the problem of violence in domestic politics.

Appendix A: data and measurement

A.1 *Archigos*: a data set of leaders

A major reason for the relative paucity of research on leaders and international conflict was the lack of systematic data on leaders. Specifically for this book – but of much broader potential use – in collaboration with Kristian Skrede Gleditsch (University of Essex and CSCW, PRIO) we collected a new data set on leaders, entitled *Archigos*. *Archigos* – the Greek word for ruler – is a database of political leaders, specifically the effective leader of each independent state (Gleditsch and Ward, 1999) between 1875 and 2004. Initially intended as a significant extension of the temporal domain of data we compiled early on in this project (Chiozza and Goemans, 2004b), *Archigos* is a comprehensive revision of the earlier data with many corrections and additions. Principal sources include Lentz (1994, 1999), Keesing's, www.rulers.org and www.worldstatesman.org, and in particular for the pre-1900 leaders, Proquest Historical Newspapers (www.umi.com/proquest). *Archigos* is continuously updated; here we rely on **Version 2.8**.

Compared to the well-known Bueno de Mesquita *et al.* (2003) data, *Archigos* contains many additional observations and variables. Bueno de Mesquita *et al.* (ibid.) identify roughly 3,000 leaders in the timespan 1816–2001 (with many duplicate observations as well as cases of multiple leaders for the same country for the same period[1]). *Archigos* contains information on not just when, but also how the leader gained and lost power. In addition, *Archigos* contains information on several personal characteristics of the leader such as birthdate or birthyear, gender, number of previous spells in office and – crucially – the leader's post-tenure fate. The data has been introduced to the scholarly

---

[1] Bueno de Mesquita *et al.* (2003) explicitly acknowledge such errors on the web page that describes their data, at www.nyu.edu/gsas/dept/politics/data/bdm2s2/ ErrorsandUpdates.htm.

community in Goemans, Gleditsch and Chiozza (2009). Because there are only 41 female leaders in the data, henceforth, when we refer to leaders in general, we use "he;" in individual cases we of course use the proper pronoun.

A.2 Dependent variables

Crisis initiation This variable measures whether the leader decided to initiate an international conflict in the international arena. An international conflict in our data is an instance in which a political leader takes a series of actions that trigger an international crisis. That is, as defined in Brecher and Wilkenfeld (1997):

(1) a change in type and/or an increase in intensity of *disruptive*, that is, hostile verbal or physical, *interactions* between two or more states, with heightened probability of *military hostilities*; that, in turn, (2) destabilizes their relationship and *challenges* the *structure* of an international system – global, dominant, or subsystem.

Each observation is coded with a dummy variable indicating whether a leader initiated an international crisis in a given year. All observations in which a country is still involved in an ongoing crisis are coded as 0. This specification allows us to model the decision to start a conflict and avoids conflating in a single framework decision processes that are likely to be distinct. Although leaders select their conflict strategies considering their chances to maintain power at the end of the conflict, the decision to continue to fight in a crisis is conceptually different from that of initiating one in the first place (Goemans, 2000b; Bennett and Stam, 2004). Data for this variable is obtained from Grieco's (2001) and Gelpi and Grieco's (2001) revised version of the International Crisis Behavior (ICB) project data (Brecher and Wilkenfeld, 1997). We updated the conflict data series using version 7.0 of the ICB data (International Crisis Behavior Project, 2007). We used this variable in Chapter 4. In our data, we list 342 instances in which a leader triggered an international crisis between 1919 and 2003 (Brecher and Wilkenfeld, 1997, 4–5).

There are no observations with missing values on this variable.

Leader's removal from office As we described at length in Chapters 3 and 4, we code when and how leaders were removed from office. We use two dummy indicators, one for regular removal, one for forcible removal. Leaders still in power as of December 31, 2003, the last year in our dataset; leaders who died a natural death; and second-term American presidents after Franklin Delano Roosevelt are coded as 0 in their last year in office; that is, these observations are considered censored. The data for these variables was originally coded in the *Archigos* data set by Goemans, Gleditsch and Chiozza (2009). We used these variables in Chapters 3 and 4.

There are no observations with missing values on the variables that measure the manner and timing of a leader's removal from office.

A.3 Explanatory variables

Domestic political institutions

Regime type We measure domestic regime type using dummy indicators that identify Autocracies, Mixed regimes, parliamentary democracies, and presidential democracies. In the regression models, Autocracies are the excluded baseline category. We code these dummy variables using the Polity IV's (2004) 21- point scale: countries scoring 7 or higher are coded as Democracies, countries scoring between −6 and 6 are coded as Mixed regimes; countries scoring −7 or less are coded as Autocracies (Jagger and Gurr, 1995, 474). The regime scores for the countries experiencing periods of interregnum, or transition – i.e. those that are coded as −77 and −88 – are converted into conventional Polity scores using the rules detailed by Monty Marshall, Director of the Polity IV project: cases of interregnum are converted to a Polity score of 0; cases of transition are prorated across the span of the transition. The cases of foreign interruption (Polity IV score of −66) are excluded from the data set.[2] In line with the coding rule developed by Chiozza and Goemans (2003), we code all the leaders who experienced, or enacted, a regime change during their office tenure by attributing to them the regime score they had for a longer period of time in the year of the regime transition.

We then distinguish between parliamentary and presidential democracies by a dummy variable indicator taken from the ACLP data set of Przeworski *et al.* (2000) for the period 1950–90, and recorded for the remaining periods from Cook and Paxton (1998), Derbyshire and

[2] These conversion rules are described in the section on the measurement of the variable "polity2" in the Polity IV codebook.

Derbyshire (1996) and the *Encyclopedia Britannica*. We folded the ACLP category of Mixed democracy into the presidential democracy category because non-parliamentary democracies can plausibly be argued to be presidential democracies for international relations purposes, since in these systems the president typically retains significant authority in foreign affairs.

There are no observations with missing values on the variables that measure regime type.

Domestic political conditions

Civil war We measure this variable using a dummy indicator coded 1 whenever a leader is in office during a civil war, and 0 otherwise. Data is taken from the latest version of the COW Intra-State War data set from Sarkees (2000) for the years from 1919 until 1946. For subsequent years, the data is taken from the PRIO data set on civil wars (version 4.2006) compiled by Gleditsch *et al.* (2002), available at www.prio.no/CSCW/Datasets/Armed-Conflict/UCDP-PRIO/.

There are no observations with missing values on this variable.

Entry This is a dummy variable that measures how a leader entered office. It is coded 0 if the leader reached power through regular means, and 1 if the leader reached power against explicit rules and established conventions of the particular state. This variable was originally coded in the *Archigos* data set by Goemans, Gleditsch and Chiozza (2009). We also include an interaction term between Entry and the leader's time in office (logged) to discount the effect of this variable over time.

There are no observations with missing values on this variable.

Days since previous elections We measure the number of days that have elapsed since the previous elections (logged). The raw data for this variable was collected from Goemans (2008).

There are no observations with missing values on this variable.

State of the economy

Economic development We measure economic development by the logarithm of the country's gross domestic product per capita. In Chapter 3, we distinguish three levels of development: (*a*) poor countries, those with a level of GDP per capita (logged) in the bottom 20%

of the distribution; (*b*) middle-income countries, those with a level of GDP per capita (logged) between the 20th and the 80th percentile in the distribution; (*c*) rich countries, those with a level of GDP per capita (logged) in the top 20% of the distribution. In Chapter 4, and in the imputation models for the missing data we use, GDP per capita is measured in 1990 International Geary-Khamis dollars from the *Historical Statistics* by Angus Maddison (available at www.ggdc.net/maddison/) for the period from 1919 to 1949 and from the Total Economy Database from the Groningen Growth and Development Centre at the University of Groningen in the Netherlands (available at www.conference-board.org/economics/database.cfm) for the period from 1950 to 2003. We supplement the Maddison and Groningen series using the GDP per capita series from Gleditsch (2002, Version 5.0). There are 968 observations (8.8%) with missing values on this variable.

Economic growth We measure this variable using the yearly change in the levels of GDP per capita. It is computed as the difference between the logarithm of GDP per capita in year t and in year t − 1. The raw data for the levels of GDP per capita comes from the same sources we used to code the levels of Economic Development. There are 1,052 observations (9.6%) with missing values on this variable.

Trade openness We measure this variable using the level of total annual trade, and standardize it by using the level of GDP in a country, where GDP serves as a proxy for a country's level of economic activity. Total trade is measured as the sum of the state's total imports plus total exports. Data is taken primarily from Barbieri, Keshk and Pollins (2008, 2009). We supplement our primary source using trade data from the International Monetary Fund's International Financial Statistics (available at www.imf.org/external/pubind.htm) and from Gleditsch (2002, Version 5.0). There are 1,366 observations (12.5%) with missing values on this variable.

Change in trade openness We measure this variable using the yearly change in the levels of Trade Openness. It is computed as the difference between the logarithm of Trade Openness in year t and in year *t* − 1. There are 1,515 observations (13.8%) with missing values on this variable.

Population size This variable measures the logarithm of the total population in each country in any given year. Data is taken from the Correlates of War *National Capabilities* dataset (version NMC 3.02). There are 168 observations (1.5%) with missing values on this variable.

Leader's features

Age This variable measures leaders' age. Data is obtained from the *Archigos* data which, in turn, based its coding on Bienen and van de Walle (1991); Lentz (1994, 1999), the www.rulers.org web page, the www.worldstatesmen.org web page, and *Encyclopedia Britannica*.

Number of days in office This variable counts the number of days that have elapsed since a leader came to power. In line with the modeling of time advocated by Carter and Signorino (2010), we include a cubic polynomial (t, t^2, and t^3). The coding of this variable is based on the *Archigos* data.
There are no observations with missing values on this variable.

Times in office This is a count variable that measures the number of times a leader has previously ruled a country. It is set to 0 in the first spell in office. The coding is based on the *Archigos* data.
There are no observations with missing values on this variable.

Conflict involvement We code the conflict record of a leader with three dummy indicators that measure whether a leader was involved in a conflict as a *Challenger*, a *Target*, or an *Inheritor*. Inheritors are leaders who entered into power when an international conflict was already underway. The excluded category (when all three dummy indicators are coded 0) identifies leaders who remained at peace. The raw data for this variable comes from the same sources used to code *Conflict Initiation* as a dependent variable. We used these three variables in Chapter 3.
There are no observations with missing values on this variable.

Conflict outcomes We code the conflict record of a leader also on the basis of the conflict outcomes he achieved. We use three indicators that measure whether a given international crisis ended in victory, defeat or draw, in line with Gelpi and Griesdorf's (2001) and the International Crisis Behavior's (2007) codings. We code the outcome of wars separate from the outcome of crisis short of war; we use the ICB four-point indicator for the severity of conflict to distinguish wars and crises: confrontations in which serious clashes, minor clashes, or no violence occurred are coded as crises, while full-scale wars are accordingly coded as wars. The outcome of the conflict is measured in the last year it was waged and in the subsequent years until there is a leadership change. We use a hyperbolic transformation to discount the effects of conflict outcomes over time. Each of the three outcome variables is coded using the following time-dependent function: $Outcome_t = 1/t$, where t represents the number of years since the termination of the conflict. Thus, in the year the outcome is realized the outcome indicator – be that victory, defeat, or draw – is coded as 1, in the second year after the end of the conflict it is coded as 0.5, in the third year as 0.333, and so on. The conflict indicators are coded as 0 for all leaders who have not fought a conflict or who were removed before the conflict ended. This coding choice reflects the intuition that the effects of the outcomes of international conflict can well linger for a long time among voters or members of the ruling coalition, but that over time the importance of such conflict outcomes will dissipate.

There are no observations with missing values on the variables that measure conflict outcomes.

Country's international political context

Major power status We identify major powers with a dummy indicator that takes on the value of 1 for all the leaders of a major power (as defined in the Correlates of War project, version 2002.1), and 0 otherwise. The following countries are identified as major powers: (1) the United States (from 1898 onwards); (2) the United Kingdom (from 1816 onwards); (3) France (from 1816 until June 22, 1940; from August 15, 1945 onwards); (4) Germany (from January 1, 1925 until May 7, 1945; from December 11, 1991); (5) Italy (from 1860 until September 2, 1943); (6) Soviet Union/Russia (from January 1, 1922 onwards); (7) People's Republic of China (from January 1, 1950 onwards); (8) Japan (from 1895 until August 14, 1945; from December 11, 1991 onwards).

There are no observations with missing values on this variable.

Military mobilization We measure this variable using a procedure developed by Alesina and Rosenthal (1995). First, we take the difference between the number of soldiers in a given year and the number of soldiers the previous year. Then, we divide this difference by the population in that given year. The variable is re-scaled by multiplying it by 100. The data for this variable is from the Correlates of War *National Capabilities* dataset (version NMC 3.02) for the period from 1919 to 2001; and from the *Military Balance* of the International Institute for Strategic Studies for 2002 and 2003.

There are 1,115 observations (10.2%) with missing values on this variable.

Number of borders This variable counts the number of land borders each nation shares with other independent nations. Data is taken from Stinett *et al.* (2002).

There are 49 observations (0.45%) with missing values on this variable.

Number of days since last crisis initiation This variable counts the number of days that have elapsed since a leader initiated an international crisis. In line with the modeling of time advocated by Carter and Signorino (2010), we include a cubic polynomial approximation (t, t^2, and t^3). The coding of this variable is based on the sources used to code Crisis Initiation as a dependent variable.

There are no observations with missing values on this variable.

Ongoing challenge This is a dummy variable that takes on the value of 1 if a leader is involved in an ongoing crisis and 0 otherwise. The year of crisis initiation is coded 0 to avoid double-measuring the dependent variable (i.e. Crisis Initiation). The raw data for this variable comes from the same sources used to code *Conflict Initiation* as a dependent variable. This variable is used in Chapter 4.

There are no observations with missing values on this variable.

Target onset This is a dummy variable coded as 1 when a leader was targeted in an international crisis in a given year, and 0 otherwise. The raw data for this variable comes from the same sources used to code *Conflict Initiation* as a dependent variable.

There are no observations with missing values on this variable.

Additional variables for the multiple imputation models

Lagged variables We include one-year lagged variables for (*1*) Economic development; (*2*) Economic growth; (*3*) Trade openness; (*4*) Change in trade openness; (*5*) Military mobilization.

Energy consumption This variable measures the levels of energy consumption on a yearly basis, and is used as a proxy for the levels of economic activity and development. The data for this variable is from the Correlates of War *National Capabilities* dataset (version NMC 3.02).

There are 632 observations (5.8%) with missing values on this variable.

Population size We include two additional measures of population size: (1) total population as reported in the Maddison and Groningen data used to code the Economic Development variable; (2) urban population (logged) as coded in the the Correlates of War *National Capabilities* data set (version NMC 3.02).

There are 925 observations (8.4%) with missing values on the first additional variable, and 643 observations (5.9%) with missing values on the second additional variable for population size.

Median duration in office This variable measures the median duration in power for all leaders in a given country, in line with Bienen and van de Walle (1991, 33). The coding of this variable is based on the *Archigos* data.

There are no observations with missing values on this variable.

Beyond median duration in office This is a dummy indicator coded as 1 for the years in which a given leader has been in power for a period longer than the median duration in office for that country, and 0 otherwise. The coding of this variable is based on the *Archigos* data.

There are no observations with missing values on this variable.

Number of days since last target onset This variable counts the number of days that have elapsed since a leader became a target of an international crisis. In line with the modeling of time advocated by Carter and Signorino (2010), we include a cubic polynomial approximation $(t, t^2, \text{ and } t^3)$. The coding of this variable is based on the sources used to code Crisis Initiation as a dependent variable.

There are no observations with missing values on this variable.

Bibliography

Acemoglu, Daron and James A. Robinson. 2000. "Why Did the West Extend the Franchise? Democracy, Inequality and Growth in Historical Perspective." *Quarterly Journal of Economics* 115(4):1167–99.

__ and __. 2001. "A Theory of Political Transitions." *American Economic Review* 91(4):938–63.

__ and __. 2006. *Economic Origins of Dictatorship and Democracy*. New York: Cambridge University Press.

Akins, James E. 1991. "Hooray? The Gulf May not be Calm for Long." *The New York Times* p. E17.

Albert, James H. and Siddhartha Chib. 1993. "Bayesian Analysis of Binary and Polychotomous Response Data." *Journal of the American Statistical Association* 88(422):669–79.

Alesina, A., S. Ozler, N. Roubini and P. Swagel. 1996. "Political Instability and Economic Growth." *Journal of Economic Growth* 1(2):189–211.

Alesina, Alberto and Howard Rosenthal. 1995. *Partisan Politics, Divided Government, and the Economy*. New York: Cambridge University Press.

Allison, Paul D. 2002. *Missing Data*. Sage University Papers Series on Quantitative Applications in the Social Sciences, 07–136. Thousand Oaks, CA: Sage.

Alvarez, R. Michael and Tara L. Butterfield. 2000. "The Resurgence of Nativism in California? The Case of Proposition 187 and Illegal Immigration." *Social Science Quarterly* 81(1):167–79.

Aquino, Enrique. 1944. *La Personalidad Politica del General José Santos Zelaya*. Managua, Nicaragua: Impreso en los Talleres Graficos Perez.

Atkins, Pope G. and Larman C. Wilson. 1998. *The Dominican Republic and the United States: From Imperialism to Transnationalism*. Athens, GA: University of Georgia Press.

Atwood, Christopher P. 2004. *Encyclopedia of Mongolia and the Mongol Empire*. New York: Facts on File.

Avirgan, Tonay and Martha Honey. 1982. *War in Uganda, The Legacy of Idi Amin*. Westport, CT: Lawrence Hill & Company.

214

Baker, Bruce. 2004. "Twilight of Impunity for Africa's Presidential Criminals." *Third World Quarterly* 25(8):1487–99.

Baker, William D. and John R. Oneal. 2001. "Patriotism or Opinion Leadership? The Nature and Origins of the 'Rally round the Flag' Effect." *Journal of Conflict Resolution* 45(5):661–87.

Bancroft, Hubert Howe. 1887. *The Works of Hubert Howe Bancroft.* Vol. III. *History of Central America, 1801–1887.* San Francisco: The History Company, Publishers.

Barbieri, Katherine, Omar Keshk and Brian Pollins. 2008. "Correlates of War Project Trade Data Set." Codebook, Version 2.0; available at http://correlatesofwar.org.

—, — and —. 2009. "TRADING DATA: Evaluating our Assumptions and Coding Rules." *Conflict Management and Peace Science* 26(5): 471–91.

Barker, Kenneth, ed. 1995. *The NIV Study Bible.* 10th anniversary edn. Grand Rapids, MI: Zondervan Publishing House.

Bearak, Barry. 2007. "Mohammad Zahir Shah, Last Afghan King, Dies at 92." *The New York Times* 24 July 2007: available at www.nytimes.com/2007/07/24/world/asia/24shah.html?_r=1&scp=3&sq=Barry ± Bearak&st=nyt.

Beck, Nathaniel, Jonathan N. Katz and Richard Tucker. 1998. "Taking Time Seriously: Time-Series–Cross-Section Analysis with a Binary Dependent Variable." *American Journal of Political Science* 42(4):1260–88.

Belkin, Aron and Evan Schofer. 2003. "Toward a Structural Understanding of Coup Risk." *Journal of Conflict Resolution* 47(5):594–620.

— and —. 2005. "Coup Risk, Counterbalancing, and International Conflict." *Security Studies* 14(1):140–77.

Bennett, D. Scott and Allan C. Stam. 2004. *The Behavioral Origins of War.* Ann Arbor, MI: University of Michigan Press.

Bienen, Henry and Nicholas van de Walle. 1991. *Of Time and Power: Leadership Duration in the Modern World.* Stanford, CA, Stanford University Press.

Bollen, Kenneth A., David K. Guilkey and Thomas A. Mroz. 1995. "Binary Outcomes and Endogenous Explanatory Variables: Tests and Solutions with an Application to the Demand for Contraceptive Use in Tunisia." *Demography* 32(1):111–31.

Bound, John, David A. Jaeger and Regina M. Baker. 1995. "Problems with Instrumental Variables Estimation when the Correlation between the Instruments and the Endogenous Explanatory Variable is Weak." *Journal of the American Statistical Association* 90(Jun): 443–50.

Box-Steffensmeier, Janet M. and Bradford S. Jones. 2004. *Event History Modeling: A Guide for Social Scientists.* New York: Cambridge University Press.

__ and Christopher J. W. Zorn. 2001. "Duration Models and Proportional Hazards in Political Science." *American Journal of Political Science* 45(4):972–88.

__, Dan Reiter and Christopher J. W. Zorn. 2003. "Nonproportional Hazards and Event History Analysis in International Relations." *Journal of Conflict Resolution* 47(1):33–53.

Brace, Paul and Barbara Hinckley. 1992. *Follow the Leader: The President and Public Opinion Polls.* New York: Basic Books.

Brecher, Michael and Jonathan Wilkenfeld. 1997. *A Study of Crisis.* Ann Arbor, MI: University of Michigan Press.

Bremer, Stuart A. 1992. "Dangerous Dyads: Conditions Affecting the Likelihood of Interstate War, 1816–1965." *Journal of Conflict Resolution* 36(2):309–41.

Brewer, Marilynn B. 1999. "Perpetrators of Prejudice; The Psychology of Prejudice: Ingroup Love and Outgroup Hate?" *Journal of Social Studies* 55(3):429–44.

Brownlee, Jason. 2002. " . . . And Yet They Persist: Explaining Survival and Transition in Neopatrimonial Regimes." *Studies in Comparative International Development* 37(3):35–63.

Bueno de Mesquita, Bruce, Alastair Smith, Randolph M. Siverson and James D. Morrow. 2003. *The Logic of Political Survival.* Cambridge, MA: MIT Press.

__, James D. Morrow, Randolph M. Siverson and Alastair Smith. 1999. "An Institutional Explanation of the Democratic Peace." *American Political Science Review* 93(4):791–807.

__ and Randolph M. Siverson. 1995. "War and the Survival of Political Leaders: A Comparative Study of Regime Types and Political Accountability." *American Political Science Review* 89(4):841–55.

__ and __. 1997. "Nasty or Nice? Political Systems, Endogenous Norms and the Treatment of Adversaries." *Journal of Conflict Resolution* 41(2):175–99.

__, __ and Gary Woller. 1992. "War and the Fate of Regimes: A Comparative Analysis." *American Political Science Review* 86(4):638–46.

Burgess, Paul. 1926. *Barrios, Justo Rufino: A Biography.* Philadelphia, PA: Dorrance and Company.

Burk, Kathleen. 1982. *War and the State: The Transformation of British Government 1914–1919.* London: Allen & Unwin.

Burns, John F. 1996. "At an Afghan Execution: It's Swift and Personal." *The New York Times* 19 December 1996: available at www.nytimes.

com/1996/12/19/world/at-an-afghan-execution-it-s-swift-and-personal.html.

Bush, George H. W. 1991. "The Gulf War; Bush Statement, Remarks to the American Academy for Advancement of Science." *Financial Times* 16 February: Section I; p. 2.

Bustamante Maceo, Gregorio. 1951. *Historia Militar de El Salvador.* 2nd edn. San Salvador, El Salvador: Publicaciones del Ministerio del Interior.

Calvino, Italo. 1988. *Under the Jaguar Sun.* New York: Harcourt Brace & Company.

Calvo, Joaquin Bernardo. 1890. *The Republic of Costa Rica.* (trans. L. de T). Chicago, IL: Rand, McNally & Company.

Campos, Alicia. 2003. "The Decolonization of Equatorial Guinea: The Relevance of the International Factor." *Journal of African History* 44(1):95–116.

Cardoso, Ciro F. S. 1991. The Liberal era, *c.* 1870–1930. In *Central America since Independence,* ed. Leslie Bethell. New York: Cambridge University Press, ch. 2, pp. 37–68.

Cardoso, Oscar Raul, Ricardo Kirschbaum and Eduardo Van DerKooy. 1987. *Falklands, The Secret Plot* (trans. Bernard Ethell). Surrey, U.K.: Preston Editions.

Carr, Edward Hallett. 1946. *The Twenty Years' Crisis, 1919–1939.* New York: Harper & Row.

Carter, David B. and Curtis S. Signorino. 2010. "Back to the Future: Modeling Time Dependence in Binary Data." *Political Analysis* 18(3):271–92.

Chiozza, Giacomo and Ajin Choi. 2003. "Guess Who Did What: Political Leaders and the Management of Territorial Disputes, 1950–1990." *Journal of Conflict Resolution* 47(3):251–78.

— and H. E. Goemans. 2003. "Peace through Insecurity: Tenure and International Conflict." *Journal of Conflict Resolution* 47(4):443–67.

— and —. 2004a. "Avoiding Diversionary Targets." *Journal of Peace Research* 41(4):423–43.

— and —. 2004b. "International Conflict and the Tenure of Leaders: Is War Still Ex Post Inefficient?" *American Journal of Political Science* 48(3):604–19.

Ciano, Galeazzo. 2002. *Diary, 1937–1943.* New York: Enigma Books.

Clapham, John Herald. 1899. *The Causes of the War of 1792.* London: C. J. Clay and Sons. Available online through Google Books.

Clark, David H. 2003. "Can Strategic Interaction Divert Diversionary Behavior? A Model of U.S. Conflict Propensity." *Journal of Politics* 65(4):1013–39.

Collier, Paul, and Anke Hoeffler. 2004. "Greed and Grievance in Civil War." *Oxford Economic Papers* 56:563–95.

Congdon, Peter. 2006. *Bayesian Statistical Modelling.* 2nd edn. Hoboken, NJ: John Wiley & Sons.

Cook, Chris and John Paxton. 1998. *European Political Facts, 1900–1996.* New York: St. Martin's Press.

Coser, Lewis A. 1956. *The Functions of Social Conflict.* Glencoe, IL: Free Press.

Craige, John Houston. 1934. *Cannibal Cousins.* New York: Minton, Balch & Company.

Croco, Sarah E. 2008. Peace at What Price? Domestic Politics, Settlement Costs and War Termination. PhD thesis University of Michigan, Ann Arbor, MI.

Cruz, Arturo J. 2002. *Nicaragua's Conservative Republic, 1895–93.* New York: Palgrave.

Dabat, Alejandro and Luis Lorenzano. 1984. *Argentina: The Malvinas and the End of Military Rule.* London: Verso.

Debs, Alexandre and H. E. Goemans. 2010. "Regime Type, the Fate of Leaders, and War." *American Political Science Review* 104(3): 430–45.

Derbyshire, J. Denis and Ian Derbyshire. 1996. *Political Systems of the World.* New York: St. Martin's Press.

DeRouen, Karl, Jr. 1995. "The Indirect Link: Politics, the Economy, and the Use of Force." *Journal of Conflict Resolution* 39(4):671–95.

___. 2000. "Presidents and the Diversionary Use of Force: A Research Note." *International Studies Quarterly* 44(2):317–28.

Diaz Lacayo, Aldo. 1996. *Gobernantes de Nicaragua (1821–1956).* Primera edición. Managua, Nicaragua: Aldilà editor.

Diehl, Paul F. 1985. "Contiguity and Military Escalation in Major Power Rivalries." *Journal of Politics* 47(4):1203–11.

Diermeier, Daniel and Randy T. Stevenson. 1999. "Cabinet Survival and Competing Risks." *American Journal of Political Science* 43(4):1051–68.

Domke, William. 1988. *War and the Changing Global System.* New Haven, CT: Yale University Press.

Downs, Anthony. 1957. *An Economic Theory of Democracy.* New York: Harpers and Collins.

Downs, George and David M. Rocke. 1994. "Conflict, Agency and Gambling for Resurrection: The Principal–Agent Problem Goes to War." *American Journal of Political Science* 38(2):362–80.

Doyle, Michael W. 1983a. "Kant, Liberal Legacies, and Foreign Affairs." *Philosophy and Public Affairs* 12(3):205–35. Part I.

___. 1983b. "Kant, Liberal Legacies, and Foreign Affairs." *Philosophy and Public Affairs* 12(4):205–35. Part II.

Efron, Bradley and Robert J. Tibshirani. 1993. *An Introduction to the Bootstrap*. Boca Raton, FL: Chapman & Hall/CRC.

El-Gamasy, Mohamed Abdel Ghani. 1993. *The October War* (trans. Gillian Potter, Nadra Morcos and Rosette Frances). The American University in Cairo Press.

Fagg, John Edwin. 1965. *Cuba, Haiti & The Dominican Republic*. Englewood Cliffs, NJ: Prentice Hall, Inc.

Farcau, Bruce W. 1994. *The Coup: Tactics in the Seizure of Power*. Westport, CT: Praeger.

___. 1996. *The Chaco War: Bolivia and Paraguay, 1932–1935*. Westport, CT: Praeger.

___. 2000. *The Ten Cents War: Chile, Peru and Bolivia in the War of the Pacific, 1879–1884*. Westport, CT: Praeger.

Fearon, James D. 1995. "Rationalist Explanations for War." *International Organization* 49(3):379–414.

___. 2004. "Why Do Some Civil Wars Last So Much Longer than Others?" *Journal of Peace Research* 41(3):275–301.

Feng, Yi. 1997. "Democracy, Political Stability and Economic Growth." *British Journal of Political Science* 27(3):391–418.

Fordham, Benjamin O. 1998a. "Partisanship, Macroeconomic Policy, and U.S. Uses of Force, 1949–1994." *Journal of Conflict Resolution* 42(4):418–39.

___. 1998b. "The Politics of Threat Perception and the Use of Force: A Political Economy of U.S. Uses of Force, 1949–1994." *International Studies Quarterly* 42(3):567–90.

Fortna, Virginia Page. 2004. *Peace Time: Cease-Fire Agreements and the Durability of Peace*. Princeton, NJ: Princeton University Press.

Fravel, M. Taylor. 2010. "The Limits of Diversion: Rethinking Internal and External Conflict." *Security Studies* 19(2):307–41.

Freedman, Lawrence and Efraim Karsh. 1993. *The Gulf Conflict 1990–1991*. Princeton, NJ: Princeton University Press.

Freese, Jeremy and J. Scott Long. 2006. *Regression Models for Categorical Dependent Variables Using Stata*. College Station, TX: Stata Press.

Gall, Sandy. 2007. "Mohammad Zahir Shah: The Last King of Afghanistan, a Patriotic but Indecisive Leader." *The Guardian* 23 July 2007: available at www.guardian.co.uk/news/2007/jul/23/guardianobituaries. afghanistan.

Gámez, José Dolores. 1889. *Historia de Nicaragua*. Managua, Nicaragua: Tipografia de "El Pais".

Gaubatz, Kurt Taylor. 1991. "Election Cycles and War." *Journal of Conflict Resolution* 35(2):211–44.

Gelman, Andrew. 2006. "Prior Distributions for Variance Parameters in Hierarchical Models." *Bayesian Analysis* 1(3):515–33.

Gelpi, Christopher. 1997. "Democratic Diversions: Government Structure and the Externalization of Domestic Conflict." *Journal of Conflict Resolution* 41(2):255–82.

___ and Joseph M. Grieco. 2001. "Attracting Trouble: Democracy, Leadership Tenure, and the Targeting of Militarized Challenges." *Journal of Conflict Resolution* 45(6):794–817.

___ and Michael Griesdorf. 2001. "Winners or Losers? Democracies in International Crisis, 1918–94." *American Political Science Review* 95(3):633–47.

Gill, Jeff. 2002. *Bayesian Methods: A Social and Behavioral Sciences Approach*. Boca Raton, FL: Chapman & Hall/CRC.

Gleditsch, Kristian S. 2002. "Expanded Trade and GDP Data." *Journal of Conflict Resolution* 46(5):712–24.

___ and Michael D. Ward. 1999. "A Revised List of Independent States since the Congress of Vienna." *International Interactions* 25(4):293–413.

Gleditsch, Kristian Skrede, Idean Salehyan and Kenneth A. Schultz. 2008. "Fighting at Home, Fighting Abroad: How Civil Wars Lead to International Disputes." *Journal of Conflict Resolution* 52(4):479–506.

Gleditsch, Nils Petter and Håvard Hegre. 1997. "Peace and Democracy: Three Levels of Analysis." *Journal of Conflict Resolution* 41(2):283–310.

___, Peter Wallensteen, Mikael Erikson, Margareta Sollenberg and Haavard Strand. 2002. "Armed Conflict, 1945–99: A New Dataset." *Journal of Peace Research* 39(5):615–37.

Goemans, H. E. 2000a. "Fighting for Survival, the Fate of Leaders and the Duration of War." *Journal of Conflict Resolution* 44(5):555–79.

___. 2000b. *War and Punishment: The Causes of War Termination and the First World War*. Princeton, NJ: Princeton University Press.

___. 2006. Territory, Territorial Attachment and Conflict. In *Territoriality and Conflict in an Era of Globalization*, ed. Miles Kahler and Barbara Walter. New York: Cambridge University Press, ch. 2.

___. 2008. "Which Way Out? The Manner and Consequences of Losing Office." *Journal of Conflict Resolution* 52(6):771–94.

___ and Mark Fey. 2009. "Risky but Rational: War as an Institutionally Induced Gamble." *Journal of Politics* 46(2):35–54.

Goemans, Henk E., Kristian Skrede Gleditsch and Giacomo Chiozza. 2009. "Introducing Archigos: A Dataset of Political Leaders." *Journal of Peace Research* 46(2):269–83.

Gowa, Joanne. 1998. "Politics at Water's Edge: Parties, Voters, and the Use of Force Abroad." *International Organization* 52(2):307–24.

Greene, William H. 2002. "LIMDEP version 8.0: Econometric Modeling Guide." Plainview, NY: Econometric Software, Inc. Vol. 1.

Grieco, Joseph M. 2001. "Repetitive Military Challenges and Recurrent International Conflicts, 1918–1994." *International Studies Quarterly* 45(2):295–316.

Guan, Weihua. 2003. "From the Help Desk: Bootstrapped Standard Errors." *Stata Journal* 3(1):71–80.

Gujarati, Damodar N. 1995. *Basic Econometrics.* New York: McGraw-Hill.

Gupta, Dipak K. 1990. *The Economics of Political Violence; The Effect of Political Instability on Economic Growth.* New York: Praeger.

Hagle, Timothy M. and Glenn E. Mitchell. 1992. "Goodness-of-Fit Measures for Probit and Logit." *American Journal of Political Science* 36(3):762–84.

Hall, Carolyn and Héctor Pérez Brignoli. 2003. *Historical Atlas of Central America.* Norman: University of Oklahoma Press.

Harrell, Frank E., Jr. 2001. *Regression Modeling Strategies: With Applications to Linear Models, Logistic Regression, and Survival Analysis.* New York: Springer.

Hastings, Max and Simon Jenkins. 1983. *The Battle for the Falklands.* New York: W. W. Norton & Company.

Hausman, Jerry and Daniel McFadden. 1984. "Specification Tests for the Multinomial Logit Model." *Econometrica* 52(5):1219–40.

Hazelwood, L. 1975. Diversion Mechanisms and Encapsulation Processes: The Domestic Conflict–Foreign Conflict Hypothesis Reconsidered. In *Sage International Yearbook of Foreign Policy Studies,* ed. P. J. McGowan. Beverly Hills, CA: Sage, pp. 213–43.

Heinl, Robert Debs and Nancy Gordon Heinl. 1996. *Written in Blood: The Story of the Haitian People 1492–1995.* Lanham, NJ: University Press of America, Inc. Revised and expanded by Michael Heinl.

Heinze, Georg and Daniela Dunkler. 2008. "Avoiding Infinite Estimates of Time-Dependent Effects in Small-Sample Survival Studies." *Statistics in Medicine* 27(30):6455–69.

__ and Michael Schemper. 2005. "A Solution to the Problem of Monotone Likelihood in Cox Regression." *Biometrics* 57(1):114–19.

Hermann, Margaret G. with Thomas W. Milburn, ed. 1977. *A Psychological Examination of Political Leaders.* New York: Free Press.

Hess, Gregory D. and Athanasios Orphanides. 1995. "War Politics: An Economic, Rational-Voter Framework." *American Economic Review* 85(4):828–46.

Hobbes, Thomas. 1996 [1651]. *Leviathan*. New York: Oxford University Press.

Horowitz, Michael, Rose McDermott and Allan C. Stam. 2005. "Leader Age, Regime Type, and Violent International Relations." *Journal of Conflict Resolution* 49(5):661–85.

Huntington, Samuel P. 1968. *Political Order in Changing Societies*. New Haven, CT: Yale University Press.

——. 1991. *The Third Wave: Democratization in the Late Twentieth Century*. Norman, OK: University of Oklahoma Press.

International Crisis Behavior Project. 2007. "ICB Version 7.0 (1918–2004)." Online, www.cidcm.umd.edu/icb/.

Jagger, Keith and Ted Robert Gurr. 1995. "Tracking Democracy's Third Wave with the Polity III Data." *Journal of Peace Research* 32(4):469–82.

James, Laura. 2005. "Nasser and his Enemies: Foreign Policy Decision Making in Egypt on the Eve of the Six Day War." *Middle East Review of International Studies* 9(2):23–44.

James, Patrick and Athanasios Hristoulas. 1994. "Domestic Politics and Foreign Policy: Evaluating a Model of Crisis Activity for the United States." *Journal of Politics* 56(2):327–48.

—— and Jean Sebastien Rioux. 1998. "International Crises and Linkage Politics: The Experiences of the United States, 1953–1994." *Political Research Quarterly* 51(3):781–812.

Jervis, Robert. 1976. *Perception and Misperception in International Politics*. Princeton, NJ: Princeton University Press.

——. 2002. "Theories of War in an Era of Leading-Power Peace." *American Political Science Review* 96(1):1–14.

Johns, Leslie. 2006. "Knowing the Unknown." *Journal of Conflict Resolution* 50(2):228–52.

Johnson, Dominic D. P. and Dominic Tierney. 2006. *Failing to Win: Perceptions of Victory and Defeat in International Politics*. Cambridge, MA: Harvard University Press.

Jones, Seth G. 2009. *In the Graveyard of Empires: America's War in Afghanistan*. New York: W.W. Norton.

Kaldor, Mary. 1999. *New & Old Wars: Organized Violence in a Global Era*. Malden, MA: Polity Press.

Kamau, Joseph and Andrew Cameron. 1979. *Lust to Kill: The Rise and Fall of Idi Amin*. London: Corgi Books.

Karnes, Thomas L. 1961. *The Failure of Union: Central America, 1824–1960*. Chapel Hill, NC: The University of North Carolina Press.

King, Gary, James Honaker, Anne Joseph and Kenneth Scheve. 2001. "Analyzing Incomplete Political Science Data: An Alternative Algorithm for Multiple Imputation." *American Political Science Review* 95(1): 49–69.

Kuran, Timur. 1991. "Now Out of Never: The Element of Surprise in the East European Revolution of 1989." *World Politics* 44(1):7–48.

Labianca, Giuseppe, Daniel J. Brass and Barbara Gray. 1998. "Social Networks and Perceptions of Intergroup Conflict: The Role of Negative Relationships and Third Parties." *The Academy of Management Journal* 41(1):55–67.

Lai, Brian and D. Reiter. 2005. "Rally 'round the Union Jack? Public Opinion and the Use of Force in the United Kingdom, 1948–2001." *International Studies Quarterly* 49(2):255–72.

Lavalle, José Antonio de. 1979. *Mi mission en Chile en 1879*. Lima: Instituto de Estudios Historico-Maritimos del Peru.

Lebow, Richard Ned. 1981. *Between Peace and War*. Baltimore, MD: Johns Hopkins University Press.

___. 1985. Miscalculation in the South Atlantic: The Origins of the Falklands War. In *Psychology and Deterrence*, ed. Robert Jervis, Richard Ned Lebow and Janice Gross Stein. Baltimore, MD: Johns Hopkins University Press, ch. 5, pp. 89–124.

Leeds, Brett Ashley and David R. Davis. 1997. "Domestic Political Vulnerability and International Disputes." *Journal of Conflict Resolution* 41(6):814–34.

Leites, Nathan. 1951. *The Operational Code of the Politburo*. New York: McGraw-Hill.

Lentz, Harris M. 1994. *Heads of States and Governments: A Worldwide Encyclopedia of Over 2,300 Leaders, 1945 through 1992*. Jefferson, NC: McFarland.

___. 1999. *Encyclopedia of Heads of States and Governments, 1900 through 1945*. Jefferson, NC: McFarland.

Levy, Jack S. 1989. The Diversionary Theory of War: A Critique. In *Handbook of War Studies*, ed. Manus I. Midlarsky. Ann Arbor, MI: University of Michigan Press, pp. 259–88.

___ and Lily I. Vakili. 1992. Diversionary Action by Authoritarian Regimes: Argentina in the Falklands/Malvinas Case. In *The Internationalization of Communal Strife*, ed. Manus Midlarsky. New York: Routledge, ch. 6, pp. 118–46.

Li, Kim-Hung, Xiao-Li Meng, T. E. Raghunathan and Donald B. Rubin. 1991. "Significance Levels from Repeated p-Values with Multiply-Imputed Data." *Statistica Sinica* 1(1):65–92.

Lian, Bradley and John R. Oneal. 1993. "Presidents, the Use of Military Force, and Public Opinion." *Journal of Conflict Resolution* 37(2):277–300.

Lipset, Seymour Martin. 1959. "Some Social Requisites of Democracy: Economic Development and Political Legitimacy." *American Political Science Review* 53:60–105.

Logan, Rayford W. 1968. *Haiti and the Dominican Republic.* New York: Oxford University Press.

Londregan, John B. and Keith T. Poole. 1990. "Poverty, the Coup Trap, and the Seizure of Executive Power." *World Politics* 42(2):151–83.

Maddala, G. S. 1983. *Limited-Dependent and Qualitative Variables in Econometrics.* New York: Cambridge University Press.

Makin, Guillermo. 1985. Argentina: The Authoritarian Impasse. In *The Political Dilemmas of Military Regimes*, ed. Christopher Clapham and George Philip. London: Croom Helm, ch. 7.

Makiya, Kanan. 1993. *Cruelty and Silence: War, Tyranny, Uprising, and the Arab World.* New York: W. W. Norton & Company.

Malanczuk, Peter. 1991. "The Kurdish Crisis and Allied Intervention in the Aftermath of the Second Gulf War." *European Journal of International Law* 2(1):114–33.

Mallar, Charles D. 1977. "The Estimation of Simultaneous Probability Models." *Econometrica* 45(7):5–39.

Mansfield, Edward D. and Jack Snyder. 1995. "Democratization and the Danger of War." *International Security.* 20(1):5–39.

— and Jack Snyder. 2005. *Electing to Fight: Why Emerging Democracies Go to War.* Cambridge, MA: The MIT Press.

Marra, Robin F., Charles W. Ostrom Jr. and Dennis M. Simon. 1990. "Foreign Policy and Presidential Popularity: Creating Windows of Opportunity in the Perpetual Election." *Journal of Conflict Resolution* 34(4):588–623.

Marure, Alejandro. 1895. *Efemérides de los Hechos Notables Acaecidos en la República de Centro América.* Guatemala.

Matibag, Eugenio. 2003. *Haitian–Dominican Counterpoint; Nation, State, and Race on Hispaniola.* New York: Palgrave Macmillan.

McGillivray, Fiona and Alastair Smith. 2000. "Trust and Cooperation through Agent Specific Punishments." *International Organization* 54(4):809–24.

Meernik, James. 1994. "Presidential Decision-Making and the Political Use of Military Force." *International Studies Quarterly* 38(1):121–38.

— and Peter Waterman. 1996. "The Myth of the Diversionary Use of Force by American Presidents." *Political Research Quarterly* 49(3):573–90.

Miller, Ross A. 1995. "Domestic Structures and the Diversionary Use of Force." *American Journal of Political Science* 39(3):760–85.

—. 1999. "Regime Type, Strategic Interaction, and the Diversionary Use of Force." *Journal of Conflict Resolution* 43(3):388–402.

Montúfar, Lorenzo. 1887. *Reseña Histórica. Centro-America.* Guatemala: Tipografia "La Union". Tomo Sexto.

Mooney, Christopher Z. and Robert D. Duval. 1993. *Bootstrapping: A Nonparametric Approach to Statistical Inference.* Thousand Oaks, CA: Sage.

Mor, Ben D. 1991. "Nasser's Decision-Making in the 1967 Middle East Crisis: A Rational Choice Explanation." *Journal of Peace Research* 28(4):359–75.

Morgan, Clifton T. and Christopher J. Anderson. 1999. "Domestic Support and Diversionary External Conflict in Great Britain, 1950–1992." *Journal of Politics* 61(3):799–814.

Morgan, T. Clifton and Kenneth N. Bickers. 1992. "Domestic Discontent and the External Use of Force." *Journal of Conflict Resolution* 36(1):25–52.

Morrow, James D., Bruce Bueno de Mesquita, Randolph M. Siverson and Alastair Smith. 2008. "Retesting Selectorate Theory: Separating the Effects of W from Other Elements of Democracy." *American Political Science Review* 102(3):393–400.

Mueller, John. 2004. *The Remnants of War.* Ithaca, NY: Cornell University Press.

Mueller, John E. 1973. *War, Presidents, and Public Opinion.* New York: Wiley.

Oakes, Amy. 2006. "Diversionary War and Argentina's Invasion of the Falkland Islands." *Security Studies* 15(3):431–63.

O'Kane, Rosemary H. T. 1983. "Towards and Examination of the General Causes of Coups d'État." *European Journal of Political Research* 11:27–44.

—. 1993. "Coups d'Etat in Africa: A Political Economy Approach." *Journal of Peace Research* 30(3):251–70.

Oliver, Christian. 2010. "North Korea: Drastic Dynastics." *Financial Times* 6 July 2010. Available at www.ft.com/cms/s/0/f0451e8a-892f-11df-8ecd-00144feab49a.html.

Omara-Otunnu, Amii. 1987. *Politics and the Military in Uganda, 1890–1985.* New York: St. Martin's Press.

Oneal, John R. and Anna Lillian Bryan. 1995. "The 'Rally 'round the Flag' Effect in U. S. Foreign Policy Crises, 1950–1985." *Political Behavior* 17(4):370–401.

___ and Jaroslav Tir. 2006. "Does the Diversionary Use of Force Threaten the Democratic Peace? Assessing the Effect of Economic Growth on Interstate Conflict, 1921–2001." *International Studies Quarterly* 50(4):755–79.

Ostrom, Charles W. and Brian L. Job. 1986. "The President and the Political Uses of Force." *American Political Science Review* 80(2):541–66.

Palmer, Frederick. 1910. *Central America and Its Problems*. New York: Moffat, Yard & Company.

Parker, Franklin D. 1964. *The Central American Republics*. New York: Oxford University Press.

Person, Roberto and Guido Tabellini. 1994. "Is Inequality Harmful for Growth? Theory and Evidence." *American Economic Review* 84(3):600–21.

Pinto, Anibal. 1921 and 1922. "Apuntes." *Revista Chilena*. No. 13: 337–73; No. 14: 112–26.

Pion-Berlin, David. 1985. "The Fall of Military Rule in Argentina: 1976–1983." *Journal of Interamerican Studies and World Affairs* 27(2):55–76.

Plummer, Brenda Gayle. 1988. *Haiti and the Great Powers, 1902–1915*. Baton Rouge, LA: Louisiana State University Press.

Polity IV Project. 2004. "Polity IV Dataset, version p4v2004d." Center for Global Policy, School of Public Policy, George Mason University and Center for Systemic Peace, available at www.systemicpeace.org/polity4.

Popper, Karl R. 1963. *The Open Society and its Enemies*. New York: Routledge.

Powell, Robert. 2006. "War as a Commitment Problem." *International Organization* 60(1):169–203.

Przeworski, Adam. 1991. *Democracy and the Market*. New York: Cambridge University Press.

___, Michael E. Alvarez, José Antonio Cheibub and Fernando Limongi. 2000. *Democracy and Development: Political Institutions and Well-Being in the World, 1950–1990*. New York: Cambridge University Press.

Quindlen, Anna. 1991. "The Microwave War." *The New York Times* p. E17.

Ramiro, Colindres. 1989. *Breve Historia de Honduras 1831–1876*. Tegucigalpa, Honduras: Graficentro Editores.

Ray, James Lee. 1995. *Democracy and International Conflict: An Evaluation of the Democratic Peace Proposition*. Columbia, SC: University of South Carolina Press.

___. 2001. "Intergrating Levels of Analysis in World Politics." *Journal of Theoretical Politics* 13(4):355–88.

—. 2003. "Explaining Interstate Conflict and War: What Should be Controlled For?" *Conflict Management and Peace Science* 20(2): 1–31.

Record, Jeffrey. 2002. "Collapsed Countries, Casualty Dread, and the New American Way of War." *Parameters* 32(2):4–23.

Reiter, Dan and Allan C. Stam. 2002. *Democracies at War*. Princeton, NJ: Princeton University Press.

Reiter, Dan and Allan C. Stam III. 1998. "Democracy, War Initiation, and Victory." *American Political Science Review* 92(2):377–90.

Rendón, Mary Catherine. 1988. Manuel Estrada Cabrera; Guatemalan President 1898–1920. Ph.D thesis Merton College, University of Oxford, England.

Richards, Diana, T. Clifton Morgan, Rick K. Wilson, Valerie L. Schwebach and Garry D. Young. 1993. "Good Times, Bad Times, and the Diversionary Use of Force." *Journal of Conflict Resolution* 37(3): 504–36.

Riker, William H. 1982. *Liberalism Against Populism*. Prospect Heights, IL: Waveland Press, Inc.

Rikhye, Indar Jit. 1978. *The Sinai Blunder: Withdrawal of the United Nations Emergency Force Leading to the Six Day War June, 1967*. New Delhi: Oxford & Ibh Publishing Co.

Rodman, Selden. 1964. *Quisqueya; A History of the Dominican Republic*. Seattle, WA: University of Washington Press.

Rodriguez, Mario. 1964. *A Palmerstonian Diplomat in Central America*. Tucson, AZ: The University of Arizona Press.

—. 1965. *Central America*. Englewood Cliffs, NJ: Prentice Hall, Inc.

Rosenau, James. 1966. Pre-Theories and Theories of Foreign Policy. In *Approaches to Comparative and International Politics*, ed. R. Barry Farrell. Evanston, IL: Northwestern University Press, pp. 29–92.

Rothenberg, Gunther E. 2007. The Origins, Causes and Extensions of the Wars of the French Revolution and Napoleon. In *Warfare in Europe, 1792–1815*, ed. Frederick C. Schneid. The International Library of Essays on Military History. Burlington, VT: Ashgate Publishing Company, ch. 3.

Rubin, Donald B. 1987. *Multiple Imputation for Nonresponse in Surveys*. New York: Wiley.

— and Nathaniel Schenker. 1991. "Multiple Imputation in Health-Care Databases: An Overview and Some Applications." *Statistics in Medicine* 10(4):585–98.

Rubinstein, Alvin Z. 1977. *Red Star on the Nile*. Princeton, NJ: Princeton University Press.

Russett, Bruce. 1993. *Grasping the Democratic Peace: Principles for a Post-Cold War World*. Princeton, NJ: Princeton University Press.

Sarkees, Meredith Reid. 2000. "The Correlates of War Data on War: An Update to 1997." *Conflict Management and Peace Science* 18(1):123–44. www.correlatesofwar.org/.

Sater, William F. 1986. *Chile and the War of the Pacific*. Lincoln, NE: University of Nebraska Press.

Schafer, Joseph L. 1997. *Analysis of Incomplete Multivariate Data*. New York: Chapman & Hall.

Scheina, Robert L. 2003. *Latin America's Wars* (2 vols). Vol. I. Washington, DC: Brassey's Inc.

Schoonover, Thomas D. 1991. *The United States in Central America, 1869–1911*. Durham, NC: Duke University Press.

Schroeder, Paul W. 1994. *The Transformation of European Politics*. Oxford: Clarendon Press.

Schultz, Kenneth A. 2001a. *Democracy and Coercive Diplomacy*. New York: Cambridge University Press.

___. 2001b. "Looking for Audience Costs." *Journal of Conflict Resolution* 45(1):32–60.

Schweller, Randall. 1998. *Deadly Imbalances: Tripolarity and Hitler's Strategy of World Conquest*. New York: Columbia University Press.

Simmel, Georg. 1898. "The Persistence of Social Groups." *American Journal of Sociology* 3(5):662–98.

___. 1955. *Conflict* (trans. Kurt H. Wolff). Glencoe, IL: Free Press.

Singer, J. David. 1961. "The Level-of-Analysis Problem in International Relations." *World Politics* 14(1):77–92.

Slantchev, Branislav L. 2004. "How Initiators End Their Wars: The Duration of Warfare and the Terms of Peace." *American Journal of Political Science* 48(4):813–29.

Smith, Alastair. 1996. "Diversionary Foreign Policy in Democratic Systems." *International Studies Quarterly* 40(1):133–53.

___. 1998. "International Crises and Domestic Politics." *American Political Science Review* 92(3):623–38.

Smith, George Ivan. 1980. *Ghosts of Kampala*. New York: St. Martin's Press.

Snyder, Richard Carlton, H. W. Bruck and Burton Sapin, eds. 1962. *Foreign Policy Decision-Making: An Approach to the Study of International Politics*. New York: Free Press of Glencoe.

Stinett, Douglas M., Jaroslav Tir, Philip Schafer, Paul F. Diehl and Charles Gochman. 2002. "The Correlates of War Project Direct Contiguity Data, Version 3." *Conflict Management and Peace Science* 19(2):67–88.

Stoll, Richard J. 1984. "The Guns of November: Presidential Reelections and the Use of Force, 1947–1982." *Journal of Conflict Resolution* 28(2):231–46.

Subercaseaux, Ramón. 1936. *Memorias de Ochenta Años*. Vol. 2. Volumes Santiago: Nascimento.

Tarar, Ahmer. 2006. "Diversionary Incentives and the Bargaining Approach to War." *International Studies Quarterly* 50(1):169–88.

Thant, U. 1978. *View from the UN*. Garden City, NY: Doubleday & Company, Inc. Appendix D, General Rikhye's Minutes of the Meeting of May 24, 1967, between the Foreign Minister of the U. A. R. and the Secretary General.

Therneau, Terry M. and Patricia M. Grambsch. 2000. *Modeling Survival Data: Extending the Cox Model*. New York: Springer.

Thornton, Richard C. 1998. *The Falklands Sting: Reagan, Thatcher, and Argentina's Bomb*. Washington, DC: Brassey's.

Thucydides. 1972. *History of the Peloponnesian War* (trans. Rex Warner). Rev. edn. London: Penguin Books.

Tullock, Gordon. 1987. *Autocracy*. Boston, MA: Kluwer.

Valenzuela, José Reina. 1984. *José Trinidad Cabañas, Estudio Biográfico*. Tegucigalpa.

Vallecillos, Italo López. 1967. *Gerardo Barrios y su Tiempo*. Vol. II. San Salvador, El Salvador: Ministerio de Educación, Derección General de Publicaciones.

Wagner, R. Harrison. 2007. *War and the State: The Theory of International Politics*. Ann Arbor, MI: University of Michigan Press.

Walt, Stephen M. 1997. *Revolution and War*. Ithaca, NY: Cornell University Press.

Walter, Barbara F. 2002. *Committing to Peace: The Successful Settlement of Civil War*. Princeton, NJ: Princeton University Press.

Waltz, Kenneth N. 1954. *Man, the State, and War*. New York: Columbia University Press.

———. 1979. *Theory of International Politics*. New York: McGraw Hill.

Welles, Sumner. 1928. *Naboth's Vineyard: the Dominican Republic 1844–1924*. Vol. 2. New York: Payson & Clarke Ltd.

WGBH. 2007. "Six Days in June, The War that Redefined the Middle East." A WGBH production in co-production with Instinct Films, Canada, Point du Jour, France, and Alma Films, Israel. ISBN No. 978–1–593757–84–7. Ilan Ziv, Director, Zvi Dor-Ner, Producer.

Wilkenfeld, Jonathan. 1968. "Domestic and Foreign Conflict Behavior of Nations." *Journal of Peace Research* 5(1):56–69.

Windmeijer, Frank A. 1995. "Goodness-of-Fit Measures in Binary Choice Models." *Econometric Reviews* 14(1):101–16.

Wolfers, Arnold. 1962. *Discord and Collaboration*. Baltimore, MD: Johns Hopkins Press.

Woodward, Ralph Lee. 1993. *Rafael Carrera and the Emergence of the Republic of Guatemala, 1821–1871*. Athens, GA: The University of Georgia Press.

Zinnes, Dina A. and J. Wilkenfeld. 1971. An Analysis of Foreign Conflict Behavior of Nations. In *Comparative Foreign Policy*, ed. W. F. Hanrieder. New York: David McKay.

Zorn, Christopher. 2005. "A Solution to Separation in Binary Response Models." *Political Analysis* 13(2):157–70.

Index